Troubling Gender in Education

This book explores new questions and lines of analysis within the field of 'gender and education', conveying some of the style and diversity of contemporary research directions. It celebrates as well as assesses the achievements of feminist work in education, acknowledging this legacy while also 'troubling' and opening up for critical reflection any potential stalemates and sticking points in research trends on gender and education. The collection has a strong cross-cultural focus, with chapters exploring experiences of students and teachers in the UK, the US, Australia, Canada, Hawaii and South Africa. The chapters examine topics relevant to both boys' and girls' education and to forms of education which span different sectors and both informal and formal spaces. Issues examined include citizenship and belonging, affect, authority and pedagogy, sexuality and the body, racism and national identity and new and emerging forms of masculinity and femininity. Across these varied terrains, each of the authors engages with theoretical work informed by a broad range of disciplinary and interdisciplinary approaches from across the social sciences and humanities, drawing variously from postcolonial, queer, and new sociological theories of modernity and identity, as well as from fields such as cultural geography and narrative studies. This collection of thought-provoking essays is essential reading for scholars and graduate students wanting to understand the current state of play on research and theory on 'gender and education'.

This book was published in a special issue of *Discourse: Studies in the Cultural Politics of Education*.

Jo-Anne Dillabough is a Reader at the University of Cambridge, UK, and an Associate Professor in the Department of Educational Studies, University of British Columbia, Vancouver. She is co-editor of *Challenging Democracy: International Perspectives on Gender, Education* and *Citizenship and Globalisation, Education and Social Change*. Her forthcoming co-authored book is entitled *Lost Youth in the Global City* (with J. Kennelly, 2009).

Julie McLeod is an Associate Professor in the Melbourne Graduate School of Education at the University of Melbourne. She is co-editor (with Andrea Allard) of *Learning from the Margins: Young Women, Education and Social Exclusion*; and co-author (with Lyn Yates) of *Making Modern Lives: Subjectivity, Schooling and Social Change*; and (with Rachel Thomson) of *Researching Social Change: Qualitative Approaches*.

Martin Mills is a Professor in the School of Education, The University of Queensland, and Visiting Professor at Roehampton University, London. He is the editor of *Discourse: Studies in the Cultural Politics of Education*. He is co-author of *Teachers and Schooling: Making a Difference* (with Deb Hayes, Pam Christie & Bob Lingard) and *Teaching Boys* (with Amanda Keddie).

Troubling Gender in Education

Edited by Jo-Anne Dillabough, Julie McLeod
and Martin Mills

Routledge
Taylor & Francis Group
LONDON AND NEW YORK

First published 2009 by Routledge
2 Park Square, Milton Park, Abingdon, Oxon, OX14 4RN

Simultaneously published in the USA and Canada
by Routledge
270 Madison Avenue, New York, NY 10016

Routledge is an imprint of the Taylor & Francis Group, an informa business

Typeset in Times by Value Chain, India
Printed and bound in Great Britain by MPG Books Ltd, Bodmin, Cornwall

British Library Cataloguing in Publication Data
A catalogue record for this book is available from the British Library

ISBN10: 0-415-46261-4
ISBN13: 978-0-415-46261-7

CONTENTS

INTRODUCTION

In search of allies and others: 'troubling' gender and education

Jo-Anne Dillabough, Julie McLeod and Martin Mills

'Gender and education' is a relatively recent category in the history and sociology of education; it has many referents – theory, empirical research, policy and practice – yet it seems to cohere as a recognisable field of enquiry. Over the last two decades, the range of work that falls within this field has expanded enormously. There are dedicated journals (*Gender and Education*), Readers and Handbooks (Arnot & Mac an Ghaill, 2006; Skelton, Francis & Smulyan, 2006), and a vast number of edited collections, monographs and articles, all of which, implicitly or explicitly, mark out the territory, the problems and the concepts which define the field of 'gender and education'.

This explosion of interest can be traced and explained in many ways, and will vary or be contested according to the disciplinary and national contexts of researchers, as well as their historical relationship to the field. To a very large extent, however, the trajectory of post-1970s educational research on gender has developed in dynamic engagement with gender studies and wider social and cultural theories and practice. In this respect, it has been strongly influenced by the insights of such debates, as well as sharing many of their impasses. Feminist educational reforms and research in the 1970s, for example, focused on questions related to equality of opportunities and the politics of representation and recognition. It then shifted to concerns about difference and inter-sectionality during the 1980s and 1990s (Dillabough, 2006), and has since turned toward the plethora of new writing about subjectivity and identity. Much of this latter influence emerged in relation to wider debates and critiques about coherent notions of 'identity' associated with European social thought, as well as vast transnational debates in cultural theory. The historical relationship between feminist theories and 'gender and education' – which will always denote more than 'theory' for theory's sake – is far more complicated than such a brief summary would suggest. The central point here is that educational research on gender has been substantially influenced by, and has contributed to, the various forms of feminist theorising that have enjoyed wide acclaim or paradigmatic dominance in the late twentieth and early twenty-first century.

Repositioning gender and education research for the new century: productive histories and their effects

As gender researchers involved in these debates, we began thinking about the current state of play of research on gender and education from a number of angles. We came with different histories of research involvement ranging across historical, theoretical and empirical sociological studies, as well as research directed towards policy and professional practice. Located in different countries, and states, we were attuned to differences as well as some commonalities in national pre-occupations. More particularly, though, we shared an interest in trying to understand the current terms of theoretical engagement with the field of gender and education, to see where it might be heading, to test any orthodoxies, and, of course, to see what new horizons might be imagined.

One substantive aim was, therefore, to 'trouble' in the most generous sense the field from the vantage point of insiders who are both identified with and also conduct research within the field, and as researchers who are interested in understanding the characteristics, the history, and effects of research – and especially theorising – on gender and education. As is now well established, feminism and gender theories in education have a long and productive history of engagement with diverse theoretical traditions (e.g., Arnot & Dillabough, 1999). However, we wanted to enquire into the state of this relationship now, and also to see where new possibilities might be emerging. We were thus concerned with questions such as: What might constitute the social and intellectual imaginaries of gender scholarship now and what theories or positions are particularly contested in education? Is *gender and education* something that we can even identify as a 'field', and, if so, what borders does it secure or transgress? Or is it a phenomenon that is better seen as a creative 'interplay of ideals, images', moral registers, dominant national locations and residual forms of 'surplus meaning' inherited from our 'diverse intellectual past' (Kearney, 2004)?

In this respect, our interests have some parallels with Raymond Williams' useful delineation of emergent, dominant and residual cultural forms, in that we view the gender and education field as similarly constituted. For example, we witness a mixture of sometimes overlapping theoretical and historical influences, some ascendant, some orthodox and others beginning to make a more substantive intellectual mark. But we were also motivated by a specific interest in working out just where it is that gender research in education has got to after so much deliberate scholarly and policy attention.

This edited collection endeavours to show some of the style and diversity of contemporary research directions, conveying both the emergence and the consolidation of important theoretical and empirical concerns for gender and education research. The collection also begins to direct our attention to the ways in which we might think about capturing a 'sense' of the field at this particular historical juncture. Of course, we are only able to decipher indirect meaning as no collection can represent the 'field' *per se*. However, through reflection on contemporary conceptual engagements and by highlighting new research, we can begin to ascertain a sense of the theoretical innovations under way, and some idea of the exciting potential of the current enlargement of the 'field'.

A secondary aim has been to draw together work which is explicitly and reflectively engaging with contemporary social and cultural theory to inform, expand and interrogate debates about gender and education. In these introductory comments, we seek to map some of the larger contexts of these reflections, and note significant trends in theoretical and policy agendas that currently constitute and are repositioning gender and education in 'new times'. The following discussions have a strong cross-cultural focus, with chapters exploring experiences of students and teachers in the UK, the US, Australia, Canada, Hawaii and South Africa. Issues examined include for example citizenship and belonging, affect, sexuality and the body, race and nation, and new and emerging forms of masculinity and femininity. Across these varied terrains, each of the authors draw upon theoretical work informed by a broad range of disciplinary orientations from within the social sciences and humanities. The chapters draw, for example, from postcolonial, queer and new sociological theories of modernity and identity, as well as from cultural geography and narrative studies. The different discussions demonstrate both the range and the significant achievements of gender studies research in education. At the same time, the authors each engage in a form of 'troubling' gender and feminist scholarship, showcasing generative processes of rewriting and repositioning the gender and education field. Each chapter thus provides a space for critically reflecting upon any potential stalemates and impasses we may encounter as gender researchers in education: such reflections are part of the ongoing project of diversifying and revitalising gender theory in education.

From the outset, then, it is apparent that we are deploying the term 'gender and education' as shorthand to capture a diverse range of scholarship that addresses gender relations, identities, inequalities, differences and the cluster of experiences, identifications, discourses, histories and forms of subjectivity that intersect with the category or sign of 'gender'. Gender has always been, and remains, an over-determined signifier, a key word in contemporary culture, which is often called upon to perform much analytic and descriptive work (McLeod, 2006). When allied with education – itself often invoking particular norms for understanding gender – it is clear that the now commonly accepted phrase 'gender and education' cannot be seen as a tightly-bound field or a narrow cluster of research interests. Nevertheless, across time and place, there are emergent and dominant characteristics in the type of research done, the questions considered most salient, and the methodologies through which they are addressed. A full history of changing themes and orientations in gender and education research is beyond our discussion and the concerns of this volume. However, it is within an historical frame, and with some recognition of temporal distance in mind, that we wish to place the following comments and chapters.

Identity, freedom and alterity: politics, sociology and change

Questions about what and who feminist accounts may have excluded and/or silenced have been a significant feature of feminist theoretical and political debates over the last two decades. The impact of what has been broadly, and often inadequately, described as 'identity politics' has been important in this regard, but so too have other trends in social and cultural theory, such as accounts of late modernity, neo-liberalism and individualism, globalisation and post-coloniality. Indeed the task of isolating a body of work as 'purely' or exclusively feminist may seem somewhat illusory when so much of contemporary feminist theorising is tied up in broader dialogues with a spectrum of theoretical and political concerns and orientations.

The work represented in this book engages with aspects of what might cautiously be called second-wave feminist theory's *others* or *allies*, encompassing theories that are both longstanding (but perhaps without substantial or sufficient recognition in education) and quite new versions or theoretical accounts of gender or gender studies scholarship. Taken together, these discussions offer many points of entry into debates currently circulating about ways of challenging elements of theoretical or substantive dominance in gender studies research (Brown, 1995; Connell, 2007), as well as providing a window onto emergent 'alterities' of master narratives that impact on associated scholarship.

This collection serves as an engagement with recent work which has been deeply affected by some of the highly influential theoretical movements of the twentieth century – psychoanalysis, various structuralisms and the remaining or re-emerging signs of neo-Marxism, poststructuralism(s), postmodernism(s), and theories of risk, individualisation, the self and cosmopolitanism. It is these theoretical struggles, and the manner in which they are woven into empirical work as a dramatic social narrative about the role of gender in everyday life, that are explored by the essays collected here. The collection is not exhaustive, but rather focuses upon concepts and related debates that mark out some fruitful territory for better understanding gender and educational research. In terms of any potential collective goal, it is toward the mediation of meaning in the field and its capacity for innovation that we turn rather than simply providing a critique or overview of any one approach.

For our purposes, we note two dominant themes in much recent research on gender and education. One has been a substantive interest in the processes of gender, subjectivity and the 'constitution of identity'. The second theme concerns the now vast responses to the 'boys' education' movement, sometimes associated with theoretical developments related to concepts of 'masculinity' and 'femininity'. Other themes and interests circulate, and these two themes, which carry different national inflections, should not be viewed as definitive characterisations of the field. But, over the last two decades, they have undoubtedly been influential, both showing the influence of broadly defined poststructuralist theories, and in different ways responding to wider gender equity and educational policy climates. But, our questions here are whether there are any stalemates in our collective thinking about these matters; how might we 'trouble' these 'taken-for-granteds', the current theoretical common-senses of the field; how might we offer some alternative or additional ways of seeing and theorising?

At the same time, questions about the status, history and effects of feminist theorising have been the focus of sustained attention, and these questions also have a major bearing on how we have come to consider research on gender in education. Wendy Brown (1995), for example, has written compellingly on the dangers of feminism's now sedimented narratives of its own history (see also Dillabough, 2008; Lather, 2007; McLeod, 2009) in which injuries associated with impasses of an earlier time are sometimes defended in the name of particular identities and associated political rationales in the present (Brown, 1995). Reflecting on the purpose of contemporary Women's Studies, Brown declares that it is confronted with the conundrum of what comes after the critique and deconstruction of 'core' concepts, such as sex and gender, and what 'comes after the loss of revolutionary feminism; it [Women's Studies] figures itself as a non-utopian enterprise with more than minor attachment to the unhappy present'. Can feminism and feminist scholarship live 'without a revolutionary horizon' (Brown, 2005, p. 99)? A question that informs her own critique of the concept of female freedom is:

> Not how we may thrive in the aftermath of the dissemination of our analytical objects, but *what are we* in the wake of a dream in which those objects were consigned to history? What does it mean for feminist scholars to be working in a time after revolution, after the loss of belief in the possibility and viability of a radical overthrow of existing social relations? (Brown, 2005, p. 99)

There are parallel questions to ask of feminist enquiry in education. If, as we have suggested, questions about the constitution of identity and the subject and its various formations have been a significant focus in recent educational scholarship, then we perhaps need to pause now and ask where that focus has taken us. What does a concentrated focus on gender identity, female freedoms or the subject elide, and what has it made possible? Following Brown's line of reasoning, are gender studies scholars in education working in a time after the loss of that which many might have imagined as a revolutionary horizon? And, equally, where might the field move following all this attention to the construction of subjectivity?

In many respects, feminist educational research can be understood as an 'agonistic space' which has been concerned in part with the deterritorialisation of paradigms and associated ideas, and with disrupting liberal conceptions of freedom which were a predominant feature of feminist post-war struggles (and its embedded history in colonial forms). As Maria Tamboukou, one of the contributors to this collection, writes:

> After all, gender and education is a theoretical and political field par excellence where striated and smooth spaces are continuously traversed and translated into each other, a site of intense struggles and antagonistic relations at play but also an open space continuously creating conditions of possibility for deterritorializations to occur, lines of flight to be released, events and nomadic subjects in their vicinities to emerge. (p. 70)

Acknowledging the impact of contested theoretical terrain and the process of 'deterritorialisation' does not mean, however, that we simply dismiss the past or intellectual history in the field. Nor do we merely pitch the apparently 'new' against the 'now apparently dated' in wider theoretical debates. Even in challenging existing traditions, the surplus meaning of theoretical ideas lives on and their original intentions must necessarily 'exceed their own frontiers' (Ricoeur, 2004) through the enduring language and symbols of earlier feminist accounts. It is both the confrontation with, and assessment of, the apparently 'new' and the traditional which provide the space for a form of theoretical displacement. Stuart Hall aptly spoke of the idea of theoretical displacement over a decade ago. He writes, 'each appropriation, each widening, [brings] new things' (Hall, 1998). In this manner, displacement (as opposed to replacement) and *rewriting* may indeed be our theoretical challenge and, as a reflexive exercise, could potentially inaugurate a generous and quite new conversation with both its allies and 'others'. As Lather writes:

> If feminist work is not to become routinized …, it must interrogate the enabling limits of its own practices … This is a sort of 'faithful transgression' that is not so much self-correction as negotiation with complexity where feminist practice is 'always already rewriting itself' … The goal is a generative undoing of a certain orthodoxy that is a necessary part of feminism making itself coherent and authoritative. Displacing fixed critical spaces enacted in earlier practices to which we are indebted, we move toward an 'iterative productivity'… that is open to permanent dynamism. (2007, p. 1)

The essays collected here do indeed negotiate with complexity and expose elements of 'education feminism' in the process of 'rewriting itself' by drawing upon a diverse range of theoretical traditions and substantive topics. It is these forms of rewriting and productive engagement that offer an important perspective both for understanding and judging the wide-reaching impact of gender studies in education from the late twentieth century onwards. Topics such as gender, religion and nation, race, 'the war on terror', global forms of neo-liberalism, the rise and fall of social class, and the highly regulative re-ordering of the state, all point to changes in the field. This is particularly so in terms of new hierarchies and configurations of gender in different spaces, places and times, and to the various forms of theoretical 'troubling' it has led to in education. In the essays we present here illustrate the ways in which the field is not only engaging with particular theoretical challenges (and presenting an ongoing need to trouble), but also with various contexts which in turn signal its complexity as an overlapping field of theory, policy and practice.

Gender policy, politics and social change

At the same time as we wish to speak to theoretical developments, we also acknowledge the ongoing salience of policy and associated political contexts in the development of gender and education. There is for example little doubt that at present, the field is still confronting a *politics of resentment* that is inhibiting the progressive agendas of the 1980s and early 1990s. These progressive agendas had 'real effects' and attempts to subvert or disrupt dominant paradigms/ discourses did, to varying degrees, constitute legitimate activity in policy terms. Indeed, in Australia, where two of us are based, and to a greater or lesser degree elsewhere, identifying issues that were impacting negatively on girls' education became a significant policy concern (e.g., Australian Education Council, 1987, 1993), particularly when seen within the context of wider cultural and political changes. The legitimacy, for example, of schools focusing on improving girls' education has been substantially diminished by the current focus on boys' education in many countries, which include countries in both the so-called global North and South (Jha & Kelleher, 2006). And claims continue to circulate in many nation-states that particular versions of feminism have reached a 'dead end' or a political nadir (Badinter, 2006) and are sometimes expressed as the 'war on boys' (Hoff Sommers, 2000) or men and boys as the new 'disadvantaged' (see, e.g., Farrell, 1993). These changes have been accompanied by equally regressive anti-feminist political ideas suggesting that social justice programs have destroyed meritocratic school outcomes, at the expense of 'white' and 'middle-class' students.

Alongside the various gender debates associated with rising political resentments and circulating moral panics, many in the 'global North' countries are witnessing the hegemony of neo-liberal educational discourses in which students are framed as forms of human capital in a competitive global market. Further, the valorising of the market within these discourses pits schools against each other as they compete for market share and market honours. This competition, as indicated by Francis and Skelton in this collection, has a significant impact on the gender order. Within neo-liberal discourses, 'failure' and 'success' are often attributed to individual efforts, thereby clearing governments of any responsibility for the distribution of, for example, low achievement scores amongst particular groups of male and female students. Paradoxically, then, within a highly masculinised schooling system where middle-class girls are perceived to be the hardest working, they are also deemed ideal 'clients' and highly perfected neo-liberal subjects (see also Burns, this volume). However, such attributions present fundamental contradictions as many of the moral registers associated with the neoliberal subject, such as risk-taking and individualism, are traditionally masculinised ones.

It is also clear that while new femininities and masculinities are appearing, some older and now sedimented forms are re-appearing as valorised constructs (e.g., Faludi, 2007). For example, in the twenty-first century, Faludi argues that 'the war on terror' carries substantial implications for contemporary gender relations in education, and for the reemergence of a regressive political agenda around gender. Following the September 11 attack in the USA in 2001 and the 2005 July 7 attacks in London, many countries identified as the 'Global North' have begun to fear the incipient 'dangers and enemies within' (Keddie & Mills, 2009). Various educational policies designed in an earlier moment to engage and value working positively with religious, racial and ethnic differences have now been placed under siege. Likewise, Muslim boys have often been represented in media and institutional contexts as dangerous and Muslim girls as oppressed by a misogynist religion. The following collection of papers offers a range of important perspectives and frameworks for examining these, and many other, contemporary theoretical, policy and social contexts.

Collection overview

The book begins with a discussion by Becky Francis and Christine Skelton of contemporary sociological and feminist theories of the self, a topic that has been at the 'heart' of much gender scholarship in education. They examine a cluster of theoretical arguments linked to accounts of late modernity, reflexivity, risk and projects of the self, including the work of Beck, Giddens and Bauman, arguing that while these theories provide new ways of seeing the self as potentially freed from tradition, they also pose particular challenges for feminist agendas, particularly regarding tendencies to 'disembed' the individual from the social. In developing this analysis they draw some revealing links to the arguments advanced by feminist theorist Judith Halberstam and her conception of 'female masculinities', which Francis and Skelton characterise as a notion that detaches gender from structural biology. While these – reflexive modernity and Halberstam – represent two quite different lines of analysis, Francis and Skelton identify some points of convergence in their 'conceptualisation of the self as to some extent freed from social structures'. The challenge for feminist scholarship in education lies, they argue, in navigating these insights – which stress agency and freedom – alongside a commitment to understanding social patterns or inequalities. These are ongoing and even obdurate problems for the sociology of education, possibly amplified in educational studies of gender which frequently straddle concerns to demonstrate power differentials and inequality alongside creative possibilities for movement and change (see also Paechter, 2007).

Related themes are explored in Mary Jane Kehily and Anoop Nayak's discussion of global femininities. Here, drawing on geographies of place and space, their analysis is developed via reflections on cross-cultural ethnographies of contemporary girlhood, and on 'how global products are consumed, [and what] their relationship to femininities and the meaning of place' might mean today. The effects of global popular culture, rather than formal or institutional learning, are examined. Against the emancipatory rhetoric of globalisation, they argue that we need to attend to how young women actually respond to these socio-cultural processes. They explore the 'global connections young women make through popular media culture' and how this gives rise to the emergence of 'new femininities'. Drawing in particular on quite new approaches in cultural studies and comparative ethnography, Kehily and Nayak's analysis avoids unhelpful binary accounts that privilege either the local or global. Instead, they outline important and compelling directions for place-based studies of gender that recognise the salience of the 'local' in relation to the persistently 'global bricolage' of popular culture. An important methodological contribution is their assessment of the value and 'imaginative appeal' of ethnography – typically associated with particularised or one-off studies of the local – as a global project that allows for examination of the 'worldwide transformations of gender and youth in late modernity'.

The impact of global popular culture is also taken up by Kellie Burns in her discussion of the relationship between globalisation, the imagination and emergent models of the girl-citizen. Adopting a Foucauldian analysis of governmentality, Burns argues for studies of globalisation to move beyond defining what globalisation is and to ask instead what it does, and particularly how it governs human subjects. To this framework she brings elements of Appadurai's account of the imagination and its role in social life, arguing that the imagination itself can be understood as a form of governing the conduct of global citizens. In Burns' analysis the 'imagination becomes a vehicle through which one attempts to locate the elsewhere . . . the otherwise of global living'. Her particular focus rests upon the ways in which young women and girls are called upon to imagine themselves as global citizens, to see themselves as, and to become entrepreneurial, life-long learners. While there has been much research on young girls' identity and identity work, Burns argues that more exploration is needed of contemporary cosmopolitanism and of the imagination in order to understand the interaction of education with new and emerging forms of girl-citizenship.

Continuing an interest in how one imagines and creates life narratives, Maria Tamboukou develops a genealogical analysis of the experiences of nineteenth-century US artist and art teacher, Mary Bradish Titcomb. This acts as a catalyst for a provoking theoretical reflection on how one might conduct historical and microsociological research through an engagement with Deleuzian concepts, and an exploration of spatial arrangements and relations. Tamboukou differentiates her approach to researching subjectivity from those that examine the construction of identity through the lens of structure/agency frameworks, which, she argues, have been dominant in gender and education and feminist studies more generally. Her Deleuzian account of subjectivity challenges this latter critical tradition and positions the self instead 'as a threshold, a door, a becoming'. Arising from this, Tamboukou outlines strategies for researching life histories and autobiographical narratives. These have been popular methodologies in feminist research, historically aligned with the task of rescuing women from obscurity. For Tamboukou, however, such narratives offer ways of 'tracing events and following lines of nomadic becoming'; and Tamboukou's discussion itself opens up possible *lines of flight* for feminist narrative enquiry in education.

Tracing the trajectories and historicity of her own pedagogical experience of teaching a graduate class in Hawaii, Hannah Tavares identifies a dramatic 'racial–ethnic–gender dynamic of identification' that can be articulated theoretically and empirically. As one response to this incident, Tavares examines the history and cultural politics of race, ethnicity, space and identity in the Pacific, and their resonance in education and teaching. The effects of power relations and gender dynamics in classrooms have been common motifs in feminist research, yet as Tavares's analysis indicates, there remains much more to be said about the complex interactions of emotion – of love, betrayal, and grief – and the associated forms of gender identification that unfold in teaching encounters. Her discussion, informed by postcolonial, feminist and psychoanalytic theories, outlines an account of the concept of embodied difference – cultural scripts of gender identification which are bound by social differentiation – and of the production of these differences 'through [the] historical processes' of colonisation.

While each of the authors in this volume may endorse, critique or develop situated analyses of subjectivity and gendered forms of identification, they achieve this in different ways. While several authors emphasise the location and mediation of subjectivity via local–global relations, others, such as Tamboukou and Tavares, are motivated by more overtly historical questions. Similarly, Sheila Cavanagh, in her contribution, invites a historical reading of lesbian-teacher sex scandals in the Canadian school context and the political and temporal complications associated with remembering and re-representing 'amorous pedagogical encounters'. Like Tavares, Cavanagh draws on psychoanalytic concepts to tease out recollections of such over-determined pedagogical relations. Engaging with a range of queer theories (e.g., Sedgwick, Halberstam, Kincaid), Cavanagh argues that heteronormative practices and forms of gendered subjectivity are regulated in part by temporal notions of childhood innocence and that lesbian-teacher sex scandals threaten to transgress and disrupt these regulatory norms. This is part of the reason why, Cavanagh suggests, such matters are currently not well conceptualised in educational studies nor are they often dealt with ethically in wider political and legal arenas. Through this historical research, we see the role played by enduring notions of gender and heteronormativity not only shaping gender relations in schools but also their part in framing both what we come to know as historical and human time through the juridical arena of the law.

Both problematising and challenging men's and boys' violence has also been a significant feminist project. However, understanding women's and girls' violence has presented challenges for those working within feminist frameworks. Another of the authors in this issue, Deevia Bhana, working in South Africa, confronts such a challenge. She argues that the ongoing silence around issues of girls' violence in South Africa has led to the conflation of the category 'girl' with attributes derived from traditional Western conceptions of the private sphere such as 'weakness' and 'vulnerability'. She argues that the high level of concerns with men's and boys' violence has served to mobilise and secure existing racist codes positioning African working-class women as objects of pity and African working-class men as misogynist savages. Drawing on ethnographic data obtained from one primary school in an African township in Durban, she demonstrates the ways in which some girls are active agents in challenging such ideas. The importance of the 'local' in understanding this violence is apparent in the discussion of the role of African women in anti-apartheid struggles; silences around women's capacity for violence have also worked to undermine the key role that working-class African women have played in the successes of that struggle.

Wayne Martino and Goli Rezai-Rashti also address issues of race and gender, in the context of a pervasive Islamophobia in North America. Whilst issues of religion and gender, and their implications for education are in no way 'new', the 'war on terror' and the contemporary and gendered construction of Muslims as the dangerous others raise difficult questions for those working within the field of gender and education. One of the most complex questions within this context, as Martino and Rezai-Rashti show, relates to the politics of veiling. The veil has come to represent a signifier of a misogynist religion for both those working within a conservative and a progressive political framework. Conservative commentators, for example in the USA and Australia, have justified the wars in Afghanistan and Iraq as wars of liberation for women and girls. These commentators have attacked feminists who do not support these wars for supposedly failing their Muslim sisters and have called upon feminists to speak out against veiling and to recognise the liberal agenda of the right's critiques of Islam. (Ironically, despite such claims, it is Muslim girls and women who have borne the brunt of public violence and harassment; Poynting & Noble, 2004.) Some feminists, as Martino and Rezai-Rashti note, have also been critical of veiling as a misogynist practice which denies, for instance, women's sexual agency. Their contribution does not seek to either justify or oppose the practice. Rather, in highlighting issues in the politics of veiling, they indicate the importance of working with and across feminist, queer and postcolonial analytic frameworks to develop an anti-racist pedagogy within the post-September 11 context.

The contributions to this book are eclectic. However, each of the authors offers an argument for developing analytical frameworks sufficiently sophisticated for addressing the complex and inter-related issues of culture, gender, sexuality, class and identity, together with their role in shaping educational exclusion under the dynamics of radically transformed gender arrangements and divisions, locally and globally. In different ways, the authors have responded to our invitation to trouble the field of gender and education, by provoking and engaging in debates and discussions within the field. They have done this, we would suggest, in nuanced, innovative and productive ways.

References

Arnot, M., & Dillabough, J. (1999). Feminist politics and democratic values in education. *Curriculum Inquiry, 29*(2), 159–190.

Arnot, M., & Mac an Ghaill, M. (Eds.) (2006). *The RoutledgeFalmer reader in gender and education*. London: Routledge.

Australian Education Council. (1987). *National policy for the education of girls in Australian schools*. Canberra: Australian Government Printing Service.

Australian Education Council. (1993). *National action plan for the education of girls 1993–97*. Carlton, Australia: Curriculum Corporation.

Badinter, E. (2006). *Dead end feminism* (J. Borossa, Trans.). Cambridge, MA: Polity Press.

Brown, W. (1995). *States of injury*. Stanford, CA: Stanford University Press.

Brown, W. (2005). *Edgework: Critical essays on knowledge and politics*. Princeton, NJ: Princeton University Press.

Connell, R. (2007). *Southern theory: The global dynamics of knowledge in the social sciences*. Crows Nest, Australia: Allen & Unwin.

Dillabough, J. (2006). Gender theory and research in education: Modernist traditions and emerging contemporary themes. In M. Arnot & M. Mac an Ghaill (Eds.), *The RoutledgeFalmer reader in gender and education* (pp. 17–32). London: Routledge.

Dillabough, J. (2008). Exploring historicity and temporality in social science methodology: A case for methodogical and analytical justice. In K. Gallagher (Ed.), *The methodological dilemma* (pp. 276–345). New York: Routledge.

Faludi, S. (2007). *The terror dream: What 9/11 revealed about America*. London: Atlantic Books.

Farrell, W. (1993). *The myth of male power: Why men are the disposable sex*. New York: Simon & Schuster.

Hall, S. (1998). Aspiration and attitude: Reflections on Black Britain in the 90s. *New Formations, 33*(1), 38–46.

Hoff Sommers, C. (2000). *The war against boys: How misguided feminism is harming our young men*. New York: Touchstone.

Jha, J., & Kelleher, F. (2006). *Boys' underachievement in education: An exploration in selected Commonwealth countries*. Vancouver, Canada: Commonwealth of Learning.

Kearney, R. (2004). *On Paul Ricoeur: The owl of Minerva*. Aldershot, UK: Ashgate.

Keddie, A., & Mills, M. (2009). Globalisation, gender justice and education: Contemporary issues and debates. In W. Ayers, T. Quinn, & D. Stovall (Eds.), *Handbook of social justice in education*. Mahwah, NJ: Lawrence Erlbaum, 107–119.

Lather, P. (2007, April). *(Post)critical feminist methodology: Getting lost*. Paper presented at the annual meeting of the American Educational Research Association, Chicago.

McLeod, J. (2006, April). *Researching historical change in the present: Gender, class, identity and Australian youth*. Paper presented at American Educational Research Association annual meeting, San Francisco.

McLeod, J. (2009). What *was* poststructural feminism in education? In M.W. Apple, W. Au, and L.A Gandin (eds.) *Routledge International Handbook of Critical Education,* New York: Routledge.

Paechter, C.F. (2007). *Being boys, being girls: Learning masculinities and femininities*. Open University Press.

Poynting, S., & Noble, G. (2004). *Living with racism: The experience and reporting by Arab and Muslim Australians of discrimination, abuse and violence since 11 September 2001* (Report to The Human Rights and Equal Opportunity Commission). Sydney: Centre for Cultural Research, University of Western Sydney.

Ricoeur, P. (2004). *Memory, history, forgetting* (K. Blamey & D. Pellauer, Trans.). Chicago: University of Chicago Press.

Skelton, C., Francis, B., & Smulyan, L. (Eds.) (2006). *The Sage handbook of gender and education*. Thousand Oaks, CA: Sage.

'The self-made self': analysing the potential contribution to the field of gender and education of theories that disembed selfhood

Becky Francis and Christine Skelton

Introduction

In keeping with the intentions of this collection, we seek to consider some novel theoretical applications in our field of work – in this case, to examine the extent to which the ideas of certain influential, contemporary social theorists can contribute to the theorising of gender and education. We have chosen to concentrate on some key theorists advancing new conceptions of selfhood with a particular focus on conceptions of the self as cut loose from social structure and biology. Hence we consider the diverse contributions of 'reflexivity theorists' (Bauman 2001, 2005; Beck 1992; Beck and Beck-Gernsheim 2002; Giddens 1991, 1998) and of 'gender theorist', Judith Halberstam (1998, 2005).

We begin by considering hegemonic explanations of neo-liberal society and particularly the emphasis on conceptions of 'individualisation' and 'individualism'. Beck's (1992) explanation of individualisation as being a state and not a choice and the corresponding conceptualisation of the 'self' as reflexive, as a project which is always in a state of becoming, has proved useful for feminist/pro-feminist educationalists in understanding the ways young people make sense of their lives. In citing Giddens' (1991) comment on the self as something we make of ourselves, McLeod (2006, p. 223) notes how this leads to 'contemporary gender identities and relations becom(ing) emblematic, representing in a kind of idealised form the possibilities of a self cut loose from tradition and required to make itself anew'. These motifs of agency and self-making – what Du Gay (1996) refers to as the positioning of individuals as entrepreneurs of the self – have been emblematic of the individualisation thesis.

At the same time we recognise the limitations and challenges of these theoretical positions: for example, the 'individualisation' thesis denotes a collapse in reference groups thus presenting a challenge for feminist agendas. For example, Beck (1992) argues that social class differences and family connections recede in importance, if not disintegrate, in an individualised society. And the privileging of agency over social structures in these theoretical positions is playing out in neo-liberal policy-making (often drawing on the highly influential work of theorists of reflexive modernity) to very directly position the individual as responsible for their trajectories and life outcomes (see e.g. Rose, 1999). Consequently, there has been a great deal of feminist critique of, as well as engagement with, such theoretical positions, both within and beyond the field of education. This has been particularly true of theoretical work analysing neo-liberal policy movements (see Davies, 2003; McLeod, 2006).

Yet the theoretical freeing up of the 'subject' that these reflexivity theorists engage has strong implications for gender identities and understandings of gender. Beck (1992, p. 111) for example, claims that women, as a group, have been released from their 'female status fate' and are symbolic of all the social changes that have occurred within the period of second (reflexive) modernity. The full implications (or challenges) of such theoretical positions have not yet been realised in empirical work in gender and education. It is also in this regard that we draw upon the theoretical promise of the work of Judith Halberstam.

Hence the initial sections of this chapter are devoted to outlining the key ideas of different proponents of the individualisation thesis, and exploring both the potential, and the limitations, of these contributions for the field of gender and education. It is argued that the individual subject evoked in the work of Beck and Giddens retains restrictive and stereotypical understandings of 'woman/women, girl/girls' (in spite of arguments to the contrary), and that as such these perspectives have limited application to the lives of women. Bauman's work is more attuned to structure in the economic sense, and we suggest that his devastating critique of neo-liberal society and its creation and pathologisation of the 'New Poor' to be highly applicable to work concerned with social justice. Yet we maintain that his lack of attention to gender will mean his work constitutes further theoretical information for feminist work, rather than a central contribution within the field.

Understandings of the self as 'disembedded' from society and its structures, and the implications for gender theory, evoke parallels with those theoretical positions in which 'gender' is detached from structural biology (Butler, 1990; Halberstam, 1998), and hence we turn to the work of Judith Halberstam in the latter part of the chapter. Some might debate the legitimacy of considering Halberstam's work alongside that of the reflexivity theorists (especially Anthony Giddens!). Halberstam positions herself as a feminist, and does acknowledge the impact of social structure (ethnicity, social class), and of the material, in some of her discussions. Likewise, while the reflexivity theorists are concerned with sociological analyses of the self in late modernity, Halberstam's work is located in cultural studies and focuses directly on constructions of gender and sexuality. However, we maintain that her work on 'female masculinity' raises similar challenges around the notions of 'choice-making', agency and self-making (in this case, regarding gender performance/

identification), and of the self as freed up from the material (in this case, from sexed bodies). Halberstam's work hence proposes an associated de-essentialising of social phenomena; and as such we argue that there are parallels between her work and that of the 'reflexivity theorists', in a shared project of disembedding the self.

Halberstam's (1998) conception of 'female masculinity' is informing, as well as being challenged by, feminist educationalists' work. The latter sections of the chapter explore some of the benefits and limitations of theories of gender as divorced from physical sex ('masculinity without men', as Halberstam puts it), arguing that this comprises an important and timely innovation which usefully challenges some of the more theoretically stagnant aspects of work on gender and education. Yet we caution that in developing such analyses we need to retain an awareness and analysis of power inequalities as central to feminist theory in education.

Notions of individualisation

Third Way theorists (such as Beck and Giddens) are specific in their use of the terms 'individualisation' and 'individualism'. 'Individualisation' is neither to be confused with individuation (the process of becoming an autonomous individual), nor emancipation. Furthermore, 'individualisation' is not shorthand for egotism, the development of a 'me-first' generation of people (Field, 2006; Giddens, 1998). However, 'individualisation' does place the ego at the centre of decision making and implies that the individual has to (and can) choose and change their social identity whilst taking risks in doing so (Reay, 2003). In defining individualism, Beck (quoted by Giddens, 1998, p. 36) writes:

> [it] is *not* Thatcherism, not market individualism, not atomisation. On the contrary, it means 'institutionalized individualism'. Most of the rights and entitlements of the welfare state, for example, are designed for individuals rather than for families. In many cases they presuppose employment. Employment in turn implies education and both of these presuppose mobility. By all these requirements people are invited to constitute themselves as individuals: to plan, understand, design themselves as individuals.

Giddens (1998) identifies the rise of 'individualisation' with globalisation processes whereby there has been a retreat in tradition such as the significance of the family, religion and politics. Beck (1992) cites three factors that have facilitated individualisation: first, the demise of social class divisions and distinctions; second, women's liberation from traditional gender roles (with the qualification that people are more 'aware' of women's equality than actually practise it); and third, changes in the nature of work. Both Beck and Giddens see this breakdown of traditional ties in a positive light as a means of providing social cohesion through 'more actively accept[ing] responsibilities for the consequences of what we do and the lifestyle habits we adopt' (Giddens, 1998, p. 37).

Applicability of individualisation to gender theory

Theories of individualism have been relatively slow to permeate feminist work on gender and education (perhaps with good reason, as we discuss below). While the neo-liberal policy environment and changed social expectations around, for example, women and work, have been discussed in relation to developments in education (see, for example, Arnot, David, & Weiner, 1999; Blackmore, 2006), until recently relatively few studies have engaged with theorists of individualisation directly to inform their analysis. (Exceptions to this include Kenway & Kelly, 2000; McLeod, 2006; Reay, 2003; Thomson & Holland, 2002; Walkerdine, Lucey, & Melody, 2001.) Critiquing Beck's work on the individualised society, Walkerdine et al. (2001) and Walkerdine (2003) have maintained that the model for the neo-liberal subject is female (though, Walkerdine observes, a specifically *middle-class* female) because attributes necessary to the subject in a neo-liberal socio-economic climate (such as flexibility, conscientiousness and so on) are feminine traits. The project of upward mobility via education and work constitute 'the feminine site of production of the neo-liberal subject' (Walkerdine, 2003, p. 238). She maintains that as well as a middle-class conservatism, neo-liberal values include those of 'emotionality, caring and introspection – the values of a psychology and interiority usually ascribed to women' (2003, p. 242). Hence Walkerdine and her colleagues argue that femininity is currently being refashioned, and they analyse the ways in which these new subjectivities are being moulded through discourses of flexibility and 'choice' which deny structural and psychic social class inequalities.

Further examples of engagement with the 'reflexivity theorists' can be found within aspects of our own work. Examples are Francis' (2006) use of Bauman's theorisation of the production and pathologisation of the New Poor in her analysis of policy shifts in relation to 'underachieving boys'; and Skelton's (2004, 2005a, 2005b) study of women in the academy, which sought to ascertain the usefulness to researchers of Beck's model of the 'individualised individual' for understanding the attitudes and actions of social actors. We elaborate these contributions below to evaluate the extent of the applicability of these theoretical approaches to the field of gender and education.

Bauman's (2005) devastating critique of neo-liberal consumerism, and the discourses of meritocracy and freedom mobilised to legitimate and perpetuate its practices, is demonstrated by Francis (2006) to be applicable to diverse aspects of neo-liberal policy (in this case, education). Bauman's work is very rich, and includes historical as well as contemporary social analysis, but a key strength is his eloquent and incisive critique of neo-liberalism. Like Rose (1999) and others, Bauman maintains that one of the benefits for the neo-liberal state in the transference of responsibility for 'failure' from the state to individuals is that these discursive practices justify a 'washing clean of hands' in relation to those not thriving in this socio-economic environment. Analysing how discourses of work ethic and meritocracy enable us to blame the poor for their social position, Bauman (2005) maintains,

> The call to abide by the commandments of the work ethic serves now as a test of eligibility for moral empathy. Most of those to whom the appeal is addressed are expected (bound) to fail this test, and once they fail they can be without compunction assumed to have put themselves, by their own choice, outside the realm of moral obligation. Society can now relinquish all further responsibility for their predicament without feeling guilty about its ethical duty. (p. 83)

And Bauman catalogues how, as the poor are discursively positioned as irresponsible rather than unfortunate, so there has been a corresponding shift in thinking about how to deal with them, resulting in the shift from a notion of 'entitlement' to that of 'obligation', which has seeped across neo-liberal policy-making internationally.[1] Hence a new approach to welfare has developed, based on a preoccupation with 'welfare dependency' and schemes to delineate the 'deserving' and 'undeserving' poor (Bauman, 2005; Mendes, 2003). This has involved the inception of a raft of punitive policies that entail the surveillance, regulation, circumscription and punishment of those deemed 'undeserving' (Bauman, 2005; Hayes & Lingard, 2003).

These practices of locating 'failure' with the individual rather than the state, and the consequences emanating from this location, are discussed by Francis (2006) in relation to the issue of 'boys' underachievement'. She argues that while an (often misogynist) 'poor boys' discourse continues to be applied to boys generally, neo-liberal policy drives are beginning to position some boys differently, with an increasingly sour note developing in English policy documents on 'failing boys'. Crucially, she maintains that we are beginning to see a policy delineation between 'deserving' and 'undeserving' boys – the latter group not unsurprisingly including working-class and Black boys, who are increasingly presented as 'beyond the pale' in neo-liberal educational policy.

Limitations of reflexive modernity theories for application to gender

On the other hand, it is notable that Francis *extends* Bauman's analysis to an aspect of gender analysis, rather than Bauman providing this angle. His focus is firmly on socio-economic movements (and within this on wealth and poverty), rather than on gender or 'race'. As such, Bauman offers ideas that prove fruitful for work on gender and education that is concerned with aspects of social class inequality, and neo-liberal policy movements, but does not have anything new to say himself about gender.

Elsewhere we have questioned Beck and Beck-Gernsheim's (2002) conception of the individualised subject as female (Francis & Skelton, 2005). Such a conception seems to support popular discourses of contemporary women as 'having it all' and their success and new-found self-confidence precipitating a 'crisis of masculinity' in men. As we have seen, Walkerdine (2003) does identify that Beck's vision evokes a specifically *middle-class*, rather than working-class womanhood, but otherwise acquiesces with Beck's description of this neo-liberal subject as a female one. Yet we argue that although the attributes which Walkerdine associates with the neo-liberal subject can be read as feminine – for example, diligence, responsibility, self-regulation (and self-blame), introspection, flexibility and self-transformation, reflexivity, care (see Walkerdine, 2003) – others may not. These might include entrepreneurism, assertion, self-confidence, 'drive', self-reliance, risk-taking, competition, and indeed individualism itself. These traditionally masculine traits are integral to neo-liberal subjecthood (Francis & Skelton, 2005).

Indeed, we used the case of the high-achieving (middle-class) girl – the subject that launched a thousand newspaper columns on 'boys' underachievement' – to demonstrate that a feminine construction of self is *not* held up as the 'ideal' version of identity, either in terms of producing educational achievement or as being an idealised expression of neo-liberal selfhood more broadly (Francis & Skelton, 2005). We argued that girls' achievement continues to be constructed as problematic, even in their out-performance of boys (as the talk is all of 'boys' underachievement', rather than 'girls' achievement'). As Walkerdine's own work has demonstrated, they tend to be constructed as performing through diligence rather than talent (and hence this diligence continues to be pathologised, even as educationalists urge boys to be *more* diligent, see Francis & Archer, 2005), and as insufficiently questioning and challenging in their learning. In other words, they are insufficiently masculine to be 'ideal students' (Cohen, 1998; Francis, Robson, Read, & Melling, 2003; Walkerdine, 1990).[2]

Skelton's (2004, 2005a, 2005b) study of two generations of female academics in which Beck's concept of the 'individualised individual' formed part of the theoretical framework revealed further limitations of its usefulness for feminists/profeminists. As was said earlier, Beck (1992) regards changes in women's position as symbolic of all the social changes that have taken place in reflexive modernity, and importantly, sees 'women' and 'men' belonging to homogenous and juxtaposed categories. Beck's idea of gender power dynamics rests solely on the public manifestation of where women are in terms of the home and labour market, thus failing to take on board a central plank of feminist/pro-feminist argument whereby power is inflected and produced by multiple aspects of social structure (e.g. gender, social class, ethnicity, age and so forth) to produce an individual's experiences and the psychic investments that contribute to constructions of identity (Reay, 2003; Walkerdine et al., 2001). At the same time, Beck's argument that the de-traditionalisation of gender has had a transformative effect on social change has garnered support from several feminists, although they stress that this is not a consistent and seamless process (see Adkins, 2002; McNay, 1999). Indeed, as Adkins (2002) argues, any recent changes in conventional understandings of masculinity and femininity are the outcome of a discontinuous process created by individuals negotiating differences in their identities within and across a range of sites of social action. The ever-increasing differentiation of 'social fields' (such as the domestic sphere and work environments) means that it is not feasible to see simplistic divisions between public (masculinity) and private (femininity) (McNay, 1999). So rather than seeing gender differentiation as 'an eternal opposition', it is more relevant to consider differentiated accounts that respect 'multiple disjuncture, overlap and conflict' (Adkins, 2002, p. 4).

The reservations expressed regarding the relevance of the concept for understanding and explaining how gender identities are experienced in this second, reflexive modernity were borne out in the study of academic women. In an interview with Jonathan Rutherford in 1999, Beck refers consistently to a period around the 1970s when transformations in terms of social movements began, thus marking the beginnings of the period of reflexive modernity. If the de-traditionalisation of gender roles did begin to occur around this time then it might be assumed that the experience and perceptions of women entering employment in higher education pre- and post-1970s would be different. However, Skelton's (2004, 2005a) research showed that there were no differences between the generations in that both earlier and later generations of academic women recounted incidents of sexism and masculinism in the academy and also identified occasions where other, often more senior feminist women had marginalised or subordinated them. This marginalisation and undermining of some women in universities by other women reflects the masculine nature of higher education (Brooks, 2001; Hearn, 2001). Masculinised organisations are part of the dominant cultural code in that masculinity inscribes and governs every aspect of institutional life from the general rules and practices through to the daily interactions of work colleagues (Adkins, 1995; Hearn, Sheppard, Tancred-Sheriff, & Burrell, 1989). While these masculinised organisational structures require support and affirmation of 'masculinity', at the same time, these are *not* sustained and reproduced by the gender of the employees (Morley, 1999). The point being made here is that in Beck's transition from a first to a second (reflexive) modernity there is no suggestion that organisational practices – including educational organisational practices – are becoming any less 'masculinised'. Thus, understandings of individualisation wherein the 'subject' is disembedded from social structures (Lash, 1994), including gender, precludes a more nuanced and representative account of gender in contemporary neo-liberal societies. As others have argued, it should not be assumed that reflexivity, in itself, brings issues of power and difference to an end (Adkins, 2002; McNay, 1999); and indeed, as our studies in this area have shown, a focus on individual agency may disguise the ongoing impact of the social on inequalities of outcome and experience, in education and elsewhere.

Gender subjectivity as severed from the sexed body

Increased awareness of the fluid and complex nature of subjectivity has of course impacted on the study of gender. That 'women/girls' and 'men/boys' have different social class, sexual, ethnic and religious identities has been increasingly acknowledged in social research; and postmodernist assaults on the humanist conception of the stable subject have challenged notions of a fixed gendered subject. This emphasis on diversity has led many researchers of gender identity to refer to 'masculinities' and 'femininities' in plural (rather than to 'masculinity' and 'femininity'), in order to reflect the multiple and diverse ways in which femininity and masculinity are constructed or performed (e.g. Connell, 1995).

However, this plural terminology has been criticised for two key (and related) reasons.[3] The first is that reference to 'masculinities and femininities' evokes typologies of masculinity and femininity, directly or by suggestion, with little attention to how these different 'sorts' of masculinity and femininity are categorised (and any similarities and distinctions between them) (Francis, 2000; MacInnes, 1998; Whitehead, 2002). In the sociology of education it has certainly been the case that some researchers have listed various 'types' of masculinity or femininity as manifesting among pupils (e.g. Mac an Ghaill, 1994; Sewell, 1997). The typological erection of categories ('types') evokes a fixity and simplicity unrepresentative of the fluid and multiple performances of gender that shift according to a discursive environment (Francis, 2002). Yet simultaneously, they do not offer adequately clear categorisations or distinctions between the different 'types' of masculinity or femininity constructed. Particularly, researchers adopting this approach rarely discuss why these various behaviours are being labelled as masculine (or feminine): as the critics above have observed, it seems to be simply assumed that the contents of these various 'types', however diverse, are either types of masculinity, or types of femininity, according to the socially-ascribed *sex* of the individual concerned. As MacInnes (1998) wryly reflects, it is tempting to conclude that the only feature linking the different 'masculinities' is the possession of a penis!

This invocation of the sexed body as the (unspoken) categoriser of femininities and masculinities exemplifies the second issue at stake here; the problematic conflation of 'sex' and 'gender' which underpins much work adopting 'gender' as a concept (Francis, 2002; Hawkesworth, 1997). Reflecting on the point made above, MacInnes (1998) observes that in the literature it is almost always boys/men that fit, or are described as performing, the various categories of masculinity; and girls/women the various types of femininity (Hawkesworth, 1997, has branded this the 'base/superstructure' model of gender). If gender is supposed to be purely notional and socially constructed, why, MacInnes asks, are women rarely described as having masculine characteristics, or expressing one of the 'types' of masculinity, and vice versa? Otherwise, gendered expression is actually intractably connected to the 'sex' of the individual subject (Halberstam, 1999). This reintroduces biological essentialism to what is ostensibly a socially constructed category (gender). Indeed Hood-Williams (1998) and MacInnes (1998) have asked why, if gender is actually linked intractably to biological sex, we actually need the concept of gender (rather than sex) at all? These criticisms may be aptly levelled at the vast majority of studies of gender in education (including some of our own previous work), and may be used to critique work that refers namely to 'multiple masculinities and femininities' without reflection on what these terms mean or how they are being applied. Halberstam (2007) speaks scathingly of those who adopt Butlerian terminology of gender performance, of 'doing gender' and so on, while simultaneously perpetuating the unarticulated assumption that males perform masculinities, and females femininities, in their analysis – hence failing to 'follow through' on Butler's thesis in deconstructing gender.

Besides the fetters of biological essentialism that such conflation of 'sex' and 'gender' involves, gender difference may be reified by such conflation. Because male non-gender-traditional expression tends not to be conceived as 'doing femininity', and female non-gender-traditional behaviour tends not to be read as 'doing masculinity', researchers of gender tend to focus rather on the gender-*traditional* behaviour of males and females. This may over-represent and hence reinforce gender difference, potentially supporting popular gender discourses based on notions of 'natural' difference, rather than working to deconstruct them (Francis, 2006, 2008a).

These issues are of course addressed theoretically by Judith Butler's (1990, 1997) work. Her poststructuralist position builds on previous articulations by researchers such as Garfinkel (1967) and Kessler and McKenna (1978) to argue that *both sex and gender* categories are entirely socially constructed: Butler maintains that this happens via binary gender discourses that inscribe bodies according to a (false) duality. Her understanding of sex/gender refuses essentialist ties to a sexed body. Instead she sees sex/gender as performative, as recognised via the acting out of (random) gender identities rather than inevitably deriving from a gendered body. Empirically, though, this refusal had scarcely been applied in research analysis prior to Judith Halberstam's use of Butler's theories to launch a profound challenge to the field. Halberstam's (1998) analysis of 'female masculinity' – the performance of masculinity by subjects discursively sexed as female – severs the umbilical link between sex and gender, queering the perception of gender as characterising the domains of exclusively sexed physical bodies. As such, Halberstam's work (1998, 2005) contests the body of research that automatically conceives men/boys as performing masculinity(ies) and girls/women as performing femininity(ies).

Halberstam has not been immune to criticism: for example, she has been accused of romanticising masculinity (Paechter, 2006), in addition to concerns that she provides insufficient clarity concerning her categorisation of masculinity (Francis, 2008b; Paechter, 2006), and incorporates inadequate consideration of the impact of embodiment and power inequalities on subject's productions of gender (Francis, 2008a, 2008b). Yet these concerns aside, Halberstam's work is both radical and pioneering in its application of Butler's ideas to specific empirical cases, and in her de-centring of the sexed body in her analysis of gender performance.

These ideas are beginning to be applied to the field of education by researchers of gender and education. For example, Mendick (2005) draws on Butler's work on gender performativity, and on Halberstam's exploration of female masculinity, to analyse the gendered subjectivities of women who excel at maths. Renold (in press) has explored the concept of female masculinity in application to her study of tom boys in primary schools. Francis (2008b) has applied the exploration of disembodied gender to the gendered performances of male teachers, identifying instances of 'male femininity'. Such work offers an exciting move away from the conflation of sex with gender, and a pleasureful exploration of gender heteroglossia. There is arguably an important contribution to be made in the field of gender and education in empirical work that avoids the potential reification of gender difference involved in tying identifications of gender performance to 'appropriately-sexed' bodies.

However, as Francis (2008b) and others have discussed, the challenges raised in seeking to apply this kind of analysis are profound. As we have seen, they relate both to the categorisation and application of masculinities and femininities when not read through the sexed body, and to the adequate recognition of the ways in which dominant discursive practices around gender and sexuality circumscribe performances of gender. In this sense, there is a parallel with problems in the application of reflexivity theories: a privileging of agency over structure/the material (in this case, the notion of 'choosing' a gender identification as disembedded from the sexed body) risks insufficient recognition of structural circumscription of such 'choice', and the related consequent potential for punishment of non-traditional 'choices'. Inscribed with power and desire as these gender/sexuality discourses are, it is no wonder that the sexed (and 'raced') body maintains a fundamental role in gender construction, even where the 'traditional' performance is eschewed by the subject concerned. The role of the spectator/reader of gender performance is seen as central – within which we include ourselves as researchers. Spectators still tend to look to the corporeal, as well as to signifiers of gender idenification such as clothing, hairstyle, posture and gait, and so on, to enable the immediate categorisation of gender that we tend to take for granted in our social interactions. We are thinking here of issues around 'passing' and 'misidentification' discussed by Halberstam (1999); of the importance of 'correct identification' to the social validity of both the subject and spectator (Speer, 2005); and of course of the policing and punishments often meted out to those seen as transgressing traditional gender/sexuality binaries. Feminist researchers of education have made an important contribution to the identification and theorisation of the ostracism, pathologisation and often bullying and harassment to which children not seen to 'fit' with traditional gender positions may be subjected by their peers (Davies, 1989, 1993; Lees, 1993; Reay, 2001; Martino & Pallotta-Chiarolli, 2003). And for a particularly extreme example of the punishments to which those 'transgressing' gender boundaries are often subject on a day-to-day basis, see Lloyd's (2005) discussion of the murder of Venus Extravaganza.

Hence this danger in elevating agency over structure in the conception of a 'disembedded self', as reflected in theories of individualisation/reflexive modernity and in Halberstam's work on 'masculinity without men', returns us to some of the old theoretical binaries that have challenged feminism in different ways throughout the decades: those of structure/determinism and agency; and those of the corporeal body and the social world (as well as the aforementioned problems of categorisation). In addition, inter-weaving all this, of course, are the tensions between a postmodern relativism and a feminist concern with power inequalities and political project. According to Weigman (2001), addressing these issues, and finding ways to negotiate a path between apparently contradictory positions, constitutes

> one of the most profound challenges for feminist theory today: not simply to address the divide between genetic bodies and discursive gender but to offer a political analysis of the socially constructed afflictions between the two. (p. 376)

Discussion and conclusions

The theorists highlighted in this chapter write from diverse viewpoints and politics, yet in spite of the strong differences in their approach, their theorisations share a conceptualisation of the self as to some extent freed from social structures (or in Bauman's view, deserted by the state), and able (or again in Bauman's terms, perhaps *left*) to make itself. As we have observed, they variously foreground agency and self-making over traditional social structure/material ties and limitations. We have illustrated how these intriguing conceptions of subjectivity have been applied to the theorisation of gender and education, to greater and lesser effect. Skelton (2004, 2005a,b) found Beck's (and Giddens') reading of the 'individualised individual' to be inadequate in accounting for gendered patterns because of the restrictive stance taken to gender power dynamics; and we have reiterated our argument that these understandings of people becoming 'entrepreneurs of the self' (Du Gay, 1996) are actually masculinised, rather than feminised. As such it is perhaps unsurprising that these theorisations of the 'reflexive individual' do not appear to 'work' in application to analysis of patterns in the behaviour of particular groups of women. (Yet here already we see a tension emerging in our text as we evoke 'groups of women' and their patterns of social expression, which we return to shortly). Bauman, meanwhile, offers a powerful critique of the contemporary state and its neo-liberal practices. His fierce critiques of neo-liberal ideology, consumerism, and the psychic as well as material violence their practices vest on disadvantaged sections of society have overlaps with some of the great feminist theorists of social material inequality (e.g. Fraser, 1997; Skeggs, 2004; and in education, Hey, 2002; Reay, 2001; Reay et al., 2005; Walkerdine, 1990; Walkerdine et al., 2001). Yet unlike these feminist theorists, Bauman does not foreground gender (or indeed other aspects of stratification and identification, such as 'race') as central to his critique.

Perhaps most theoretically innovative and exciting for the field of gender and education has been the contribution of Halberstam's work in moving forward understandings of gender production and performance. Weigman (2001) has elegantly heralded this work as 'inaugurated by a refusal to accede to the domain of the biological as the prior condition for gender's construction, as the "natural material on which gender dimorphically depends"' (p. 371). We believe that this contribution is important in reinvigorating the field and in disturbing tired theoretical cop-outs of 'masculinities and femininities' as related exclusively to one gender or the other. Yet here again, we have highlighted the 'risks' in this vision of gender as detached from the corporeal body – as agentically constructed free from material designations – for the feminist project of analysis of inequality in gender and education. As with the application of 'reflexive individualisation' theses, these risks particularly relate to the potential lack of recognition of the impact of social structures and practices in circumscribing 'choices', and punishing 'wrong choices'. Hence, elsewhere Francis (2008a) argues that the challenge in developing Halberstam's ideas is to do so while simultaneously maintaining an analysis of the impact of the material body and (relatedly) of power. There are material implications to inhabiting bodies defined as female, and as Weigman (2001) observes, social and psychic costs of 'living under the organizational sign *woman*' (p. 379). We need to be able to explore gender diversity while simultaneously holding on to the point that social structures produce patterns of behaviour and inequality across the group 'women'.

The challenge for us as feminists, then, is to address the new discursive productions of subjecthood practised within society and its institutions (such as education), and in particular to take forward analysis of masculinity and femininity as not inevitably belonging to one 'sex' or 'the other', without losing sight of the feminist endeavour to identify – that we can work against – patterns of inequality.

Notes

1. The New Labour administration in the UK has been preoccupied with 'Something for Something' (rather than the supposedly prior 'something for nothing') welfare policies. In Australia this has been referred to as 'Mutual Obligations' (and the ensuing catch-phrase 'no rights without responsibilities').

2. As Archer and Francis (2007) have shown, such constructions of high-achieving groups as pathological also extends to some minority ethnic groups such as British-Chinese (and Indian) pupils, who are also produced in a Western educational construction as *too* diligent and conformist (i.e. insufficiently masculine).
3. These and other critiques are outlined more extensively in Francis (2008a).

References

Adkins, L. (1995). *Gendered work*. Buckingham, UK: Open University Press.

Adkins, L. (2002). *Revisions: Gender and sexuality in late modernity*. Buckingham, UK: Open University Press.

Archer, L., & Francis, B. (2007). *Understanding minority ethnic achievement: Race, gender, class and 'success'*. London: Routledge.

Arnot, M., David, M., & Weiner, G. (1999). *Closing the gender gap*. Cambridge, UK: Polity Press.

Bauman, Z. (2001). *Community: Seeking security in an insecure world*. Cambridge, UK: Cambridge University Press.

Bauman, Z. (2005). *Work, consumerism and the new poor*. Buckingham, UK: Open University Press.

Beck, U. (1992). *Risk society*. London: Sage.

Beck, U., & Beck-Gernsheim, E. (2002). *Individualisation*. London: Sage.

Blackmore, G. (2006). Unprotected participation in lifelong learning and the politics of hope: A feminist reality check of discourses around flexibility, seamlessness and learner earners. In C. Leathwood & B. Francis (Eds.), *Gender and lifelong learning* (pp. 9–26). London: Routledge.

Brooks, A. (2001). Restructuring bodies of knowledge. In A. Brooks & A. Mackinnon (Eds.), *Gender and the restructured university* (pp. 15–44). Buckingham, UK: Open University Press/SRHE.

Butler, J. (1990). *Gender trouble*. London: Routledge.

Butler, J. (1997). Performative acts and gender constitution. In K. Conboy, N. Medina & S. Stanbury (Eds.), *Writing on the body: Female embodiment and feminist theory* (pp. 401–417). New York: Columbia University Press.

Cohen, M. (1998). A habit of healthy idleness: Boys' underachievement in historical perspective. In D. Epstein, J. Elwood, V. Hey & J. Maw (Eds.), *Failing boys?* (pp. 19–34). Buckingham, UK: Open University Press.

Connell, R.W. (1995). *Masculinities*. Cambridge, UK: Polity.

Davies, B. (1989). *Frogs and snails and feminist tales*. Sydney: Allen & Unwin.

Davies, B. (1993). *Shards of glass*. Sydney: Allen & Unwin.

Davies, B. (2003). Death to critique and consent? The policies and practices of new managerialism and of 'evidence-based practice'. *Gender and Education*, *15*, 91–103.

Du Gay, P. (1996). *Consumption and identity at work*. London: Sage.

Field, J. (2006). *Lifelong learning and the educational order*. Stoke-on-Trent, UK: Trentham Books.

Francis, B. (2000). *Boys, girls and achievement: Addressing the classroom issues*. London: RoutledgeFalmer.

Francis, B. (2002). Relativism, realism, and reader-response criticism: An analysis of some theoretical tensions in research on gender identity. *Journal of Gender Studies*, *11*(1), 39–54.

Francis, B. (2006). Heroes or zeroes? The construction of the boys' achievement debate within neo-liberal policy discourse. *Journal of Education Policy*, *21*(2), 187–199.

Francis, B. (2008a). Engendering debate: How to formulate a political analysis of the divide between genetic bodies and discursive gender. *Journal of Gender Studies*, *17*(3), 211–223.

Francis, B. (2008b). Teaching manfully? Exploring gendered subjectivities and power via analysis of men teachers' gender performances. *Gender and Education*, *20*(4), 109–121.

Francis, B., & Archer, L. (2005). Negotiating the dichotomy between Boffin and Triad: British-Chinese constructions of 'laddism'. *Sociological Review*, *53*, 495–522.

Francis, B., Robson, J., Read, B., & Melling, L. (2003). Lecturers' constructions of gender and undergraduate writing. *British Journal of Sociology of Education*, *24*, 357–373.

Francis, B., & Skelton, C. (2005). *Reassessing gender and achievement*. London: Routledge.

Fraser, N. (1997). *Justice interruptus: Critical reflections on the 'postsocialist' condition*. New York: Routledge.

Garfinkel, H. (1967). *Studies in ethnomethodology*. Englewood Cliffs, NJ: Prentice-Hall.

Giddens, A. (1991). *Modernity and self-identity*. Cambridge, UK: Polity.

Giddens, A. (1998). *The third way.* Cambridge, UK: Polity.

Halberstam, J. (1998). *Female masculinity.* Durham, NC: Duke University Press.

Halberstam, J. (1999). Masculinity without men (Anna Marie Jagose interviews Judith Halberstam). *Genders, 29.* Retrieved from http://www.genders.org/g29/g29_halberstam.html

Halberstam, J. (2005). *In a queer time and place.* New York: New York University Press.

Halberstam, J. (2007, March 14). The anti-social turn in queer theory. Keynote speech at the launch of the Centre for the Study of Gender and Sexualities, Roehampton University.

Hawkesworth, M. (1997). Confounding gender. *Signs, 22,* 649–685.

Hayes, D., & Lingard, B. (2003). Introduction: Rearticulating gender agendas in schooling: An Australian perspective. *International Journal of Inclusive Education, 7*(1), 1–6.

Hearn, J. (2001). Academia, management and men: Making the connections, exploring the implications. In A. Brooks & A. Mackinnon (Eds.), *Gender and the restructured university* (pp. 69–89). Buckingham, UK: SRHE/Open University Press.

Hearn, J., Sheppard, D., Tancred-Sheriff, P., & Burrell, G. (1989). *The sexuality of organization.* London: Sage.

Hey, V. (2002). Getting over it? Reflections on the melancholia of reclassified identities. *Gender and Education, 18,* 295–308.

Hood-Williams, J. (1998). Stories for sexual difference. *British Journal of Sociology of Education, 18,* 81–99.

Kenway, J., & Kelly, P. (2000). Local/global labour markets and the restructuring of gender, schooling and work. In N. Stromquist & K. Monkham (Eds.), *Globalisation and education* (pp. 173–197). Lanham, MD: Rowman and Littlefield.

Kessler, S., & McKenna, W. (1978). *Gender: An ethnomethodological approach.* Chicago: University of Chicago.

Lash, S. (1994). Reflexivity and its doubles: Structure, aesthetics, community. In U. Beck, A. Giddens, & S. Lash, *Reflexive modernization* (pp. 110–173). Cambridge, UK: Polity.

Lees, S. (1993). *Sugar and spice.* London: Penguin.

Lloyd, M. (2005). *Beyond identity politics: Feminism, power and politics.* London: Sage.

Mac an Ghaill, M. (1994). *The making of men.* Buckingham, UK: Open University Press.

MacInnes, J. (1998). *The end of masculinity.* Buckingham, UK: Open University Press.

Martino, W., & Pallotta-Chiarolli, M. (2003). *So what's a boy?.* Buckingham, UK: Open University Press.

McLeod, J. (2006). Working out intimacy: Young people and friendship in an age of reflexivity. In M. Arnot & M. Mac an Ghaill (Eds.), *The RoutledgeFalmer reader in gender and education* (pp. 223–237). London: RoutledgeFalmer.

McNay, L. (1999). Gender, habitus and the field: Pierre Bourdieu and the limits of reflexivity. *Theory, Culture and Society, 16*(1), 95–117.

Mendes, P. (2003). *Australia's welfare wars.* Sydney: University of New South Wales Press.

Mendick, H. (2005). A beautiful myth? The gendering of being/doing 'good at maths'. *Gender and Education, 17,* 205–219.

Morley, L. (1999). *Organising feminisms: The micropolitics of the academy.* Basingstoke, UK: Macmillan.

Paechter, C. (2006). Masculine femininities/feminine masculinities: Power, identities and gender. *Gender and Education, 18,* 253–263.

Reay, D. (2001). 'Spice girls', 'nice girls', 'girlies' and 'tomboys': Gender discourses, girls' cultures and femininities in the primary classroom. *Gender and Education, 13,* 153–166.

Reay, D. (2003). A risky business? Mature working-class women students and access to higher education. *Gender and Education, 15,* 301–317.

Renold, E. (in press). Tomboys and 'female masculinity': (Dis)embodying hegemonic masculinity, queering gender identities and relations. In W. Martino, M. Kehler, & M. Weaver-Hightower (Eds.), *The problem with boys: Beyond recuperative masculinity politics.* New York: Haworth.

Rose, N. (1999). *Powers of freedom.* Cambridge, UK: Cambridge University Press.

Sewell, T. (1997). *Black masculinities and schooling.* Stoke-on-Trent, UK: Trentham.

Skeggs, B. (2004). *Class, self, culture.* London: Routledge.

Skelton, C. (2004). Gender, career and 'individualisation' in the audit society. *Research in Education, 72,* 91–108.

Skelton, C. (2005a). The 'individualised' (woman) in the academy: Ulrich Beck, gender and power. *Gender and Education, 17*, 319–332.

Skelton, C. (2005b). The 'self-interested' woman academic: A consideration of Beck's model of the 'individualised individual'. *British Journal of Sociology of Education, 26*, 3–14.

Speer, S. (2005). The interactional organization of the gender attribution process. *Sociology, 39*(1), 67–87.

Thomson, R., & Holland, J. (2002). Imagined adulthood: Resources, plans and contradictions. *Gender and Education, 14*, 337–350.

Walkerdine, V. (1990). *Schoolgirl fictions.* London: Verso.

Walkerdine, V. (2003). Reclassifying upward mobility: Femininity and the neoliberal subject. *Gender and Education, 15*, 237–247.

Walkerdine, V., Lucey, H., & Melody, J. (2001). *Growing up girl: Psychosocial explorations of gender and class.* London: Macmillan.

Weigman, R. (2001). Object lessons: Men, masculinity and the sign. *Signs, 26*, 355–388.

Whitehead, S. (2002). *Men and masculinities.* Cambridge, UK: Polity.

Global femininities: consumption, culture and the significance of place

Mary Jane Kehily and Anoop Nayak

Introduction

Globalisation is said to offer young people possibilities for new forms of subjectivity and belonging, seemingly free from the immediate ties of family, peer group and geographic location (Beck, 1992; Giddens, 1991; Lash & Urry, 1999). For young women in particular, globalisation may provide opportunities for the emergence of new femininities. Within this framework young women have been positioned as the ideal neo-liberal subjects for post-industrial times, taking centre stage in the reconfiguration of labour patterns, consumption practice and gender roles (Aapolo, Gonick, & Harris, 2005; McRobbie, 2002; Walkerdine, Lucey, & Melody, 2001). It could be agued here that late modernity unshackles women from the patriarchal past. No longer subservient to the male breadwinner, the new female subject is economically independent, liberated from the confines of the domestic sphere and, with the help of new reproductive technologies, can realise the possibility of 'having it all' and 'doing it all'. The fuschia-pink hue of late modernity can be seen as part of the prevailing Zeitgeist, giving young women licence to become agentic, assertive and 'out there'. Where once the lives of young women were relegated to the margins, in the contemporary period they appear: their visibility is part of their unassailable presence in the new girl order (McRobbie, 2006).

This gender portrait of agency and opportunity is certainly seductive. However, far less is known about how young women respond to these changes and the role that new global media play in their lives. To address this we aim to consider globalisation from *below* by looking at young women and consumption. By focusing upon the cultures of youthful femininities, we aim to explore young women's relationship to the global and particularly the ways in which the products of a globalised media culture feature in their lives. In exploring young women's negotiations with cultural globalisation, we seek to illustrate the ways in which the global flows of objects, signs, media images and music may be appropriated, adapted and subverted within the texture of their everyday lives. Our discussion draws attention to the significance of place in the production and appropriation of youthful femininities. It indicates that places and institutions carry meaning and ways of being that may give rise to specific 'communities of interpretation' (Radway, 1984). We suggest that these 'communities of interpretation' can also be seen as local–global conversations in which young women speak back to late modern conceptualisations of new femininities. Such locally embedded practices shape gendered subjectivities and the possibilities afforded by the glamorous commodities of cultural globalisation. In this way young women may be seen to be involved in the scripting of individual biographical projects of the self (Giddens, 1991), but these remain connected to places, institutions and peer communities that are rooted in the contemporary social mores of the local.

The study points to the significance of school as a grounding feature of the local landscape that frames young women's encounters with the products of cultural globalisation. While school may exist as a regulatory force within young women's lives, global media provide a glimpse into celebrity culture and cosmopolitan spaces beyond the school where moral imperatives appear more relaxed and opportunities more plentiful. In this respect school is contradictorily placed in late modern times as simultaneously the route to cosmopolitan citizenship and the delimiting local institution replete with the conservative values of an older gender order. Educational practitioners and policy makers have largely overlooked the cultural as a sphere for the 'doing' of gender. We suggest that cultural studies accounts of music, television and media technologies have a great deal to impart when it comes to understanding the performance of gender in 'new times'. Our focus upon young women's engagements with cultural globalisation points to the importance of local–global negotiations to the making of gender. Furthermore, young women's participation in global media consumption across different sites indicates that many of the 'opportunities' for young women appear to exist beyond the school in the reconfigured labour and leisure patterns of late modern culture. It is our contention that exploring young women's interactions with global culture is a means of 'troubling' the more parochial understandings of gender in late modernity.

Comparative ethnographies

The paper draws upon data from a series of intermittent but nevertheless intensive periods of ethnographic fieldwork undertaken between 1993 and 2003. The data form part of a multi-site analysis that took place in four English state schools in different, largely working-class neighbourhoods.[1] It involved participant observation and interaction with young people as well as recorded interviews with students and teachers, complemented by field diaries and local sources pertaining to these areas. Although the ethnography provides close-in descriptions of young women's relationship to consumer goods, we are especially keen to interpret these practices alongside ethnographic studies undertaken in other countries. Our school-based study of femininities in the UK is then placed alongside studies of young women in South Africa, Northern Ireland, the Netherlands, Trinidad, Slovenia, China and Iran.

The value of a comparative ethnography is that it enables us to situate our accounts alongside a global literature on gender, youth and cultural studies to make connections across time and place (Nayak & Kehily, 2008). It also allows us to better understand the difference that *place* makes to understandings of gender and consumption. Looking globally enables us to reflect upon the place-specific dimensions of our work and the need to internationalise debates on gender and youth. This allows us to better explore local–global relations and interpret the coming-into-being of global femininities. Finally, comparative ethnography provides a means of critiquing Western assumptions of gender and globalisation by enabling us to elaborate upon, or speak back to the established theories and meta-narratives of social change.

In pursuing our research questions we have been influenced by recent debates concerning the status of ethnography in an interconnected world (Burawoy et al., 2000). This move gestures towards a more open-ended sense of place and a global way of looking. It contrasts with much early ethnographic approaches that tended to focus upon the detailed anthropological construction of a community, gang, village or 'tribe' (e.g. Malinowski, 1922; Whyte, 1943). This spatially 'bounded' way of looking features in most school ethnographies that have foregrounded the role of the institution to the making of race, gender, class and sexuality (Mac an Ghaill, 1994; Thorne, 1993; Willis, 1977). Recognising young people as global citizens suggests that their gender practices and identifications may reach beyond school gates. For Doreen Massey (1994) 'progressive sense of place' has the potential to prise open the local to recognise the multiple identifications and interconnections that can be made with the global. In particular modern diasporas, migrations and media cultural 'flows' permeate everyday spaces and pull apart the idea of place as a securely bounded entity.

In exploring this potential we attempt to follow the global connections young women make through popular media culture in order to understand how it may give rise to the emergence of 'new femininities'. It is our contention that looking globally need not eradicate some of the fine-grain texture of local school ethnographies. Instead, it may allow theory to travel and yield new insights on the question of gender, consumption and the contemporary conundrum of place. For if we are to argue that culture is an important site for the doing of gender then this inevitably entails a dialogue with the global. As high consumers young women regularly interact with a global bricolage of media signs, commodities, music, film and magazines. These global products have a bearing on who they are and how they wish to present in school and neighbourhood cultures. We remain compelled by the imaginative appeal of ethnography as a global project that allows us to think beyond the local and examine the worldwide transformations of gender and youth in late modernity.

In order to unsettle tightly bounded institutional readings of gender we address three research questions: How do young women engage with and consume global cultural products? How can these practices of consumption help us to understand new femininities? In what ways is place and social context significant to the relationship between new femininities and cultural consumption? The paper begins by discussing gender and local–global styles of consumption. We then turn to comparative ethnographies to explore the relationship between new femininities, cultural globalisation and practices of consumption across three sites. This includes an analysis of television soaps, film and romance; contemporary music and dance; and new media technologies.

Consuming locally and globally

Globalisation has had a much discussed impact upon youth and culture. A commonly held view suggests that globalisation in the cultural sphere produces Western hegemonic structures at the expense of local cultures. Cultural globalisation has been characterised as the flow of ideas, products and practices from the Western 'core' to the 'periphery' of non-Western locations. A recurrent theme of globalisation points to the emergence of social inequalities based upon the ability to consume and the ability to move. While middle-class young women exercise cultural capital and accrue social mobility to craft 'choice biographies' aimed at getting noticed in the global market place, working-class young women remain rooted to their locality, unable to access opportunities in education or work and prone to early pregnancy, single motherhood and social exclusion. Walkerdine et al. (2001, p. 209) argue that middle-class and working-class young women exist as 'each other's Other', cautionary examples of an alternative version of girlhood that is strange and undesirable. Class-based accounts of new femininities cast a shadow over the coming-of-age party for girls in new times, powerfully indicating that a place on the guest-list is not available to *all* young women. Skeggs (2004) suggests that globalisation offers the possibility of cosmopolitan citizenship, marked by participation in the global capitalist economy. Full citizenship and access to cosmopolitan spaces, she contends, appears to rest with some groups rather than others, the working-class and particularly working-class women forming the commonly excluded category. Empirical studies, however, suggest a more complex melange marked by reconfigurations of the local and the global in which individuals rework connections with family and community while undergoing personal change and social mobility (Thomson & Taylor, 2005; Henderson, Taylor, & Thomson, 2007).

An identifiable theme in Skeggs' work is a concern with the negative associations surrounding working-class femininity. Femininity can be understood as a class-based property premised upon appearance – what you look like serves as shorthand for who you are, defining at a glance feminine identity, behaviour and morality. Skeggs argues that appearance operates as a condensed signifier of class in which negative value is attributed to working-class forms of embodiment and adornment. Seen from this perspective, class exists as a process that works through evaluation, moral attribution and authorisation. Within the symbolic economy working-class women are commonly assumed to embody a style of feminine excess, denoting an overly abundant and unruly sexuality that places them dangerously close to the reviled figure of the prostitute. The fecundity of young working-class women, particularly, is viewed as excessive and morally reprehensible. Skeggs claims that the respectable/unrespectable binary that served to evaluate the working class in industrial times now works in different ways to construct certain vices as marketable and desirable while others retain no exchange value. Young working-class mothers provide a striking illustration of a group whose embodied vice is not recoupable for exchange. 'Even in the local context her reproductive use value is limited and limits her movements … white working-class women are yet again becoming the abject of the nation' (Skeggs, 2004, p. 23). In contrast to theories of individualisation, Skeggs suggests that mobility exists as an unequal resource, offering different points of access to different social groups. In

Skeggs' analysis mobility becomes a classed and gendered affair that confines working-class femininity to the local, offering little opportunity for movement.

Young women, however, are not only positioned by cultural commodities; they also engage in the representational sphere and produce meanings for themselves. Ethnographic studies can point to moments of ambivalence and fragmentation that challenge the Western idea of 'global community' and cosmopolitan citizenship. For example, Salo's (2003) study of gender and personhood in the new South Africa offers a closely observed and richly nuanced account of the ways in which cultural flows may be incorporated into local practices and given new meaning. The focus of her study is Manenberg township, Cape Town, a predominantly coloured neighbourhood where motherhood was regarded as the epitome of femininity. Under apartheid, adult women exercised moral authority over young people's position in the community and their transition to adulthood. In the post-apartheid era the influence of adult women was in decline and young people were looking to other sources for a developing sense of personhood. Salo demonstrates that the media and public transportation offered young people access to a cosmopolitan style that had a transformative effect upon their lives. Watching television 'transformed these domestic locales into transgressive hybrid spaces from which new ideas and practices of divergent new feminine identities emerged' (2003, p. 356). In a locality where male violence remained a routine feature of sexual relationships, television offered young women alternative images of gender relations based upon pleasure, desire and mutual respect. Through televisual portrayals, young women 'imagined gender relations beyond the narrow choices their mothers proscribed' (2003, p. 358). Television programmes such as soaps placed emphasis upon individuality, connections with peer group and the dismantling of older, apartheid-styled signifiers of race. Watching these programmes gave young women a glimpse of new forms of cultural capital, inspiring some to seek cosmopolitan experiences in other parts of the city – an agentic move that usually brought both new forms of freedom and constraint. Salo cites the example of Chantel, a 17-year-old respondent who traded upon her good looks and fashionable style in order to gain access to cosmopolitan spaces and social experience beyond her local community. Her mobility was made possible through the exchange value of youthful femininity suggesting that, in her case, working-class femininity/sexuality can carry symbolic value and may not necessarily exist as a barrier to cosmopolitan citizenship.

Although our focus in this chapter is upon young femininities, a brief comparison with their male counter-parts is indicative of the new spaces of gender mobility. Like young women, young men also sought alternative spaces for themselves in Manenberg. Youthful male activity in the neighbourhood centred round the hokke, a building that served as the gang headquarters, local shop, radio station and social club. Through the functions of the hokke, young men in the locality were more visible than women, having a public presence that was broadcast through local media. These men were heavily influenced by African-American rap culture, adopting the gangland style and practices of inner-city US neighbourhoods. Their activities challenged the authority of senior women in the community while establishing the position of 'gangster' as an alternative means of achieving status in the local context. Ironically, while young women looked outside the neighbourhood to realise new forms of femininity and sociality, young men's attempts at new style masculinity further rooted them in their locality as their gangland status depended upon notions of fixed territoriality and remaining local.

McGrellis (2005) reports a similar pattern in her study of youth transitions in Northern Ireland. Young women appeared able and willing to access cosmopolitan culture in urban spaces beyond the local, while young men remained rooted in sectarian structures that harnessed them within local boundaries. Interestingly it is this aspect of Salo's study and McGrellis' work that runs counter to Skeggs' argument that working-class women remain among the most excluded and vilified of groups. Salo argues that local meanings of personhood were reformulated through young people's engagement with global youth culture. Consumer culture and new cosmopolitanism played an important part in deconstructing and reconfiguring gender relations and racial divisions. Far from imposing Western hegemony, globalised youth culture offered young people in non-Western contexts alternative structures and practices for refashioning gender identities.

A sense of place transforms cultural globalisation in significant ways. The ethnographies discussed above suggest that class, femininity, cosmopolitan citizenship and mobility may not be as fixed as Skeggs claims. It is possible to suggest that some cultural characteristics may be highly valued in the symbolic economy to be successfully utilised by working-class subjects. It is also possible that high exchange value may be attached to 'hot' qualities and attributes that traverse class boundaries such as beauty, style, sporting ability, musicality or ICT wizardry. Here working-class and once-colonised subjects with the appropriate symbolic capital can entertain the possibility of 'passing' in terms of class or ethnicity, a move enabled by the prioritisation of their high exchange value qualities. A sense of place and the dynamics of local culture become important in young people's configuration of relationships between local and global (Nayak, 2003; Pilkington et al., 2002). Through the local, processes of cultural globalisation have an impact on citizenship, cosmopolitanism and social mobility which, in turn, take on shifting meanings for young people, offering different and sometimes unanticipated points of connection and desire.

Soap, film and the ideology of romance

Television soaps and film are global commodities assembled through a technology of production that includes the availability of hardware, software, financial resources, artistic input, state regulation and marketing. They can be located in Johnson's (1986, p. 283) elaborate 'circuit of culture' as texts that are open to complex practices of consumption and may elicit fantasy and collective forms of identification. A number of soaps can be placed within the broad cultural context of young women's lives as a mass-produced, globally marketed and publicly shared media form, which speak to girls in particular ways. They are commonly regarded as a cultural resource for young women that they can, at different moments, 'talk with' and 'think with' (Nayak & Kehily, 2008).

The global impact of television soaps can be traced in the complex 'communities of interpretation' that emerge around them. Ien Ang's (1985) cultural studies account of the popular 1980s American soap opera *Dallas* reveals how readers in the Netherlands may derive emotional pleasure by situating texts within their own lives. To research *Dallas*, Ang drew upon 42 letters she received (39 from women and girls), after advertising for responses in a magazine. It may seem strange how a soap essentially based upon the elite families of multimillionaire Texas oil barons could have such global appeal. Amidst the wealth, Stetsons, Cadillac cars and swimming pool cocktail parties, Ang discovered viewers were implicated in complex modes of identification. She found that for her mainly female Dutch audience *Dallas* offered 'emotional realism' as readers came to associate with what Ang depicts as a 'tragic structure of feeling' that connects with the ups and downs of their own everyday lives.

This theme is reworked by Danny Miller (1992) while conducting ethnographic research in Trinidad where he was struck by the way in which everyday life came to a standstill while the US soap *The Young and Restless* was broadcast for an hour. Rather than fostering an Americanised cultural imperialism, the soap was rapidly resituated into the rhythms of island life. Miller found that viewers did not use the soap as a window on the West but felt it resonated with the idea of 'bacchanal' – where hidden truths are exposed through scandal – a theme of that is replayed in Jamaican Carnival. The oil boom in the Trinidadian economy witnessed the rise of a large nouveau riche whose fragile pretensions were to implode when recession set in. Miller documents how many middle-class dwellings were repossessed by banks with financial ruin only becoming known through rumours and when phone lines were cut off in response to unpaid bills. In this way, the soap had an unanticipated aspect functioning as a global product that inadvertently could offer a critique of local conditions in a way that state-controlled media could not. Here, a seemingly homogenous global product is transformed into a highly distinctive Trinidadian commodity that is part and parcel of an enduring but ever-changing national culture.

The importance of looking globally is reflected in emerging scholarship on soap opera that challenges Western feminist readings. The popular US show, *Ally McBeal*, which focuses upon the sad but funny plight of a hapless young lawyer whose romantic dalliances and daydreams underscore her professional persona to tragic-comic effect, has been roundly condemned by some British feminists. Angela McRobbie (2002) has been particularly scathing of the presentation of a post-feminist, pre-pubescent image of regressed girlhood she claims shows like *Ally McBeal* and *Sex and the City* propagate. However, audience-based research undertaken by Vidmar-Horvat (2005) in post-socialist Slovenia articulates a very different reading of gender relations. In Slovenia *Ally McBeal* appeals to a number of female viewers as it resists post-Socialist attempts to draw women back into the home. Where women had been active workers under the Soviet regime they are now being recast as homemakers whose identity rests with family duties and domesticity. Watching Ally's scatty, rambling but often honest and moving court performances enables young Slovenian women to re-think their own place in the world. This reinterpretation of gender and work suggests that young women can perform as independent and able workers and that this does not have to come at the cost of being thought of as unfeminine.

Young women we spoke with were invested in many different media forms, the most popular and ubiquitous being soap opera. Story-lines and characters from soaps provided a common talking point for a range of issues and events. As with teen magazines, the open structure of soaps invites multiple forms of dialogue and interactivity (Barker, 1998; Buckingham & Bragg, 2003). Just as *Dallas*, *The Young and the Restless* and *Ally McBeal* may appeal across national borders, young women in our research were equally drawn to US programmes, Australian and British soaps. They were aware of the dramatic scope of soaps, associating popular prime-time programmes such as *Home and Away* and *Neighbours* with themes aimed at a child audience, while *Coronation Street*, *Emmerdale*, *Brookside* and *EastEnders*,[2] placed later in the schedule, risked sensitive and controversial adult themes such as sex and drugs:

> Lucy: [*Brookside*] deals with it all really strictly.
> Imogen: Like *Neighbours* and *Home and Away*, it's like, nothing happens like that.
> Claire: Just fantasy.
> Lucy: All the girls are like innocent little goody goodies and all the boys would never take advantage ...

Claire: Yes, none of them smoke or drink. But in *Brookside* it's all realistic and that. It's like they've done things like drug abuse and everything.
Imogen: Yes, and then there's the lesbians.

The realism of the 'adult' soaps and their incorporation of issues such as drug use and sexuality forms part of the appeal for young people. They contrast with the 'goody goody' image of childhood femininity Lucy is critical of lunchtime and early evening soaps. Instead 'adult' soap operas provided a form of fandom where the performance is everyday life. Following the soaps involved an evaluative appraisal of their ability to capture the rhythms and texture of 'real life'. Soap operas, and identifications with the characters within them, have the potential to challenge young people's views and opinions. They also offer spaces in which new femininities can be performed through the relatively safe mediated genres of television fiction. In a discussion of lesbianism, Emma remarked 'Since watching *Brookside* – and now *EastEnders* have got them – I don't feel as bad as I used to now'. Here, gay and lesbian characters may become 'familiar neighbours' in the televisual imaginaries of young people. This suggests that young women's negotiation of global cultural texts remains responsive to the mores of local environment, establishing simultaneously an awareness of normative values and a way of acting upon them.

For many young women, television, cable and satellite is one of the most immediate portals for global interconnection. Australian soaps and American television shows aimed at a teenage audience such as the *OC* and *Buffy the Vampire Slayer* (the latter includes a 'phallic' young woman as the lead character and her friend who is a teenage lesbian) extend the repertoire of youthful sexual knowledge and incite a wider proliferation of femininities with the potential to elicit a more cosmopolitan outlook.

Barker's (1998) study of British Asian girls' television viewing practices in the UK also suggests that soap operas provide young women with resources to discuss issues that may not be sanctioned within some of the religious and cultural spaces they inhabit. Of particular significance to young women in his study is the development of moral identities or what Dwyer (1999) terms 'appropriate femininities', once again suggesting that self-generated notions of respectability inform youthful femininities in significant ways (Kehily, 2002; Skeggs, 1997). Barker found that young women's 'soap talk' provided them with a set of tools to make moral and ethical judgements. Girls were concerned with morally disciplining characters in soaps for bad behaviour and simultaneously to 'make themselves' through such discourses of incitement. Significantly, girls in his study appeared to reserve the full weight of their condemnation for female characters who acted like 'sluts'. In keeping with Skeggs (1997), girls rework moral values for themselves; however, their refashioning of gender values may draw upon many of the traditional and conservative features of dominant versions. Barker's (1998) media study of British Asian girls and soap operas and our own discussions with young women indicate that soaps are woven into the fabric of young lives and read within the context of their immediate environment. Like magazines, soaps certainly provide a site for the refashioning of gender identities, offering opportunities for styling and adaptation, but these imaginaries are anchored in the local peer-group cultures of daily life.

While soaps offered many opportunities for active viewing we found that girls in our study also spoke of Hollywood film in similar ways. For many young women romantic film more than other media provided a cinematic template for relationships:

Mary Jane: When you were a bit younger and you imagined relationships, did you imagine them to be a certain sort of way?

Vicky: Yeah, off the telly, never argue, never fight.
[all laugh]
Catrina: Well I used to think that you used to walk down the street holding hands and he bought you all these gifts ...
Mary Jane: What's the reality been like?
Vicky: Much more arguments and fights, get presents, but not all the time. In the films you always get the idea it's all –
Catrina: Happily ever after ...
Vicky: The man trying to please the girl who is nasty to him and I used to think that I had to be nasty too ... I'm nicer now ... We used to fight when I couldn't have my own way.
Catrina: You know what I got from films? You know when they have an argument and the woman starts to cry, I says whenever I have an argument with one of my boyfriends I wouldn't cry like they do on the telly.

The comments of young women in our study illustrate Winship's (1987) point – reading romantic text is a pleasurable, interactive activity producing collaborative acts of interpretation. Young women integrate their reading into the texture of daily life and make points of connection between media texts and their own experiences (Hermes, 1995). Second, such practices have implications for gender identity. For young women, collective viewing or discussion offers an opportunity for femininities to be produced, defined and enhanced. Here peer group relations play a part in the mediation and regulation of cultural commodities, where embracing and repelling characters can be viewed as a *gender display* intended to purvey a particular femininity in dialogue with commercially produced forms but shaped by local norms and values.

In discussion with young women we found that popular tropes of the romance genre are juxtaposed with their own experiences of intimate relationships. The romantic gestures of the form and the promise of future happiness are exposed as 'tricks' that do not retain their illusory power in real life. Themes of romance and trickery are further explored in Gill's (2006) study of 'chick lit' and post-feminism. Gill considers whether the burgeoning of this genre aimed at young women and spearheaded by the success of *Bridget Jones* can be seen as an endeavour to rewrite romance fiction for a new generation of women. Gill notes the intensification of romance in late modernity (see Blackman, 2004), evidenced in an increasingly lucrative wedding industry and the general revival of interest in 'girly' and romantic themes such as hen parties, pamper weekends, Valentine gifts and dinner for two. She suggests that chick lit as text has much in common with its romantic predecessor, the Mills and Boon-style novel. Chick lit heroines may be sexually experienced and economically independent with a job, a mortgage and/or a child; however, they largely conform to the values of normative femininity in their search for romance, marriage and long-term happiness with a male partner. The formulaic development of the plot inevitably includes a 'rescue scene' in which the heroine is saved from the ravages of single life/ workaholism/single parenthood/dead end job by a man who melts her heart with true love.

And yet, we might wonder, do readers of romantic fiction consume the ideology of romance and the 'preferred' meanings encoded? If Vicky and Catrina's viewing of romantic Hollywood film is anything to go by, these global products and the gender identities they represent can be challenged, resisted and read 'against the grain'. As Radway (1984) and Walkerdine (1990) have demonstrated, romantic fiction creates spaces for individuals that may be occupied in diverse and unanticipated ways. As Hall (2000, p. 17) discloses, because identification involves the psychoanalytic engagement of fantasy and desire it can never be complete, 'There is always "too much" or "too little" – an over-determination or a lack, but never a proper fit, a totality'. This does not render the text meaningless. On the contrary, romantic fiction, soap opera and film provide pleasure and opportunities for 'magical' thinking; offering women potential resolutions to the lived contradictions of femininity. Versions of femininity in romantic films are rehearsed in personal encounters in the here and now, tried on, adapted and repelled. Engagement with cultural commodities is inevitably mediated by the context in which these encounters take shape, in schools, homes and leisure spaces. Through these interactions the global can be imaginatively rearticulated.

Music, dance and the cosmopolitan

The global flow of music, image, style and media signs are thought to have a 'disembedding' effect upon youth cultures in late modernity. They offer possibilities for more cosmopolitan forms of belonging and postmodern styles of consumption that transgress the boundaries of the local (Featherstone, 1998). However, global ethnographies of youth suggest a complex melange in which gender and race signs are still subject to place and geographical context. Through detailed observations of *di-si-ke* (that is, Chinese disco) in Shanghai and beyond, Farrer (1999) provides a fascinating insight into the global spectacle of gender performance amongst young people in China. According to Farrer, *di-si-ke* is a fantasy space that allows young people to travel beyond the mundane world of neighbourhoods, work or family life. It enables young women to participate in what Farrer depicts as a 'glamorous modernity', where 'one does not distinguish oneself by class or locality' (1999, p. 149), but instead can lose oneself in the immediate and intense spectacle of dance. The cosmopolitan spaces of *di-si-ke* become sites for new sexual and gendered imaginaries in which the global is not so much resisted but appropriated, localised and transfigured into new modes of being.

Chinese disco culture operates here as a colander-like sexual arena in which Western migrants, global videos, urban music and other commodities leak and pass through. Rather than being the passive conduits of Westernisation Chinese youth decipher, pilfer and make anew these mediated signs of global culture. By drawing upon the sexualised imagery of dance, dress and musical lyrics, Farrer suggests that Chinese girls may perform as sexual cosmopolitans. Here, scantily dressed 'young women – whose modesty had been encouraged in Chinese society – simulate sexual excitement with lithe pelvic motions' (1999, p. 159). This simulation of image and sound occurs by mimicking the media signs of Western video and the cacophony of musical and cultural forms that interplay and overlap across one another. This heady, sexual 'inter-textuality' between music, pop stars, dancers and youthful bodies reveals Shanghai *di-si-ke* to be a multilayered arena in which Chinese young women are adept 'textual poachers' of Western images using these resources to reflexively enhance their own projects of self. This is not simply a taking on of global mass media images. Instead, as Farrer reflects, 'Foreigners became the objects of sexual fantasy and occasional sexual adventures, but even more so were the mirrors for the construction of a cosmopolitan sexual self-image' (1999, p. 157). Evidently Westerners and Western sexual imagery can each be transformed into mutable props through which a new cosmopolitan sexuality can transpire. It would appear that in a world of signs, 'image is everything'. Here, 'The disco is a place for the visual consumption of others but even more for offering oneself up for visual consumption' (1999, p. 162), a willing transformation of subjects into objects, selfhood into signs.

In our ethnographic discussions with young women in Britain it is also apparent that global musical forms are consumed in ways that have personal meanings to those concerned and can be deployed to negotiate new femininities. Tina, who was of mixed-heritage, developed a strong identification with the singer Whitney Houston. This desire could be embodied through consumption, 'I had all her records, I even had a leather jacket the same as hers'. She goes on to add, 'I think she's ever so pretty and she's got a good singing voice'. However, for Tina and her best friend Samantha, the singer Madonna represented a more problematic and at best partial identification, due to her ambiguous sexuality and what they perceived as a sexually assertive, excessive femininity that needs to be held in check.

> Tina: I used to like Madonna, but I think Madonna is a ****.
> Samantha: I used to like Madonna, but I don't like the image she's got now [this is prior to Madonna's more recent demure look].
> Anoop: And you don't like her anymore, what it is about her you don't like?
> Tina: Her's showing herself up now. Her's using ... like this was in a magazine I had the other day, she just uses her body to get attention.
> Samantha: She's using her stardom to get attention, her used to make good songs an' that.
> Tina: In my magazine I got the other day it had got pictures of her how she is. Remember when she used to sing 'Holiday', she didn't look nice but she looked better compared to them silly pictures where she's just changed. You want to see how she's changed.
> Samantha: I got all her records.
> Mary Jane: Her body's changed a lot hasn't it?
> Tina: Dyed hair, no end of colours.
> Anoop: What image of Madonna did you like best?
> Tina: When she did 'Vogue'. I thought she looked really nice when she did 'Vogue'.
> Samantha: Yeah, she did. I got a video of her when she did the 'Like a Virgin' tour when her was young and I got her Italian tour.
> Tina: I tell you which one she looks weird on, her new one 'Erotica'. When she's got her hair all slicked down like that, her looks like a ... like a man. And it was on the telly the other day, and she went to a fashion show and she was a celebrity and she walked on. She'd got a dress and had cut out the holes round there [indicates to breasts] and nobody realised until she took off her jacket. And she was standing round like that with her hands on her hip.
> Mary Jane: Do you think she might've been deliberately trying to shock?
> Tina and Samantha: Yeah!
> Samantha: I think its 'cos not many people liked her again, 'cos her started looking like a whore and her wanted to make a comeback.
> Tina: I still like her records but I don't like her act at all.
> Samantha: I don't like her act – I don't like 'Erotica'.

It is interesting to consider this extract in the light of Madonna's more recent history and the manner in which she is technically proficient in the marketable reinvention of self. In the 1980s Madonna went from sexy pin-up girl to no-nonsense 'Material Girl' in the blink of an eye. In the 1990s Madonna self-consciously flirted with the borders of the allegedly 'perverse', including S/M imagery, lesbianism, black sexuality and a gambit of illicit sexual signifiers that construed her as the 'dirty-sexy-bad-girl' of pop that Tina and Samantha are so repelled by. The manner in which past images of Madonna have been marketed through a fetishisation of black, lesbian and S/M iconography is further testimony to the ways in which 'difference' is incorporated, transfigured and sold back to us as titillating. However, if we look at Madonna today her lived sexual biography is much more mundane and far less 'out there' than may be imagined. She opted for a traditional marriage with a multi-millionaire, has entered middle-age, given birth, written children's books, attends English elocution lessons and professes to aspects of religious spiritualism. Despite these practices, Madonna is an indisputable global icon. She is adept at 'working the sign', seamlessly producing her 'self' as the soft-focus, desirable cinematic sex symbol for popular music video.

As the ethnographic illustration reveals the identity of Madonna materialises through a series of global commodities including music, magazines, clothes, videos, DVDs and a dense scattering of mediated signs and images. For Bauman consumerism has replaced work as the main instrument of social cohesion to become 'the hub around which the life-world rotates' (1988, p. 76). He suggests that consumption appears to offer individuals choice, pleasure and seemingly endless 'model identities' to inhabit, but in actuality exerts a controlling force over individual freedom. However, it is interesting to note in this context that young women are not 'cultural dupes' but generate meanings from the commodities they acquire. Evidently Tina and Samantha use local peer-group cultures of femininity to assert a 'moral order' over what is acceptable and unacceptable in the making of new femininities. It is apparent that they are in part performing their femininities through active identification and dis-identification with Madonna and other global celebrities. These gender productions take place across the body of Madonna which, it is alleged, she uses to get attention. This can be achieved through hairstyles 'dyed ... no end of colours', dress and a sexually provocative 'hands on her hip' posture. The process of dis-identification is discursively enacted when Madonna's image is constructed as bad taste, revealed in 'silly pictures' in which 'she looks weird', 'like a man' and behaves, in sexually explicit fashion, 'like a whore'. Ideas of taste have been further explored by Bourdieu (1984) who suggests that identities are produced through practices of 'distinction', allowing individuals to differentiate themselves from others. Through the practices of consumption individuals and groups exercise cultural capital, express taste and articulate a sense of identity. Such practices point to the potential for consumption to become a 'moral project' (Miller, 1997, p. 47), a vehicle for the expression of identity.

In the end Samantha and Tina negotiate their femininities through these contradictory cultural representations, partially resolved through making distinctions between Madonna's old image where 'she looked really nice' and her Erotica performances. The careful regulation of gender is seen where a balance must be struck between lacking femininity (looking 'like a man'), and the enactment of an excessive, hyper-sexualised femininity (looking 'like a whore'). These comparisons enable Tina and Samantha to demarcate between liking Madonna's music while hating her act; a gendered and local–global split that enables them to perform a particular femininity fashioned through and against these complex contradictions. These interactions can productively be read alongside those of the young sexual cosmopolitans discussed by Farrer (1999) in Shanghai. They each demonstrate the energetic role of music to incite multiple identifications. In particular, they demonstrate how gender is performed through simulated acts of embodiment frequently achieved though an interplay of media signs and the acquisition of material goods. In such a reworking of the global there are possibilities for fantasy, identification and dissimulation to co-exist.

Virtual girls: new technologies, electronic media and cyber-feminism

For writers such as Baudrillard (1983) contemporary postmodern culture is characterised by endless simulation, image hallucination and simulacra. The eclectic plethora of images that abound in film, advertising and other media communication come to form a 'blizzard of signs' in which image and reality are indistinguishable. For Baudrillard this has given way to a type of 'hyper-reality' in which media signs have come to replace the meaning of objects and events, leading to what Featherstone (1998, p. 65) refers to as the 'aestheticization of everyday life'. Thus, in one of his most notorious statements Baudrillard (1995) boldly declared that the first Gulf War did not happen – referring instead to the way in which our experience of armed conflict is mediated through television, newspaper and other technologies that ultimately become the 'event' itself. In this way reality is said to be disposable in a world where signs, symbols and images become the ultimate media spectacle. Indeed, the act of modern warfare is often a simulated experience that takes place at a geographical remove and is signed through the use of computer images, virtual reality and technologies that permit distant 'surgical strikes' of unseen people and territories. Baudrillard's argument is that reality has been displaced, or transcended through such hyper-real events. In a postmodern world with no abiding meta-narratives we are caught within the 'eye of the storm', lost in a depthless culture where endless floating signifiers, artifice and affective intensities pervade.

In contrast to Baudrillard's focus on the dehumanising 'white noise' of electronic media, feminist theorists are exploring the possibilities for new media technologies to offer sites for the emergence of alternative ways of living and being. Here, the act of 'doing girl' is no longer restricted to the body or the physical confinement of a 'bedroom culture' (McRobbie, 1978) which necessitates face-to-face interaction. In a study of Australian girls, Bloustein (1998) has explored the bedroom as a space saturated by global merchandising notably through musical cultures. Aapola et al. (2005) further argue that the Internet has become an important site for girls to express themselves as individuals and, through dialogue with other girls, develop a collective identity and social attitude. The radical potential of virtual realities are further celebrated by 'cyberfeminists' such as Sadie Plant (1996, p. 182) who suggests cyberspace provides 'a dispersed, distributed emergence composed of links between women, women and computers, computers and communication links, connections and connectionist nets'. For Plant (1996), the ones and zeros of machine code resist the phallic economy of patriarchal binaries and can be productively compared to the type of fused replication envisioned in Donna Haraway's (1990) postmodern, hybrid and open-ended idea of a 'Cyborg Manifesto'. For Haraway the attraction of the cyborg lies in its inauthentic nature functioning as 'a kind of disassembled and reassembled, postmodern collective and personal self' (1990, p. 205).

The possibilities of virtual interactions are seen in Aapolo et al.'s (2005) description of the US 'Riot Grrrls' scene which comprises mainly white middle-class young women.

> In addition to face to face meetings, gigs, workshops and conventions, the Riot Grrrls network through zines … The writings take up a full range of themes and styles: angry, supportive, advice-giving, on issues like relationships, harassment, mental, physical and verbal abuse, and rape … Zines are often attempts to forge new communities beyond their locales. The capacity to build a global grrrl movement through these media is critical to many zine creators. (pp. 20–22)

The prevalence of websites and personal blogs suggests that young women have new media resources with which to develop identities and social networks. In this way the constrained space of the bedroom, once the sole refuge for girls on the margins of male-dominated youth culture, is transformed into a globally connected site, networked with other young women poised to challenge the gender order. The proliferation of electronic magazines, written by and for girls, points to a level of energy and agency active in redefining feminine identities, providing a commentary on the emergence of the 'virtual girl' of contemporary times.

However, ethnographic research suggests that while postmodernist notions of cyborgs, mutants and other replicants may be generative of new theories and ideas, we should not over-write the manner in which social relations are embedded in place. In a parallel study of grrrl zines in the UK and the US, Leonard (1998) also suggests that e-zines encourage young women to engage with new technology and establish a presence on the Internet. However she cautions that despite the ability to transcend place, the virtual world of new femininities is redolent with the rhetoric of geography and location. Girls refer to their activities in cyberspace as building a home, 'rearranging the furniture' (1998, p. 112), establishing a hideout and setting up a clubhouse – indicating that the metaphor of place retains meaning in the subterranean virtual networks of the digital age. This is particularly evident in Lincoln's (2001, pp. 7–8) ethnographic study of UK teenage girls where she claims, 'The bedroom is a biographical space. The posters, flyers, photographs, framed pictures, books, magazines, CDs and so on catalogue a teenage girl's youth cultural interests'. In this respect girl's bedrooms may well be connected to a global elsewhere but they are also material spaces of daily habitation.

Despite the possibilities afforded by new assemblages and bio-technologies it is clear that the relations between gender, computers and bodies are more complex in late modernity than previously imagined. The Internet has, for example, emerged as a dominant sphere for pornography and the transformation of women's bodies into a high-tech spectacle that blurs the virtual with the real, but in rather different ways to those anticipated by the corpus of cyber-feminists. Looking globally, we find that in Islamic countries like Iran where Sharia law is practised new media mobile communications are reconstituting sexual relationships for young women. Young couples, who are expected to refrain from sex until marriage, are deploying 'phone sex' as a new practice of intimacy to traverse distance and the bed-hopping hazard of getting found out. As Shahidian (1999) discovered in research with immigrant Iranians in Canada, older women are also not immune to the proliferation of mediated sexual cultures. With eye-opening astonishment, a 65-year-old Iranian woman recalls how Western media led to a new sexual awakening.

> All my life I lay underneath and my husband on top. A while ago, I was visiting some relatives and accidently watched a video which showed a couple making love. She was on top and he was lying under her. So it *is* possible to do it another way. (p. 204)

Such accounts inform us of the value of global ethnographies and their potential for rethinking gender across time and place.

Even so the meshing of gender relations, media technologies and bodies is not always as sexually liberating as it might appear and has been seen to engender high risk forms of sexual activity. For example, Iran is also witnessing a marked rise in the increase of HIV/ AIDS amongst new generations. In Tehran money, consumption and mobile technologies may enable more exploitative sexual relations to transpire. It is estimated that around 300,000 Iranian women work as prostitutes and many target boutique clothes shops where designer-wear, mini-skirts and skimpy tops are sold.

> Ahmed Reza, 23, admitted having accepted such offers. 'I was sitting outside the shop when two women came and said they wanted to try various manteaus [overcoats]', he said. 'They asked for a bargain and I offered them the standard discount. But they said, 'We cannot pay that – if you give us a good discount and your mobile number, we will serve you'. So I gave them more discount and got their numbers. (*The Guardian*, 3 January 2007)

These remarks provide a context for the more resplendent possibilities of the digital future initially envisaged by cyber-feminists. In youth cultures, technology and cyberspace though liberating in some aspects are also found to have powerful regulatory devices. Electronic bullying by text messaging, the irate disparagement of individual reputations through 'flaming' on e-message boards and, most notably, the phenomena of 'happy slapping', in which young people use mobile phone and computers to record other youth being beaten up, exist as the darker side of these virtual assemblages (see Kehily, 2007). Despite their appeal to global interconnectedness new technologies may also be more locally rooted than at first appears. It could be argued that the virtual scenes of MySpace, Facebook or Bebo, while suggesting new possibilities for female friendship, are themselves constrained by domestic geographies that give rise to an enhanced 'bedroom culture' which has long been a spatial prerequisite for modern girlhood leisure.

Young women are increasingly positioned as the ideal neo-liberal subjects of late modernity – flexible, technologically savvy, open to change and in control of their destiny. However, the contradictions of new media technologies are apparent where webcams, Skype and mobile phones may offer forms of communication and connectedness for young women but can also be seen as modern modes of governance and surveillance. The development of e-zines, message boards, virtual communities, text messaging, computer gaming and mobile communications suggest new ways of performing femininities but they have not necessarily signalled a break with the anxieties of the past. In popular media discourse when it comes to young women, fears persist about 'gossiping' on the phone, the unwarranted advances of sexual predators on the Internet or the threat of sexist text-messaging from young peers. If our observations are anything to go by young women must continue to live and rework the contradictions of femininity in the digital age if the fluid potential of virtual girl and cyborg feminism is to be realised.

Concluding comments

In this paper we have sought to understand global femininities as a gendered performance styled to fit the contours of late modern social practice. We have explored the local–global connections young women make through engagement with popular media culture. In looking at the relationship between new femininities and the products of global culture, we place our own UK school-based data alongside ethnographic studies from other geographical locations. Looking across differently situated accounts has enabled us to locate our study within the wider landscape of globalisation and social change. In order to extend beyond the spatially bounded practice of institutional approaches we have sought to follow some of the connections young women make with global commodities and consider how this impacts upon their understandings of subjectivity. In discussing these themes we have considered the impact of cultural globalisation from below by focusing upon the texture of young women's everyday encounters and their engagements with mediated versions of femininity. To return to our original research questions – concerned with how global products are consumed, their relationship to new femininities and the meaning of place – we found that global media cultures play an integral part in young women's lives and are an important resource for creating meanings, shaping identities and forging relationships. Through an engagement with the 'flow' of cultural signs and material objects, young women appropriate, adapt and subvert globally marketed versions of femininity. In doing so, they work through and speak back to the tropes of cultural globalisation in particular ways. This has meaning for the youth cultures and the schooling communities they inhabit.

In considering gender as a global project we have been inspired by ethnographies that draw attention to the significance of place and the bearing this has upon 'doing girl' in late modernity. We have used these international insights to broaden the geographies of gender. It is here that the value of looking at young femininities globally can be seen. Television, film, music, dance and new media technologies form part of the global circuit of culture where gender signs are transmitted and through which new femininities are imaginatively conveyed. Subject positions made available though global encounters may then be reworked in ways that respond to the values and norms of the local environment, offering points of negotiation, connection and dissonance. This would indicate that media signs cannot be extrapolated from everyday life, to be hygienically decoded outside of their daily contexts. Global femininities rely upon place-based forms of recognition and action in order to become locally meaningful. They are further dependent upon the youthful communities of interpretation that interact with and serve to trouble gender anew.

Notes

1. Beginning with our collaborative research on gender and sexuality in the early 1990s, based in two large comprehensive schools in the West Midlands conurbation, interviewing and observing young people aged 14–15 years and 16–17 years (see Kehily & Nayak, 1997; Nayak & Kehily, 1996). The paper also includes data gathered independently from one another, in the West Midlands (14–15 years) and a further school in London (14–16 years).
2. Many of the British soap operas are fictionalised through a strong regional or local dimension which has a powerful appeal on the national imagination. For example, *Coronation Street* is associated with Manchester, *Emmerdale* with rural Yorkshire, the now defunct series *Brookside* with Liverpool and *EastEnders* with London's East End. Although these representations are of course imaginative constructions the focus on place and 'ordinary' working-class folk is an attempt to achieve authenticity within the realist format.

References

Aapola, S., Gonick, M., & Harris, A. (2005). *Young femininity, girlhood, power and social change.* Basingstoke, UK: Palgrave.

Ang, I. (1985). *Watching Dallas: Soap opera and the melodramatic imagination.* London: Methuen.

Barker, C. (1998). 'Cindy is a slut': Moral identities and moral responsibility in the 'soap talk' of British Asian girls. *Sociology, 32*(1), 65–81.

Baudrillard, J. (1983). *Simulations.* New York: Semiotext(e).

Baudrillard, J. (1995). *The Gulf War did not take place.* Sydney: Power Press.

Bauman, Z. (1988). *Freedom.* Milton Keynes, UK: Open University Press.

Beck, U. (1992). *Risk society: Towards a new modernity.* London: Sage.

Blackman, L. (2004). Self help, media cultures and the production of female psychopathology. *European Journal of Cultural Studies, 7*(2), 219–236.

Bloustein, G. (1998). 'It's different to a mirror 'cos it talks to you': Teenage girls, video cameras and identity. In S. Howard (Ed.), *Wired up: Young people and electronic media* (pp. 115–133). London: UCL Press.

Bourdieu, P. (1984). *Distinction: A social critique of the judgement of taste.* Cambridge, MA: Harvard University Press.

Buckingham, D., & Bragg, S. (2003). *Young people, sex and the media: The facts of life?.* Basingstoke, UK: Palgrave.

Burawoy, M., Blum, J.A., George, S., Gille, Z., Gowan, T., Haney, L., Klawiter, M., Lopez, S.H., Riain, S.O., & Thayer, M. (2000). *Global ethnography: Forces, connections, and imaginations in a postmodern world.* Berkeley: University of California Press.

Dwyer, C. (1999). Negotiations of femininity and identity for young British Muslim women. In N. Laurie, C. Dwyer, S. Holloway & F. Smith (Eds.), *Geographies of new femininities* (pp. 135–152). Harlow, UK: Pearson.

Farrer, J. (1999). Disco 'super-please leave culture': Consuming foreign sex in the Chinese disco. *Sexualities, 2*(2), 147–166.

Featherstone, M. (1998). *Consumer culture and postmodernism* (2nd ed.). London: Sage.

Giddens, A. (1991). *Modernity and self identity: self and society in the late modern age.* Cambridge: Polity.

Gill, R. (2006, April). *Re-writing the romance? Chick lit and post feminism.* Paper presented at the ESRC New Femininities seminar, Milton Keynes, UK.

Hall, S. (2000). Who needs 'identity'? In P. du Gay, J. Evans, & P. Redman (Eds.), *Identity: A reader.* London: Sage/The Open University.

Haraway, D. (1990). A manifesto for cyborgs: Science, technology and socialist feminism in the 1980s. In L.J. Nicholson (Ed.), *Feminism/Postmodernism.* London: Routledge.

Henderson, S., Taylor, R., & Thomson, S. (2002). In touch: Young people, communication and technologies. *Information, Communication and Society*, 5, 494–512.

Hermes, J. (1995). *Reading women's magazines.* Cambridge: Polity.

Johnson, R.J. (1986). The story so far. In D. Punter (Ed.), *Introduction to contemporary cultural studies.* Harlow: Longman.

Kehily, M.J. (2002). *Sexuality, gender and schooling: Shifting agendas in sexual learning.* London: Routledge.

Kehily, M.J. (2007). Playing. In M.J. Kehily (Ed.), *Understanding youth: Perspectives, identities and practices* (pp. 249–281). London: Sage/The Open University.

Kehily, M.J., & Nayak, A (1997). Lads and laughter: Humour and the production of heterosexual hierarchies. *Gender and Education*, 9, 69–87.

Lash, S., & Urry, J. (1999). *Economies of signs and space* (2nd ed.). London: Sage.

Leonard, M. (1998). Paper planes: Travelling the new grrrl geographies. In T. Skelton & G. Valentine (Eds.), *Cool places, geographies of youth cultures* (pp. 101–118). London: Routledge.

Lincoln, S. (2001). *Teenage girls bedroom cultures: Codes versus zones.* Unpublished manuscript, Manchester Metropolitan University.

Mac an Ghaill, M. (1994). *The making of men.* Buckingham, UK: Open University Press.

Malinowski, B. (1922). *Argonauts of the Western Pacific.* London: Routledge.

Massey, D. (1994). *A global sense of place, in space, place and gender* (2nd ed.). Oxford: Polity Press.

McGrellis, S. (2005). Pure and bitter spaces: Gender, identity and territory in Northern Irish youth transitions. *Gender and Education*, *17*, 499–514.

McRobbie, A. (1978). Working class girls and the culture of femininity. In *Centre for Contemporary Cultural Studies, Women take issue.* London: Hutchinson.

McRobbie, A. (2002). Notes on 'What not to wear' and post feminist symbolic violence. *Sociological Review, 52*(2), 97–109.

McRobbie, A. (2006, February). *Top girls: Young women and the post feminist social contract.* Paper presented at ESRC Identities and Social Action public lecture, Milton Keynes, UK.

Miller, D. (1992). The young and the restless in Trinidad: A case study of the local and global in mass consumption. In R. Silverstone & E. Hirsch (Eds.), *Consuming technologies.* London: Routledge.

Miller, D. (1997). Consumption and its consequences. In H. MacKay (Ed.), *Consumption and everyday life.* London: Sage/The Open University.

Nayak, A. (2003). *Race, place and globalisation: Youth cultures in a changing world.* Oxford: Berg.

Nayak, A., & Kehily, M.J. (1996). Playing it straight: Masculinities, homophobias and schooling. *Journal of Gender Studies, 5*(2), 211–230.

Nayak, A., & Kehily, M.J. (2008). *Gender, youth and culture: Young masculinities and femininities.* Basingstoke, UK: Palgrave.

Pilkington, H., Omel'chenko, E., Flynn, M., Bliudina, U., & Starkova, E. (2002). *Looking West? Cultural globalisation and Russian youth cultures.* University Park: Pennsylvania State University Press.

Plant, S. (1996). On the matrix: Cyberfeminist simulations. In R. Shields (Ed.), *Cultures of the Internet: Virtual space, real histories, living bodies.* London: Sage.

Radway, J. (1984). *Reading the romance: Women, patriarchy and popular literature.* Chapel Hill: University of North Carolina Press.

Salo, E. (2003). Negotiating gender and personhood in the new South Africa. *European Journal of Cultural Studies, 6*, 345–365.

Shahidian, H. (1999). Gender and sexuality among immigrant Iranians in Canada. *Sexualities, 2*(2), 189–222.

Skeggs, B. (1997). *Formations of class and gender: Becoming respectable.* London: Sage.

Skeggs, B. (2004). *Class, self, culture.* London: Routledge.

Thomson, R., & Taylor, R. (2005). Between cosmopolitanism and the locals, mobility as a resources in the transition to adulthood. *Young, 13*, 327–342.

Thorne, B. (1993). *Gender play: Girls and boys at school.* Brunswick, NJ: Rutgers University Press.

Vidmar-Horvat, K. (2005). The globalisation of gender: Ally McBeal in post-socialist Slovenia. *European Journal of Cultural Studies, 8*, 239–255.

Walkerdine, V. (1990). *Schoolgirl fictions.* London: Verso.

Walkerdine, V., Lucey, H., & Melody, J. (2001). *Growing up girl: Psychosocial explorations of gender and class.* Basingstoke, UK: Palgrave.

Willis, P. (1977). *Learning to labour: How working class kids get working class jobs.* Farnborough, UK: Saxon House.

Winship, J. (1987). A girl needs to get streetwise: Magazines for the 1980s. *Feminist Review, 2*, 25–46.

Whyte, W.F. (1943). *Street corner society: The social structure of an Italian slum.* Chicago: Chicago University Press.

(re)Imagining the global, rethinking gender in education

Kellie Burns

Introduction

> ... a partially coherent set of practices ... is starting to be produced by the cultural circuit of capital, a kind of instrumental phenomenology which can produce subjects that disclose the world as uncertain and risky but also able to be stabilized (in profitable ways) by the application of particular kinds of intense agency that are creative, entrepreneurial and businesslike. (Nigel Thrift, *Knowing Capitalism*, 2005, p. 98)

> Margaret Thatcher articulated deep dissatisfacton with prevailing standards of education. She saw high standards of education (defined in terms of qualifications) as increasingly important if Britain was to compete in the global economy, and deregulation as the only means of reversing what she saw as the worst aspects of post-war collectivist education policy. Thus the raising of standards and the modernizing of the UK entrepreneurial culture constituted the main government agenda for education – an agenda described by some as neo-liberalism. (Madeline Arnot, Miriam David, & Gaby Weiner, *Closing the Gender Gap: Postwar Education and Social Change*, 1999, p. 84)

> Young women are leading examples of DIY citizenship, but they are also invested in as key players in the comforting narratives of national continuity in times of change, mass movements of people around the world, and the loosening of traditional social bonds within communities. (Anita Harris, *Future Girl: Young Women in the 21st Century*, 2004a, p. 80)

Each of the epigraphs above speaks to the ways in which entrepreneurial language now permeates both state policy and the everyday practices of individual citizens. As government policy becomes increasingly corporatised and underscored by neo-liberal visions of an entrepreneurial society, so too do various other socio-cultural institutions such as public education. This type of economic rationalisation is justified by governments, at least in part, as an important measure for ensuring national citizens are equipped with the right 'skills' to cope with the changing conditions associated with living in an increasingly 'global' world (Arnot, David, & Weiner, 1999). Contemporary citizens become what Nigel Thrift (2005) refers to as 'mineral resource[s] with attitude ... self-willed subject[s] whose industry will boost the powers of the state to compete economically, and will also produce a more dynamic citizenry' (p. 98). Being productive, resourceful and self-managing is what makes individuals successful and viable community members within the current neo-liberal governmental order. As such, citizens take on the task of being 'creative', 'imaginative' and 'entrepreneurial' and deploy a range of strategies for self-management in order to remain, on the one hand, adequately mobile, flexible and adaptable, and, on the other hand, aware and in control of the risks associated with living more 'globally'.

A growing body of research asks how these carefully prescribed skill sets have influenced the production of gendered subjectivities in educational contexts (Arnot, 2002; Arnot et al., 1999; Davies & Saltmarsh, 2007; Harris, 2004a, 2004b, 2006; Hopkins, 2002; McLeod, 2004; Youdell, 2006). Educational reform in the 1980s and 1990s (which, these various authors explain, was one part of a much broader neo-liberal reform of public and welfare services) discredited social justice frameworks and policies aimed at identifying the systemic inequities experienced by certain minoritarian groups (Arnot et al., 1999). 'Equality' was no longer achieved through policies that held the state responsible (economically and/or ideologically) for social injustices, but rather through the implementation of policies and practices that defined the state as the great equaliser of *economic* opportunities. In schools this was achieved through the implementation of more rigidly standardised models of teaching, learning and assessment (Apple, 2006; Arnot, 2002; Arnot et al., 1999; Marginson, 1997; McLeod, 2004; Whitty, Power, & Halpin, 1998). Of course, with these standards came a much broader overhaul of 'school values' that focused on training young people to become self-managing individuals with an eye to their economic futures.

With time a 'gender gap' emerged in most western schooling contexts, with girls[1] achieving much better test scores than they had in previous decades in comparison to boys (Arnot et al., 1999). The number of girls achieving in traditionally 'male' curriculum areas also increased, and it appeared that girls were harnessing post-school opportunities in greater numbers. If one allows the logic of these educational reforms to run its 'natural' course, a set of assumptions about girls' gendered subjectivities emerge. School curriculum standards are invested in a knowledge economy that is intimately bound to the market. Achievement is possible by honing a range of self-management skills that encourage individualism and valorise consumption. Girls in schools are achieving higher standards in greater numbers. Achieving certain skills at school and becoming self-managing and economically self-sustainable young adults grants a greater number of young women passage into the national fold. As intelligible national citizens, these girls become actors in an increasingly significant global marketplace. According to the logic of these reforms, the act of constituting oneself as girl-subject 'at school' is inextricably linked to the capacity to imagine oneself as a certain type of global citizen-subject beyond one's schooling years. An idealised model of the girl-student emerges; she is self-motivated and self-managing and is working to ensure her inclusion both in her national citizenry and in the broader global marketplace.

This chapter focuses on understanding not only the cause-and-effect relationships neo-liberal reforms in schools construct between gender-based achievement, citizenship and global living, but also the mechanisms with which these types of linear relationships are produced and governed. In particular, it is concerned with the role the *imagination* plays in producing and managing normative meanings around gender and global citizenship both 'at school' and within the broader cultural practices of everyday living. The chapter argues that as a technology of governance, the *imagination* is bound to a range of self-managing strategies individuals must deploy in order to become intelligible 'global' subjects. For girls, the imagination operates as an important tool with which they can construct and manage their global selves alongside normative meanings around gender and sexuality.

However, before beginning to understand how girls' sexed/gendered subjectivities are mediated through the 'global imaginary', one must first consider the critical weight of the word 'globalisation'. So much of the scholarly work done around globalisation and education presumes to know what globalisation *is*. This paper takes a step back, not only to rethink what globalisation *is* but also to ask what globalisation *does* – what it produces, normalises, assumes or limits. As such, the first two sections of the discussion focus on establishing a new theoretical framework for 'thinking the global' in relation to studies of gender and education. These sections make two important critical contributions: for one, they stress the importance of questions of government (Foucault, 1991) to research on 'globalisation', and, for another, they begin to map out how the imagination might be understood as a governmental technology that limits the possibilities of what it means to be a global citizen-subject. The final section of the paper demonstrates the merits of this new critical framework to studies of gender and education by beginning to tease out the ways in which the global imagination produces and governs the relationships between girls' schooling achievements and their role as actors and agents in a 'global world'.

Globalisation as governmentality

As suggested above, the aim of this first section is to establish how Foucault's analytics of governmentality (1991) enriches and extends studies of 'globalisation' (Larner & Walters, 2002, 2004). Foucault's concern for government is about tracing the uneven operations of power relations that 'conduct the conduct' of individuals and normalise the practices of everyday living. He identifies what Colin Gordon refers to as particular 'systems of thinking about the nature of the practice of government (who can govern; what governing is; what or who is governed)' (Gordon, 1991, p. 3) and argues that a functional 'art of government' is one 'capable of making some form of that activity thinkable and practicable both to its practitioners and to those upon whom it was practised' (1991, p. 3). In other words, for Foucault, an 'art of government' is one that not only functions logically for those administering order, but also for those upon whom practices of order are being enacted. As the introductory reflections of this chapter suggest, neo-liberalism is a very good example of an effective 'art of government'. It emphasises individual responsibility and self-care such that individuals take up the task of ensuring their own social and economic wellbeing. It assumes that all citizens have 'equal' opportunities regardless of their differences and that economic and social 'success' is simply about taking responsibility for oneself and one's community. Financial, social or health-related deficiencies cannot be blamed on government policy or practice, but rather on the individual and his or her inability to (self-)manage appropriately (Rose, 1999). Neo-liberalism's appeal, and indeed its success, rests with its promise to reward individuals' hard work and with the idea that one's economic and social well-being is inextricably linked to one's level of self-efficacy.

Governmentality studies, with their concern for mapping certain 'arts of government', are useful in rethinking how we come, critically speaking, to studies of the global. Wendy Larner and William Walters (2002) suggest that too often critical work around globalisation sets out to 'capture the substance of [global] change along one or several axes' (p. 1). These works ask what globalisation *is* rather than considering what it *does* or how it *acts*. Conversely, introducing questions of governance allows one to focus on the mentalities of the global, how globalisation acts to organise, discipline, normalise, expand and shrink at the level of 'the local' or the individual subject. In doing so, analyses shift away from questions concerned with the *why* of power and allows one to think about the *how* of power. Less concern is given to understanding why certain spaces or people are affected by new waves of global change. Instead, they ask how these 'waves' are produced as 'new' and 'evolving' conditions of the present and how individuals define and organise themselves as global subjects from within these 'novel' configurations.

Larner and Walters also argue that while reactions to globalisation are plentiful, globalisation theories are anchored to a relatively narrow set of ontological starting points. They argue that much of the current thinking around globalisation tends to be somewhat repetitive, offering a rather narrow set of responses to both the macro- and micro-level changes that are taking place around the world. Very complex economic, cultural and ideological shifts are captured by much less diverse sets of theoretical approaches. Furthermore, these shifts are often tied to a narrow set of spatial and temporal metaphors that envision the world as either being dissolved into a single space or expanded in infinite directions. These two approaches to 'the global' commonly characterise it within a homogeneous/heterogeneous binary (Appadurai, 1996; Grossberg, 1996; Larner & Walters, 2002).

Theories of homogeneity personify the global as a set of forces that takes over, imposes upon, Americanises, Westernises, (neo-)Colonises or Imperialises the national and/or local. Marshall McLuhan and Bruce Power's (1989) 'global village' epitomises this critical position as it envisions local cultures becoming assimilated into a transnational cultural monolith. The notion of a global village implies that a world once organised into geographically, economically, culturally and politically distinct nation-states is slowly seeing the demise of its regulated territorial borders. The rising power of multinational corporations, the large-scale migration of people from the Third World to the First World have become symbols of globalisation's homogenising impact.

In contrast to theories of homogeneity, theories of heterogeneity describe the intensifying pastiche that marks global living. Living in a global world means living in a world where everything is so multiply coded, endlessly diverse and irregular that one can no longer claim to belong to a fixed place or to have a clear sense of identity. From this critical perspective the spatial and temporal effects of globalisation do not necessarily thrive on the erasure of difference and the swallowing up of borders, as suggested by theories of homogeneity, but, instead, globalisation is seen as a set of practices that multiply and intensify cultural differences, modes of production, geographic territories and ways of communicating. Whereas McLuhan suggests that difference is erased by the blanketing force of the global, the shrinking of the world into a single space, theories of heterogeneity maintain that difference is lost to the speed and intensity through which objects, events and ideologies are (re)produced. Theories of this kind construct a world whose order is so various that it is difficult to maintain clarity around the notions of culture or identity. Local or national identities can no longer be understood as bounded constructs, but rather are merely mediations within a rapidly changing and borderless world. Images and ideas are so overlapping and various that to speak of 'culture' as something distinct or tangible, or of 'nations' as somehow contained within geographical boundaries or borders is meaningless.

Both of these critical perspectives have been widely critiqued. While it is beyond the scope of this discussion to overview all of these critiques, a brief engagement with some of the key criticisms is useful in highlighting how governmentality studies offer a critical space 'beyond' homogenising/heterogenising theories of the global. Perhaps the most significant charge against theories of homogeneity is the failure to account for the ways in which power remains unevenly distributed. Viewing the global as a singular and unidirectional force and positioning the nation-state as being under attack fail to recognise that in many cases the borders and divisions between nations have *deepened* over the past three decades, with citizens clinging to nationalist and patriotic discourses in times of greater mobility, instability and change. Similarly, heterogenising models of the global are critiqued for the power they afford to the global. The mourning of lost identities, be they cultural, national or sub-cultural, is problematic for it re-inscribes each of these as a contained or stable entity. In particular, it positions the nation as a fixed and entirely tangible structure and undermines minoritarian critiques of the nation as a social and political entity whose regulatory practices exclude those who do not adhere to certain norms. Suggesting that nation-states and identities are lost entities infers that both of these somehow existed *before* globalisation in a pure and essential manner. This upholds a linear nostalgia for 'the way things used to be', and the global becomes somehow unearthly, extra-territorial or omnipotent (Larner & Walters, 2002).

Whether one is describing globalisation as a process of homogenisation or hetero-genisation, the repetition of this dichotomy positions globalisation in a predatory role, linking the inevitable repercussions of global living with the inability of minoritarian cultures to produce an effective counter-hegemonic polity. According to Larner and Walters (2002), in the repetition of these types of binary narratives, the term 'globalisation' essentializes, singularises and ontologizes irregular and contradictory sets of transnational conditions that eventually come to constitute 'the [globalization] story we all know' (Larner & Walters, 2002, p. 1). Their concern is therefore with the ways in which the bodies of knowledge used to make sense of globalisation translate into modes of being that produce the grounds upon which objects (e.g. the nation, the local, the global, capital) and subjects (e.g. the global citizen, the national citizen, and, in the case of this chapter, global standards, national curricula, global students, global schools, etc.) are produced and governed. In other words, Larner and Walters ask how globalisation *governs*.

Unlike both theories of homogeneity and theories of heterogeneity, understanding globalisation as governmentality encourages a range of new ontological starting points for studying 'the global'. Rather than describing what globalisation *is*, one begins to ask how everything we have come to know as 'globalisation', including theories of globalisation themselves, brings with it new modes of order and regulation that directly impact upon the lives of individuals or certain populations. In focusing on how the global governs, Larner and Walters (2002) introduce a second important conceptual shift; they suggest that globalisation can be viewed as an assemblage or *dispositif*. The *dispositif*[2] is a term borrowed from Foucault, who approaches concepts, terms or institutions such as sexuality, capitalism, the prison, the hospital and madness as overlapping and conflicting assemblages (Larner & Walters, 2002; Rabinow & Rose, 2003). For Foucault (1994), a *dispositif* is:

a resolutely heterogeneous grouping composing discourses, institutions, architectural arrangements, policy decisions, laws, administrative measures, scientific statements, philosophic, moral and philanthropic propositions; in sum, the said and un-said, these are elements of an apparatus. The apparatus itself is the network that can be established between these elements. (p. 298)

The *dispositif* becomes a useful tool for studies of governmentality because it allows relations of power within a given socio-political terrain to be viewed as diffuse and uneven. One no longer goes searching for the essence or substance of a social structure or event (in a way that symptomatic readings, psychoanalysis or semiotics might for instance) in order to understand what it *is*. Instead one seeks to understand what it *does*, how it operates as 'a machinic contraption whose purpose in this case is control and management of certain characteristics of a population' (Rabinow and Rose, 2003, p. x).

Viewing globalisation as a *dispositif* turns a singular term like globalisation into a web-like network of mechanisms and effects that are never entirely tangible. Rather than seeing globalisation as a finite or linear set of processes it becomes a vast assemblage of competing and contradictory forces that organise and manage populations. All of the work one does in globalisation studies is thus a part of the globalisation apparatus. How one critically speaks or writes about globalisation contributes to the defining, ordering and regulation of the parameters around what is 'knowable' about the global. As Larner and Walters (2002) explain, the *dispositif* demands that researchers interrogate the processes and practices of naming and theorising, questioning 'the conditions of truth and practice under which [globalization] acquires a certain positivity' (p. 6).

Viewing globalisation as a *dispositif* disrupts 'the story we all know' about the 'global', 'globalisation' and about what it means to be a global subject. Where this paper's broader focus on the relationships between gendered subjectivities at school and globalisation are concerned, the presumed linearity between girls' school success and their capacity to become viable global citizens is unsettled and a series of important questions emerge: When schools are 'preparing' young girls to become suitably 'global', what is the global assumed to be? How do the assumptions one makes about what globalisation *is* presuppose the skill sets young people are being asked to acquire at school? In working to become viable global citizen-subjects, what practices of self-management must young people take up? How are these 'global' skill sets and the practices of self-management they demand gendered? How are girls in particular expected to imagine themselves as active and agentic global citizen-subjects? Finally, how are these skills and self-management strategies linked to broader neo-liberal governmental policies and practices?

Before addressing specific questions of this kind, there is a great deal more that needs to be stated concerning how, that is, through what tactics and techniques, the global *governs*. The section that follows focuses specifically on how the *imagination* operates as one of a number of tools or technologies used by individuals in their attempt to constitute themselves as intelligible global citizen-subjects.

Imagining the global otherwise

Arjun Appadurai (1996) argues that the number and variety of reactions to the term globalisation are indicative of the ways in which it features as a source of anxiety for various people around the world. When one speaks or writes about globalisation one is engaging with a concept that is articulated in multiple directions, for a variety of reasons and is emotionally underscored by a variety of symbolic and material implications, all of which, in the words of Appadurai (1996), have left globalisation 'marked by a new role for the imagination of social life' (p. 31).

It is worth resting for a moment on Appadurai's use of the imagination and the imagined in relation to the shifts and changes in 'global living'. He argues that, 'the image, the imagined, the imaginary – these are all terms that direct us to something critical and new in global cultural processes: *the imagination as a social practice*' (Appadurai, 1996, p. 31, emphasis added). He acknowledges that the transnational movements that mark contemporary living are by no means new phenomena – many other periods over the past two centuries have experienced equally as significant changes in the production, circulation and distribution of capital, peoples and goods. While he makes this point clear, he does insist that electronic mediation and the mass migration of peoples 'create a new force field for social relations globally' (Appadurai, 1999, p. 230). Moreover, Appadurai (1996) argues that in this current phase of global living there *is* a new role assigned to the imagination and that this change should inspire new theoretical approaches to the global:

> The imagination has become an organized field of social practices, a form of work (in the sense of both labor and culturally organized practice), and a form of negotiation between sites of agency (individuals) and globally defined fields of possibility. This unleashing of the imagination links the play of pastiche (in some settings) to the terror and coercion of states and their competitors. The imagination is now central to all forms of agency, is itself a social fact, and the key component of the new global order. (p. 31)

Appadurai extends Benedict Anderson's notion of 'imagined communities' (Anderson, 1983) to suggest that it is now more appropriate to say that we live in 'imagined worlds' (Appadurai, 1996, p. 33). Imagined worlds are composed of various irregular flows that are never uni-directional and never wholly tangible. He puts forth a framework to describe the landscape of these imagined worlds that involves five overlapping -*scapes*. These -*scapes* embody the 'fundamental disjunctures between economy, culture, and politics that ... have only begun to [be] theorise[d]' (p. 31): *ethnoscapes, mediascapes, technoscapes, financescapes* and *ideoscapes*. The head noun -*scape* describes fluid landscapes that speak to a broad set of global trends as far-reaching as financial or capital flows, to styles and fashions that circulate worldwide. The simultaneity of openings and closures, surpluses and deficits, consumers and producers articulated in Appadurai's conceptualisation of -*scapes* counter earlier approaches that understand globalisation in binary terms. He moves away from over-simplified analyses of globalisation as he attempts to analyse the complex and contradictory relationships that mark the symbolic and material flow of people, ideas, images and cultures in various directions around the world. The global is no longer positioned as an all-encompassing external power for in his estimate, viewing globalisation as a unidirectional entity fails to account for the pace at which various ideas or trends introduced from particular metropolises are immediately culturally contextualised – what he calls 'indigenized' (Appadurai, 1996, p. 32) – by minoritarian cultural groups.

Appadurai also stresses that imagined worlds act as sites for resisting dominant ruling forces. He contends that people can utilise their positionality within a given imagined world to, 'contest and sometimes even subvert the imagined worlds of the official mind and of the entrepreneurial mentality that surround them' (Appadurai, 1996, p. 33). As the 'official mind' and the 'entrepreneurial mentality' imagine normative models of global citizenship, individuals and communities can imagine their (global) worlds otherwise – in opposition to these dominant forces of power. The imagination thus becomes a tactic for resisting and/or surviving the messiness of global living.

While clearly significant in moving away from traditional critical readings of the global, there are some limitations with Appadurai's notion of *imagined worlds* and with his description of global *-scapes*. In his own attempt to theorise globalisation outside existing homo-/heterogenising binaries, Lawrence Grossberg (1996) suggests that while Appadurai's *-scapes* are arguably more fluid than previous models of global living, they are still modular in form. Grossberg queries the need to name and frame the irregularity of global living in such absolute terms. What, he asks, gets accounted for within new theories of the global and what gets elided? In other words, how did Appadurai (1996) arrive at five particular *-scapes* when what he is describing is an irregular assemblage of endlessly shifting processes and forces? Grossberg also argues that the relationship between 'the global' and 'the local' remains under-theorised in Appadurai's work. He maintains that Appadurai focuses on reworking the content of 'the global' and providing a revised model of the global that is simply more deterritorialised, rhizomatic and chaotic. In doing so Appadurai repositions the local as a *place* of resistance, while the 'global' remains a large and omnipotent space that continuously impacts upon the actions of local lives – albeit a less-locatable and more fractured one. Grossberg argues that what needs to be theorised is less the *content* of the global (*what it is*) and more the changing relationships *between* the global and the local (*what it does*).

Appadurai's suggestion that the imagination has become 'an organized field of social practices' through which individuals and/or communities oppose and/or survive the conditions of global living also sits uneasily with Grossberg. Of most concern to him is that Appadurai's notion of 'imagined worlds' relies heavily on Anderson's idea of the nation as an 'imagined community'. Grossberg problematises Anderson's idea that the nation is an entirely social and cultural fabrication built on the commonalities of its citizen-constituents. To this end he asks: 'Why is the nation not a *real* community, always built on the basis of imagined commonalities? Or is there even another possibility for understanding such communities?' (Grossberg, 1996, p. 174, emphasis added). Grossberg's questions imply that there is more than one way of understanding the relationships between the national community and the realm of the 'imaginary'. He suggests that it might be more productive to rethink the nation as a *real* entity, that is, as the material outcome and/or effects of *imagined* commonalities between various groups of people. In making this shift, customs, nostalgia, memories and longings for place fold into an imaginary set of commonalities that with time and a great deal of investment shape nations in *real, material* ways and inform normative definitions around citizenship and nationhood. The nation thus becomes less a fictive template upon which cultures write themselves, and instead becomes the material outcomes of imagined identities, histories, geographies and so on.

The shift that Grossberg makes in his critique of Appadurai's work is a subtle but important one, and one that returns this discussion to questions of government. Like Larner and Walters, Grossberg identifies a need to interrogate the critical tools scholars use to make sense of globalisation. He argues that too often the global is married to a series of presuppositions that determine in advance what the global is, where the global is or when the global acts. Appadurai's 'alternative' morphology of the global demonstrates that the demands for order and structure engendered in most dominant modes of thought are difficult if not impossible to escape. Grossberg insists that it is not enough to simply formulate new theories that describe the global in more chaotic and irregular terms. In his estimate, there is a need to make theories themselves chaotic and irregular enough that they are able to respond to the shifting dynamics that have come to be named 'globalisation'. He argues that new questions need to be generated around those concepts and constructs of 'the global' that have become the most familiar – nation, culture, place, space, local, global and so on. Given Larner and Walters' concern for how the global governs, and Grossberg's critique of Appadurai's *imagined worlds*, how might the notion of the global imagination be approached differently? Moreover, how might thinking the global imagination otherwise shift the questions we ask about the relationships between globalisation and gender within critical education studies?

To begin to address these two questions a couple of additional observations about Appadurai's use of the imagination are necessary. It seems that for him the imagination operates as both the space of dominant 'imagined' ideologies and as the 'faculty' through which individuals resist or subvert the impositions of global living, if sometimes only fleetingly or momentarily. The imagination engenders the hope and potentiality of becoming otherwise or of inhabiting an elsewhere. It is both that which imposes sanctions on citizens and communities and that which opens up a space for new ways of constituting one's identity. In his description of the push and pull of the global imaginary there is a sense that resistance or survival within the global requires new forms of labour, the ability to *imagine* outside or against the boundaries of the dominant social imaginary. Whether intentional or not, there seems to be a dichotomy created between the real and the imaginary where the imagination becomes both a space for political reconstitution and the impetus or force behind creative practices of resistance.

In contrast, the *imagination* can be said to operate within a broader set of neo-liberal imperatives that both produce and govern normative and desirable models of global subjectivities. In making this shift, the *imagination*, in particular the promise for personal and political agency and the transformation it engenders, is a modality of governance that reinforces a neo-liberal, market-driven logic that sees the global citizen-subject as an entrepreneur and manager of the self, and of others. The imagination functions as a mechanism of order and regulation that demands that global subjects constantly imagine themselves in various new ways (or in 'old ways' couched in 'the new'). So while for Appadurai the imagination seems to offer the space 'in between' in which one is called upon to *be* and in which one *becomes* through processes of resistance, for the purposes of this argument the imagination is understood to be a tool or technology of (global) governance and a site for regulating the conduct and actions of so-called 'global citizens'. The imagination becomes a vehicle through which one attempts to locate the elsewhere, the beyond, the otherwise of global living through various practices of self-regulation. Although never explicitly stated, Appadurai seems to designate the imagination as a biological or psychological faculty of some sort such that drawing upon the imagination is about making use of some natural or psycho-social dimension of the self. For the purposes of this discussion, the imagination is not biological or psychological, rather it is technical.

Having established the importance of asking how the global governs and having suggested that the imagination is a key mechanism with which individuals produce and govern themselves as intelligible global citizen-subjects, the chapter now considers the significance of these theoretical shifts to rethinking the relationships between globalisation, education and the production of gendered subjectivities. The section that follows makes two key arguments: first, it suggests that girls' gendered identities (both at school and beyond) are increasingly mediated through discourses of the global imaginary and by the discourses of self-governance and consumption bound to the imaginative; second, it argues that asking what role the imagination plays in the project of 'making' and 'managing' global citizen-subjects is vital to understanding emergent models of girl-citizenship both within and outside schooling contexts.

Becoming global girl-citizens

The questions posed here about the global imagination contribute to an existing body of scholarly work concerned with the ways in which girls' citizenship is mediated through discourses of economics and consumption. This work highlights how girls are expected to forego basic social and civil rights in exchange for new sets of consumptive rights and freedoms (see, for instance, Best, 2004; Harris, 2004a, 2004b, 2006; Hopkins, 2002; McRobbie, 2000). Girls are asked to manage the 'uncertain' conditions of contemporary global living by investing in a range of entrepreneurial, self-management strategies in order to become 'responsible self-made citizens' (Harris, 2006, p. 268). 'Being a girl' and 'becoming a young woman' are mediated through discourses of leadership, responsibility and self-sufficiency. However, a girl's sense of responsibility and personal direction are less about repositioning herself as a more active public citizen, and more about ensuring her economic independence from the state. Apart from being economically self-sufficient, the idealised girl-citizen is also called upon to be creative, inventive, and flexible enough to capitalise on the new forms of freedom and choice afforded to her in this so-called 'global' age.

The values assigned to the new girl-citizen are reproduced in schooling policies and practices in a variety of ways.[3] Emergent models of consumer citizenship have become increasingly linked to academic performance at school. A young person's economic success and her or his capacity to be an active agent in the broader global economy are presumed to be directly linked to 'doing well' at school. School prospectuses promise to prepare students to be responsible citizens and full participants in a changing global marketplace. The challenge girls' schools face is to prepare 'new types of girls' to meet the demands faced by a new generation of 'global' women. To this end, schools must commit to 'producing' young women who will play a much more active role in public life than have previous generations of women (Arnot et al., 1999). But again, women's activity in the public realm is primarily validated through consumption and (self-)enterprise. As such, the skills girls 'need' to become full, active (global) citizens are unashamedly linked to entrepreneurial practices of self-invention and consumption.

But what role does the imagination play in these projects of self-management and self-work? How are girl-citizens called upon to *imagine* themselves as a globally-minded actors and/or consumers? Johanna Wyn (2000) argues that the demands of contemporary living produce young 'subjects who can *imagine* themselves as free to make choices about their lives, and who see themselves as autonomous subjects who will willingly reinvent themselves' (p. 63, emphasis added). Wyn's use of the imagination, although perhaps accidental, returns us to the critical framework established earlier in this paper. It can be said that the imagination signifies a type of self-taught foresight or vision; it is a tool for 'knowing' and governing oneself as an intelligible, productive young citizen-subject. The imagination conjoins with neo-liberal discourses of freedom and choice and operates as a resource for reinventing oneself in order to accommodate the changing conditions of contemporary living.

For girls, the imagination is positioned as an important tool for constructing new ideals of 'femininity' and 'womanhood'. It is mobilised in girls' efforts to 'get smart', 'become entrepreneurial', 'make money', 'envision new choices', and 'consume more widely and responsibly', all practices that involve varying degrees of self-work. Inherent in these practices of (self-)labouring is a commitment to getting to know one's self, a practice that is ongoing or 'lifelong'. Nikolas Rose (1999) links self-determination, self-knowledge and self-enterprise to the notion of 'lifelong learning', a concept that since the 1970s has been invested in a broader neo-liberal project that emphasises the role of the individual in maintaining governmental order. Becoming a lifelong learner means committing to reinventing oneself on an ongoing basis so to minimise one's burden on the state. Becoming a lifelong learner is important within the current 'global' context as living more 'globally' is associated with new sets of risks and uncertainties. Individuals can be expected to change careers multiple times, travel more widely and interact with rapidly changing technologies. Imagining oneself as an ongoing project, a subject in the process of perpetual reinvention, allows individuals to remain future-oriented, flexible, mobile and responsive to new forms of risk (e.g. 'global warming', 'global terrorism', global disease).

For girls and young women, becoming globally-minded lifelong learners is about imagining a variety of ways of capitalising on *themselves*. They must identify their strengths and weaknesses early and use this self-knowledge to forge socially and economically successful futures. Imagining and harnessing one's personal capital as a girl-citizen requires a commitment to ongoing practices of labour and consumption. Almost every facet of a young woman's personal life – family, relationships, shopping, work, leisure time, food, exercise, sex, health, education, travel (the list is endless) – is framed by a political economy of personal preoccupation. What she acquires for herself and what she does to herself in relation to these facets of everyday living, determine both her immediate experiences and establish options or outcomes for her future.

Discourses of self-knowledge and lifelong learning operate powerfully in educational discourse. Schools are constructed as sites for making responsible, self-managing citizens and curriculum focuses on providing students with life skills and habits that they can call upon at various points throughout their lifetime. Preparing girls as lifelong learners entails helping them imagine how their lives can or will unfold and equipping them with the skills to translate the imaginable into material outcomes. This generation of girls and women have a wider range of options and opportunities than previous generations of women have had and the aim is to help them gain the appropriate skills with which they can actualise these new possibilities. A variety of school and community-based schemes such as girl-only leadership programs, entrepreneurial retreats and ambassadorial programs aim to do just this (Harris, 2006). In different ways these schemes teach young girls to construct their bodies and their lives alongside discourses of self-esteem, self-help, healthism and post-feminist discourses such as 'girl-power'. In turn, each of these is linked to a range of consumer items (self-help books, gym memberships, alternative health therapies, etc.) that position spending as an important way of working on the self. These consumptive rituals encourage girls and young women to see the maintenance of well-being as a personal and private enterprise rather than a public one. Imagining and working on oneself as a 'lifelong' project is thus about participating in a class-based system that sees the freedom to consume as evidence of hard work and positions those 'without' as lacking in self-care and self-efficacy. Furthermore, although the project of helping girls and young women imagine themselves as globally-oriented, self-managing subjects seems to challenge traditional meanings of 'womanhood', in the end the ultimate reward for the self-managing woman is to participate fully in a global capitalist economy that relies on the heteronormative family as one of its core cultural units (Chasin, 2000).

The project of constructing global girl-citizens both in schools and beyond is also invested in helping girls imagine themselves as cosmopolitan citizens with access to a broader range of 'cultural' experiences. At a very basic level, being 'cosmopolitan' means being open and able to interact with a variety of world cultures (Hannerz, 1990); it describes a group of people who have 'become seemingly more diverse, more international, more *worldly*' (Latham, 2006, p. 92). Being cosmopolitan is often associated with 'mixing' with a range of people from different cultural backgrounds as part of everyday experiences.

Increasingly, schools are being described as institutions that promote a cosmopolitan worldview (Elkind, 2000). Globalisation is said to have significantly changed 'average' classroom demographics, especially in large cities, and a wider range of cultural and class backgrounds in schools is said to be unsettling white, middle-class values. In addition, gender roles are said to be shifting with 'traditional differences between male and female roles' being overturned (Elkind, 2000, p. 13). The cosmopolitan classroom is defined by its 'natural' diversity and the role it plays in challenging traditional 'provincial' values and social norms.

However, through the lens of governmentality, cosmopolitanism can be viewed as a set of qualities or skills mobilised by a class of 'global citizens' who live in urban centres and/ or have access to global travel. This shift recognises an entire political economy from within which certain cultural and consumer practices define and govern what it means to be a cosmopolite (Beck, 2004; Latham, 2006). This shift does not simply name and describe the qualities or characteristics of the cosmopolitan citizen. Consideration is also given to the discursive and material (though these are by no means independent of one another) processes and practices against which one comes to name or describe oneself as cosmopolitan. Being a cosmopolitan citizen becomes a 'classed phenomenon' that is about acquiring certain forms of knowledge and cultural capital; it is 'being worldly, being able to navigate between and within different cultures, [it] requires confidence, skill and money . . . a cosmopolitan disposition is most often associated with transnational elites that have risen to power and visibility in the neo-liberal era' (Binnie, Holloway, Millington, & Young, 2006, pp. 8–9).

Preparing young citizens to become cosmopolitan entails developing the appropriate skills such that they gain access to a certain type of education, particular socio-cultural norms, particular experiences of urban living, specific types of consumption and so on. The aim is to help young people recognise and be part of a global creative class (Binnie et al., 2006), which is characterised by certain life-style interests and experiences. Neo-liberalism thrives on the idea of a select, creative class, and entrepreneurialism emphasises the importance of finding creative and innovative ways of coping with the changing conditions and contexts of contemporary living. In the global context, the ability to creatively integrate a range of cultural practices into the way urban spaces are organised, business is done and human socialisation is played out, contributes to the neo-liberal agenda of 'making' individuals more resourceful, flexible, and mobile. For young girls, access to this creative class has become important not only for imagining themselves as viable global citizens, but in producing and governing themselves as new types of *women* in a new type of global world.

Conclusion

This chapter introduced a new critical framework for understanding the global that focuses on how globalisation governs the conduct and actions of individuals and certain populations. Reading Appadurai's (1996, 1999) notion of the 'global imagination' alongside questions of government, it suggested that within the current global milieu, the imagination operates as a mechanism with which individuals produce and govern themselves as intelligible global citizen-subjects. This critical shift was used to ask specific questions about the ways in which the idealised 'girl-citizen' is produced and governed alongside discourses of global living. It argued that girls and young women are encouraged to *imagine* themselves as active agents within an increasingly global world by acquiring a range of entrepreneurial and self-management skills that position them as lifelong learners and as cosmopolitan global consumer-citizens.

There is a great deal more that can and must be said about the governance of girl-citizens today, and about the ways in which discourses of the global inform normative constructions of 'girlhood' and 'womanhood'. There is also a great deal more that needs to be explored around the idea of girls as global *cosmopolitan* citizens. Ulrich Beck (2004) suggests that the idea of a cosmopolitan citizen or creative class, feeds an economy of excess that depends on the fetishisation and consumption of the Other. For Beck, the desire to be more cosmopolitan, to acquire the quality of 'being worldly', is about making a number of consumer choices – travelling to certain 'exotic' places, watching certain anthropological television documentaries, eating in certain 'ethnic' suburbs – that overlook the operations of power and give majoritarian cultures cause and permission to consume the minoritarian Other. Studies concerned with the relationships between globalisation, girlhood and educational discourse should also consider the ways in which the body of the 'Other' lends weight and credibility to the skills and choices of global girl-citizens. In other words, in imagining herself as adequately 'global', how does the girl-citizen participate in certain political and cultural economies that allow her to consume experiences of non-White, Third World and Indigenous 'Others', and how is this consumption validated as part of her broader entrepreneurial agenda of global self-making?

Notes

1. I use the term 'girl(s)' throughout the paper to call attention to the way it functions as a homogenous category in a great deal of educational discourse. However, I recognise that this category is highly problematic. There is not, of course, only one way to be a 'girl'. Furthermore, using categories like 'boy' and 'girl' reinforces the normative gender order and ignores the multitude of ways in which young people construct their sexed/gendered selves beyond these simple binary categories (Burns, 2004).
2. While some scholars apply Foucault's notion of the assemblage or the *dispositif* to their works, an actual textual reference that indicates when Foucault first used these terms is difficult to trace. Paul Rabinow and Nikolas Rose (2003) suggest that while the concept of an assemblage is used in various places throughout his work before 1975, it was in an (unspecified) interview in 1975, following the publication of *Surveiller et Punir*, that he first used the term *dispositif*.
3. Of course this is not a new phenomenon. Previous 'generations' were morally and socially 'shaped' by dominant schooling policies and practices (McLeod, 2001, 2006; Wyn, 2000).

References

Anderson, B. (1983). *Imagined communities: Reflections on the origin and spread of nationalism.* London: Verso.

Appadurai, A. (1996). *Modernity at large: Cultural dimensions of globalization.* Minneapolis: University of Minnesota Press.

Appadurai, A. (1999). Globalization and the research imagination. *UNESCO*, 229–238.

Apple, M. (2006). *Educating the 'right' way: Markets, standards, God and inequality* (Rev. ed.). London: RoutledgeFalmer.

Arnot, M. (2002). *Reproducing gender: Essays on educational theory and feminist politics.* London: Routledge.

Arnot, M., David, M., & Weiner, G. (1999). *Closing the gender gap: Postwar education and social change.* Cambridge, UK: Polity Press.

Beck, U. (2004). Cosmopolitan realism: On the distinction between cosmopolitanism in philosophy and the social sciences. *Global Networks*, *4*, 131–156.

Best, A.L. (2004). Girls, schooling, and the discourse of self-change: Negotiating meanings of the high school prom. In A. Harris (Ed.), *All about the girl: Culture, power, and identity* (pp. 195–204). New York: Routledge.

Binnie, J., Holloway, J., Millington, S., & Young, C. (2006). Conclusion: The paradoxes of cosmopolitan urbanism. In J. Binnie, J. Holloway, S. Millington & C. Young (Eds.), *Cosmopolitan urbanism* (pp. 246–253). London: Routledge.

Burns, K. (2004). Pedagogical dysphoria: Teaching genetics and (trans)gender. Review essay. *Discourse: Studies in the Cultural Politics of Education*, *25*, 495–506.

Chasin, A. (2000). *Selling out: The gay and lesbian movement goes to market*. New York: St. Martin's Press.

Davies, B., & Saltmarsh, S. (2007). Gender economies: Literacy and the gendered production of neo-liberal subjectivities. *Gender and Education*, *19*, 1–20.

Elkind, D. (2000). The cosmopolitan school. *Educational Leadership*, *58*(4), 12–17.

Foucault, M. (1991). Governmentality. In G. Burchell, C. Gordon & P. Miller (Eds.), *The Foucault effect: Studies in governmentality* (pp. 87–104). London: Harvester Wheatsheaf.

Foucault, M. (1994). *Dits et écrits* (Vol. III). Paris: Editions Gallimard.

Gordon, C. (1991). Governmental rationality: An introduction. In G. Burchell, Colin Gordon & Peter Miller (Eds.), *Foucault effect: Studies in governmentality* (pp. 1–51). Chicago: The Chicago Press.

Grossberg, L. (1996). The space of culture, the power of space. In I. Chambers & L. Curti (Eds.), *The postcolonial question: Common skies, divided horizons* (pp. 169–188). New York: Routledge.

Hannerz, U. (1990). Cosmopolitans and locals in world culture. *Theory, Culture & Society*, *7*(2), 237–251.

Harris, A. (2004a). *Future girl: Young women in the 21st century*. New York: Routledge.

Harris, A. (2004b). Jamming girl culture: Young women and consumer citizenship. In A. Harris (Ed.), *All about the girl: Culture, power, and identity* (pp. 163–172). New York: Routledge.

Harris, A. (2006). Citizenship and the self-made girl. In M. Arnot & M. Mac An Ghaill (Eds.), *The RoutledgeFalmer reader in gender and education* (pp. 268–282). New York: Routledge.

Hopkins, S. (2002). *Girl heroes: The new force in popular culture*. Sydney: Pluto Press.

Larner, W., & Walters, W. (2002, July). *Globalization as governmentality*. Paper presented at the International Studies Association Congress, Brisbane, Australia.

Larner, W., & Walters, W. (2004). *Global governmentality: Governing international spaces*. London: Routledge.

Latham, A. (2006). Sociality and the cosmopolitan imagination: National, cosmopolitan and local imaginaries in Auckland, New Zealand. In J. Binnie, J. Holloway, S. Millington & C. Young (Eds.), *Cosmopolitan urbanism* (pp. 89–111). London: Routledge.

Marginson, S. (1997). *Markets in education*. St. Leonards, Australia: Allen & Unwin.

McLeod, J. (2001). When poststructuralism meets gender. In K. Hultqvist & G. Dahlberg (Eds.), *Governing the child in the new millennium* (pp. 259–289). London: RoutledgeFalmer.

McLeod, J. (2004). Neo-liberal agendas and gender equity: From social justice to individual performance. *Redress: Journal of the Association of Women Educators*, *13*(3), 1–8.

McLeod, J. (2006). Citizenship, schooling and the sex role in Australia: Making up students for the future. In T.S. Popkewitz, K. Petersson & U. Olssen (Eds.), *The future is not what it appears to be* (pp. 220–241). Stockholm: University of Stockholm Press.

McLuhan, M., & Powers, P.R. (1989). *The global village: Transformation in world, life and media*. New York: Oxford University Press.

McRobbie, A. (2000). *Feminism and youth culture* (Rev. ed.). London: Macmillan.

Rabinow, P., & Rose, N. (2003). Foucault today. In P. Rabinow & N. Rose (Eds.), *The essential Foucault: Selections from the essential works of Foucault, 1954–1984* (pp. vii–xxxv). New York: New Press.

Rose, N. (1999). *Powers of freedom: Reframing political thought*. Cambridge, UK: Cambridge University Press.

Thrift, N. (2005). *Knowing capitalism*. London: Sage.

Whitty, G., Power, S., & Halpin, D. (1998). *Devolution of choice in education: The school, state, and the market*. Buckingham, UK: Open University Press.

Wyn, J. (2000). The postmodern girl: Education, 'success' and the construction of girls' identities. In J. McLeod & K. Malone (Eds.), *Researching youth* (pp. 59–70). Hobart, Australia: Australian Clearinghouse for Youth Studies.

Youdell, D. (2006). *Impossible bodies, impossible selves: Exclusions and student subjectivities.* Dordrecht, The Netherlands: Springer.

Machinic assemblages: women, art education and space

Maria Tamboukou

Introduction

> M. Bradish Titcomb paints and receives friends in one of the most fascinating of the truly
> Bohemian atmospheres. The studio window that appears in part in several of her important
> works might easily look out over the Latin quarter of Paris ... Sketches made in Spain and
> France are stacked on the old balcony which is connected with the main studio by a quaint
> stairway. Fragrance is in the air of the China white narcissus blooms, which arranged under the
> old window with a figure seating at the desk, make the composition of her gem 'The Writer'.
> (Barbee-Babson, cited in Jarzombek, 1998, pp. 8–9)

On 1 March 1914, this is how Barbee-Babson was presenting Mary Bradish Titcomb to the
readers of the Bostonian *Sunday Herald* in her article 'Studios of some who have made
Boston famous in the world of art'. The article and 'The Writer', a self-portrait of the artist
in a studio/room of her own (Figure 1) compose an idealistic image: an intellectual woman
writing in the calmness of a bohemian décor – part of a wider artists' community, the
Grundman studios in Boston – and surrounded by paintings, art objects and paraphernalia
of her European travels. The story is seductive for readers then and now. It is not accidental
that both the article and the self-portrait were included in the catalogue of an exhibition of
Titcomb's work, held by the Vose Galleries in Boston between May and July 1998 and this
exhibition catalogue was filed in the archives of the Massachusetts College of Art
(MassArt, Boston) where I found it in March 2006, while working there for a genealogy of
women artists.[1] What was not included in the newspaper article is the fact that Mary
Bradish Titcomb worked as a teacher in New Hampshire, Boston and Brockton for over 25
years (1875–1901) and that becoming an artist was a life-long project, a difficult journey
in-between geographical, social and cultural spaces. This significant omission is a telling

Figure 1.   Mary Bradish Titcomb: 'The Writer', c.1912, oil on canvas, 30 × 25 inches, private collection (reproduced with owner's kind permisssion).

example of the inevitable partiality of reading and writing about the lives of others. But is this partiality necessarily problematic? In this paper I want to challenge an image of narratives as unified representations of lives and subjects; at the same time I am arguing for their importance in opening up microsociological analyses that focus on processes, deterritorializations, becomings and lines of flight, rather than striated spaces and structures, institutional segmentarities and motionless or fixed identities.

Deterritorialization, reterritorialization, lines of flight, striated spaces and smooth spaces are central notions in Deleuze and Guattari's philosophical writings, particularly elaborated in their collective work, *A Thousand Plateaus* (1980/1988). A common aspect in all these notions is the importance of the relations we have with space in general and the earth in particular. We experience the world as a continuum of striated and smooth spaces: 'smooth space is constantly being translated, transversed into a striated space; striated space is constantly being reversed, returned to a smooth space' (Deleuze & Guattari, 1988, p. 474). Striated spaces are hierarchical, rule-intensive, strictly bounded and confining, whereas smooth spaces are open, dynamic and allow for transformations to occur. In this light, 'all becoming occurs in smooth space' (p. 486). As a matter of fact we constantly move between deterritorialization – freeing ourselves from the restrictions and boundaries of controlled, striated spaces – and reterritorialization – repositioning ourselves within new regimes of striated spaces. As Deleuze and Guattari warn us: 'You may make a rupture, draw a line of flight, yet there is still a danger that you will reencounter organizations that restratify everything, formations that restore power to a signifier, attributions that reconstitute a subject' (1980/1988, p. 9). However, in the context of Deleuze and Guattari's geophilosophy, where we start from or where we end up – beginnings and endings – are not so important. In their writings, they have actually put forward nomadic modes of existence: 'other ways of moving and traveling: proceeding from the middle, through the middle, coming and going, rather than starting and finishing' (p. 25). What is critical in the experience of freedom is our movement in-between, when we follow lines of flight or escape, the intermezzo, the process of becoming other.[2]

By destabilizing the very notion of identity and indeed the subject and further problematizing conventions around representation and agency, the Deleuzo-Guattarian approach inevitably challenges a critical tradition in the field of feminist studies in general and the area of gender and education in particular, that has drawn on women's forgotten and marginalised auto/biographical narratives to revisit the agency/structure relation and show how studying women's lives can offer rich insights into the socio-historical relations interwoven in the constitution of female subjectivities.[3] I am aware of this tension, but in taking the Deleuzo-Guattarian route, I follow a long-standing tradition of criticizing socio-historical formations, discourses, practices and the subject itself, a strand that is most recognizable today in Foucault's redeployment of the Nietzschean genealogy.

A genealogical approach to narratives rejects the search for hidden meanings, truths, characters and biographical subjects and looks closely at how narratives work, the discourses that traverse them, the ways they connect with other stories in shaping meanings and forming perceptions, and the power/knowledge relations they enter.[4] Rather than representing lives or subjects, narratives emit signs[5] of how subjects respond to real and imagined experiences; they are both discursive effects and sites of discursive production. In this sense, narratives carry traces of genealogical events, discontinuties and ruptures, throwing light on the microphysics of power and desire, the minutiae of the subtle and open processes that subjects and their social milieus are bound together.

Although working along genealogical lines I, however, am once again bending their trails, going beyond Foucault's configuration of the self as an effect of power relations interwoven with certain historical and cultural practices or *technologies* (1988). In following Deleuze–Guattarian (1980/1988) lines of flight I am considering the self as a threshold, a door, a becoming between multiplicities, an effect of a dance between power and desire. Instead of prioritizing battles and conflicts that are central in Foucault's analysis of power, I am rather focusing on deterritorialization and lines of flight, critical notions, as I have already discussed, in how Deleuze and Guattari conceive and analyse nomadic subjects and their social milieus. It is therefore tracing events, open processes and nomadic becomings by way of narratives that this chapter is about, troubling the waters of how narratives have been used and analysed in the field of gender and education and rethinking desire as a constitutive force of the social.

In the context of problematizing narratives, what is particularly intriguing with the stories that comprise Titcomb's archive is that with the exception of a few letters, she left no personal documents – diaries, memoirs, journals or anything that could be registered as a 'life document'. It is only through her paintings, some official reports, as well as journal articles and photographs of the period recounting some events of her life and times that the genealogist can re-imagine Mary Titcomb. In addition, her case is largely sidelined by the feminist project of restoring women's place in the history of art.[6] Celebrated in her own times, Titcomb was forgotten soon after her death, constituting herself as the grey dusty figure of genealogical research. Having left no personal documents she is thus an elusive figure, a becoming-imperceptible woman artist, difficult to be registered in dominant regimes of signs and systems of taxonomies; she is continuously evading our definitions, being always elsewhere, laughing at us as we are trying to pin her down, in the way Foucault himself had imagined the author in her playful vanishing and unexpected reappearances (1969/1991, p. 17). Thus, in focusing on Mary Titcomb, I am not interested in drawing her portrait or constructing a biographical narrative, not even a feminist one. In looking into narratives revolving around her life and work, I consider them as useful analytical tools illuminating connections between women, art education and spatial relations. Instead of constructing coherent or unified images around subjects and their lives, narratives offer rich insights into how lives, images, and stories are intertwined in multifarious and complex ways. As Norman Denzin has argued: 'the study of narrative forces the social sciences to develop new theories, new methods and new ways of talking about self and society' (2000, p. xi).

If Titcomb's subjectivity, her inner self, the truth or essence of what she was, cannot become an object of knowledge, the spaces and places that she inhabited can be more easily invaded by the researcher's gaze. In thus reflecting on Michel de Certeau's insights on 'penetrating the obscurity of ways of doing things' (1988, p. xi), I look at how a woman teacher at the dawn of the 20th century reinvents herself in the world of art by deterritorialization and movement along real and imaginary spaces. Although I am tracing these practices in biographical narratives, I agree with de Certeau that 'the question at hand concerns modes of operation or schemata of action and not directly the subjects ... who are their authors or vehicles' (1988, p. xi). I am therefore interested in the how of spatial practices, rather than the psychologization of these practices and their connection to a particular character or persona. This approach makes connection with the Deleuzian concept of the individual as a plane wherein thought takes place as an event and not necessarily as a conscious process: 'the individual is rather a series of processes that connect actual things, thoughts and sensations to the pure intensities and ideas implied by them' (Williams, 2003, p. 6). What therefore appears critical in the discussion of this chapter is an attention to space that opens up paths for an analytics of becomings, processes and nomadic subjectivities in the field of gender and education.

Mapping Titcomb

Mary Titcomb (1856–1927) was born and grew up in Windham, New Hampshire, where she stayed till the age of 28 working as a teacher and living with her mother and younger brother since her father had died when she was only 12. She moved from Windham to Boston in 1886, one year after her mother's death, determined to take a break from teaching and train as an art teacher in the Massachusetts Normal Art School (MNAS; 1886–1887). This career/life change became possible for Titcomb since MNAS would waive fees for students on the condition that upon their graduation, they would reside in Massachusetts and teach in public schools. This is actually what Titcomb did after graduation: she became Director of Drawing for Brockton public schools in 1887.

Training art teachers was the central mission of MNAS. Indeed, it was founded in 1873 as a response to the growing demand for art teachers after the 1870 Industrial Drawing Act that made art education compulsory for all children in public schools in the USA: 'The specific aim at present is to prepare instructors to teach and superintend industrial drawing in the schools of the state'.[7] It goes without saying that women comprised the majority of the body of teachers to be trained in art education and consequently of the student population of MNAS (Massachusetts College of Arts Archive, 1998, p. 3). As Diana Korzenik has noted, Walter Smith, the first principal of MNAS who moved from England to Boston to take up his post, believed that 'there is an unworked mine of untold wealth among us in the art education of women', and he therefore hoped that 'there shall be absolutely no distinction made concerning the eligibility or disqualification of sex in the students' (cited in Korzenik, 1987, p. 33). Suffice to know that as recorded in the booklet that was published to celebrate the first 30 years of MNAS, even from the first year that the school run, in a total of 133 students enrolled there were '47 Gentlemen and 86 Ladies' (Dean, 1924, p. 6), while in the first 30 years of the school there were 898 women and only 219 men who received certificates for at least one art specialty (Korzenik, 1987, pp. 33–34). MNAS has therefore been presented and indeed celebrated as a progressive educational institution that made art education accessible to the masses:

> Massachusetts Normal Art School revolutionized *who* could study art in this country. As a normal school, it was one of the institutions created as part of a movement to improve the quality of teachers, but as a normal *art* school, it was unique in this county. At that time many people associated art with affluence and privilege. At this fledging school, art was reinterpreted as the legitimate domain of working people. (Korzenik, 1987, p. 33)

Hand in hand with this revolution, however, went a specific vision of what art in general and art education in particular should be about when offered or made accessible to the masses. According to the pioneering project of Walter Smith:

> The thing we have to do for children is to teach them to think and think rightly; to develop the ability to analyze and compare; to distinguish between the right and the wrong, between the beautiful and that which is not beautiful, between the true and the false; and to incline them to choose the right, the beautiful and the true by their own mental action. That is education; and the process and manual exercise through which it is done is only the means, never the end. What we are trying to do in our lessons is to make the children know how to draw and not how to make drawings and I hope you see the distinction. And the great reason for them to draw is, that the process of drawing makes ignorance visible – it is a criticism made by ourselves on our perceptions, and gives physical evidence that we either think rightly or wrongly, or even do not think at all. For a bad or incorrect drawing is never an accident; it is an uncomfortably accurate mirror of our thoughts and fixes the stage of mental development and civilization at which we have arrived. (Dean, 1924, pp. 7–8)

There is indeed an interesting matrix of social attitudes, educational practices, pedagogical discourses and ethico-aesthetic orientations comprising Smith's philosophy of art education, which need to be seen in the context of his overall involvement in the aesthetics and politics of the Arts and Crafts movement. Indeed his vision was to popularize and enshrine art, a project that he was attempting to transfer from South Kensington to Boston. As Stankiewicz has noted, 'a number of art education historians place the work of Walter Smith as promoting industrial drawing in the context of the British South Kensington System of Art Education' (1992, p. 165). And despite our terror of an image of thought that takes art as a power to discipline the mind and soul, what is particularly interesting for the analysis of this chapter is Smith's focus on art education as an open process rather than a closed and definitive project. I think it was this openness that inflicted cracks in the segmentarity of governing the mind and soul through art and created conditions of possibility for art teachers to imagine themselves as artists, appropriating the vision of the Romantic figure of the artist who rises beyond earthy conventions and material concerns (Davidoff, 1995, p. 234). While working in the archives of the MassArt in Boston, I found an interesting dossier of poems entitled as *L' Atelier Frivole.* The 'Frivolous Studio' was a society of 15 MNAS students, formed in 1909: they would gather weekly in the studio of one of their teachers to write and read poems, and imagine their future beyond conventions and taken-for-granted expectations. In the following extract a student, figuring herself as *Alice in Wonderland*, is trying to find out what the future holds:

> Through dark mysterious regions we wandered until suddenly a black cave loomed before us. I peered cautiously into the darkness, I saw a bony hand stretch out from some unknown region.

All seemed uncanny and I was about to flee when suddenly there flamed strange sullen lights and I saw a large placard which read:

'Out of the door into the wall
Big or little, little or small
The truth I will tell you all
Poetry a dime; Prose a nickel.'
(*L' Atelier Frivole*, MassArt Archives)

As forcefully expressed in the poems of *L' Atelier Frivole*, Smith's disturbing view of art as a power to discipline was continuously contested and challenged by the artists and students of MNAS. Within the paradox of modernity that Foucault has so influentially analysed, disciplinarian strategies and democratic trends were interwoven in a complex network of power/knowledge relations and forces of desire. MNAS, as a project of *Art for all*, was counterposing the gradually emerging highbrow–lowbrow distinction and the discursive construction of hierarchies in American culture that Lawrence Levine has written about (1988). In the context of this socio-cultural division, Paul Dimaggio (1982a, 1982b) has particularly focused on how in the period between 1870 and 1900, the forming years of MNAS, the social elite of the Boston Brahmins institutionalized cultural hierarchies through the establishment of the Museum of Fine Arts (1870) and the Boston Symphony Orchestra (1881), as the Bostonian elite cultural institutions par excellence:

> The culture of an elite status group must be monopolized, it must be legitimate and it must be sacralized. Boston's cultural capitalists would have to find a form able to achieve all these aims: a single organizational base for each art form; institutions that could claim to serve the community, even as they defined the community to include only the elite and the upper middle class; and enough social distance between artist and audience, between performer and public, to permit the mystification necessary to define a body of artistic work as sacred. (Dimaggio, 1982a, p. 38)

Mary Titcomb was therefore striving to become an artist within the turbulence of cultural wars waging around power/knowledge and antagonistic relations and discourses at play. As the traces of her movements across a range of geographical, social and cultural spaces indicate, she must have been somehow conscious if not fully aware of this intensity. Indeed, what I argue is that her life unfolds as a logbook of travels, a sophisticated system of spatial and cultural practices tactically deployed in the process of her becoming-artist. Titcomb, the artist, slowly emerges in between the gaps and interstices of striated spaces – the social and cultural institutions of the elite and the less rigidly bound art spaces that MNAS had opened up for her.

In considering Titcomb's spatiality as a configuration of spatial elements, relations and tactically deployed practices, I draw of course on de Certeau's (1988) conceptualization of tactics as guerilla-like subversive practices of everyday life, associated with the advantage of the unexpected moment, the particular time that explosions occur. The tactic, de Certeau has written, 'operates in isolated actions, blow by blow ... it takes advantage of opportunities ... and depends on them' (1988, p. 37). In taking up tactics, however, I am more sceptical in theorizing them within the binarism of strategies–tactics that de Certeau's thought has introduced. As Doreen Massey has commented, in relating strategies with power and tactics with subversion, de Certeau's strategies–tactics dichotomy views power as much more coherent and monolithic than it appears in its actuality and instead of 'empowering the weak' – as it claims to do – it actually reduces them to a situation of the rebellious powerless (2005, p. 45).

Indeed in looking closer into the conditions of possibility for Titcomb's becomings, one cannot really discern 'a passage from the dull fields of teaching to the colourful landscapes of art'. As a matter of fact, such a binarism hardly exists and the boundaries between strategies and tactics are really blurred. Becoming other is an open process without discursively constructed abject beginnings – being a teacher – and or celebrated ends – being an artist. Although Titcomb's emergence as an artist was an effect of the deployment of a specific set of spatial tactics – her move to Boston, her European and American travels – there was already a depository of social networks and cultural strategies that supported and geared her tactics, creating possibilities for transformations to occur and keeping open the process of continuously reinventing herself. While her father was a manufacturer, her mother was a teacher and writer for local newspapers. It is therefore no surprise that 'Mary was well educated, learned some French and even took elocution lessons as a young woman' (Jarzombek, 1998, p. 2). Her mother was therefore instrumental in the creation of a depository of cultural strategies that Mary would rely on in moving through geographical, social and cultural spaces even if it was after her mother's death that 'real' movement actually happened. However, can we really freeze the moment of Titcomb's deterritorialization? When were her lines of flight set into motion? When she left New Hampshire or when she started imagining herself elsewhere? The question therefore arises: how can one analyse the process of Titcomb's deterritorialization? Is it just a problem of social mobility that can be attributed to different forms of capital, be these social, cultural or emotional and the flows in between them in a Bourdieuisian image of thought – a significant trend in the field of gender and education? Not that it is wrong to talk about Titcomb's cultural, social, emotional, or even corporeal capital as many strands in feminist research have recently suggested.[8] What I argue, however, is that although useful in explaining social reproduction, Bourdieu's concepts are not particularly effective in the unravelling of the microphysics of power and desire intertwined in Titcomb's becoming, which unfolds as a continuous process not necessarily linked to a series of causalities or sequential orders, but rather emerging as a series of events.

Clearly, the notion of the event here should not be conflated with the commonsense meaning of something that has happened – Titcomb moved to Boston, then she enrolled in MNAS. It draws on a line of philosophical thinking that has seen it as a glimpse into the unreachable, the yet to come (Nietzsche, 1895/ 1990); a transgression of the limitations of the possible (Foucault, 1987); a flash in the greyness of the virtual worlds that surround us (Deleuze, 1969/2001). As Deleuze has poetically put it: 'The event is not what occurs (an accident), it is rather inside what occurs, the purely expressed. It signals and awaits us . . . it is what must be understood, willed and represented in that which occurs' (1969/2001, p. 170). Departing from good sense, the event sticks out from the ordinary, marks historical discontinuities and opens up the future to a series of differentiations. Titcomb's move to Boston is an event expressing her pure desire to transgress the boundaries of what was given, to imagine herself otherwise, to become other than what she had found herself to be. 'Becoming an artist' should thus be analysed as a process, a series of events, expressing the desire of effectuating material and cultural changes in a woman's life. In this light, when did Titcomb 'become an artist'? Was it when she enrolled in MNAS or when she started travelling and painting in Europe during her summer vacations? Maybe it was when she resigned from her job as a teacher, but what about when she simply started imagining herself as an artist? Becoming an artist cannot be pinned down within a specific space/time block; it would rather be seen as a continuum that needs to be mapped on a grid of intelligibility, a machinic rather than a linear model of transformations, that allows for rhizomatic connections to be seen working together. But here again, what exactly is a machine?

Unlike closed organisms and fixed identities, *machines* in Deleuze and Guattari's philosophy are assemblages without any organising centre, who can only function as they connect with other machines in a constant process of becoming: 'a machine may be defined as a *system of interruptions* or breaks ... Every machine, in the first place, is related to a continual material flow (*hylè*) that it cuts into' (1972/1984, p. 36). The machine has no ground or foundation: 'it is nothing more than the connections and productions it makes; it is what it does; it therefore has no home; it is a constant process of deterritorialization, or becoming other than itself' (Colebrook, 2002, p. 56). Colebrook further explains that 'there is no aspect of life that is not machinic; all life only works and is in so far as it connects with some other machine; ... so life is a proliferation of machinic connections' (2002, p. 56). The concept of the machine allows for the possibility of open configurations, continuous connections and intense relations, incessantly transforming life: 'everywhere there are breaks-flows out of which desire wells up, thereby constituting its productivity and continually grafting the process of production onto the product' (Deleuze & Guattari, 1972/1984, p. 37).

In thus facing the need of making sense of events, transpositions, social relations in flux and subjects in becoming, what I suggest is that the Deleuzo-Guattarian concepts of the assemblage, the machinic and the nomadic and their focus on chaotic and non-hierarchical organizations – open processes, rather than predefined entities or closed circuits – are useful and effective theoretical tools. Drawing on the microsociology of Gabriel Tarde, a theoretical project that was taken over by the Durkheimian focus on 'social facts', order, stability and purity, Deleuze and Guattari have argued that society is not so much defined by its molar formations and their dialectic oppositions but rather by what has escaped them, not the molar socio-cultural entities, but the molecular counter-formations, its lines of flight:

> It is wrongly said (in Marxism in particular) that a society is defined by its contradictions. That is true only in the larger scale of things. From the viewpoint of micropolitics a society is defined by its lines of flight, which are molecular. There is always something that flows or flees, that escapes the binary organizations, the resonance apparatus and the overcoding machine: things that are attributed to a 'change in values', the youth, women, the mad, etc.'. (Deleuze & Guattari, 1980/1988, p. 216)

What makes Tarde's microsociology distinctive is his attention to the monad and his assertion that the social is a consequence rather than a cause, it does not hold any explanatory power; it is actually what mostly needs to be explained. As Bruno Latour (2002) points out, in Tarde's thought the micro/macro distinction does not enable the analysis of how human societies emerge and function. As a matter of fact the smallest entities are always richer in difference and complexity than their aggregates:

> For since everything in the world of facts proceeds from small to great, everything in the world of ideas, which reflects it as though reversed in the mirror, naturally proceeds from great to small and in the course of its analysis comes upon the elementary facts and real explanations only at the end of its journey. (Tarde, 1899, p. 111)

It is Tarde's theorization of difference as an ontological condition and his rejection of the very notion of identity that has inspired Deleuze's philosophy of difference and repetition (1968/2004) and has geared his engagement with the distinctiveness of Tardean microsociology:

To exist is to differ; difference, in one sense, is the substantial side of things, what they have most in common and what makes them most different. One has to start from this difference and to abstain from trying to explain it, especially by starting with identity, as so many persons wrongly do. Because identity is a minimum and, hence, a type of difference, and a very rare type at that, in the same way as rest is a type of movement and the circle a type of ellipse. (Tarde, 1895, 2006, p. 355)

In this light, Paul Patton has commented that the difference between macropolitical and micropolitical levels of social analysis 'is not simply a difference in scale but a difference in kind' (2006, p. 30). It is an analytical path oriented towards complex and multifarious modalities of living in the interstices and ruptures of molar social entities and amongst the minutiae of socio-cultural and affective relations, the micro-spaces where power and desire meet in producing realities and indeed the subject. As I have elsewhere argued (Tamboukou, 2003b), it is within the consistency of the genealogical project that the concept of *machinic assemblages* becomes a useful analytical tool and it is the specific analytics of this chaper that I hope will further throw light on the richness of Tarde's microsociological project, that Foucault and Deleuze and Guattari have followed.

Following lines of flight

In retracing storylines again, I will now leap into the years after Titcomb completed her studies at MNAS (1886–1887) and took up a position as Director of Drawing for Brockton public schools. Numerous journals and newspaper articles of the period have recorded her successful career in her new post and the way she had been inculcating Smith's philosophy on art education in the schools of her remit: 'There is hope and good reason for believing that education on the subject of drawing will elevate the standard of action, for the frequent recurrence of the mind and eye to the beautiful and symmetrical stamps an impression, which is enduring and effective'.[9] Beyond her professional practice it seems indeed that 'the frequent recurrence' of Titcomb's 'mind and eyes to the beautiful' had already geared a set of practices that were deterritorializing the educator and unleashing lines of flight for the artist.

During her teaching years in Brockton (1886–1901), Titcomb was involved in a vigorous community of the single 'independent women' that Martha Vicinus (1985) has written about. Together with her friend and fellow teacher Sylvia Donaldson 'who was outspoken on issues of women's rights' (Jarzombek, 1998, p. 3), she became an active member of the Brockton's Women's Club and lived a life immersed in the pursuit of cultural interests, the love for art and the passion for travelling around America and Europe. I have written elsewhere about women teachers' travelling practices and their passionate attachment to art as a heterotopic space in the constitution of their subjectivity (Tamboukou, 2003a).

Titcomb's passion for a life immersed in art is therefore an event in what Deleuze and Guattari would call deterritorialization of the self in the process of becoming other. This passion, however, was not an individualistic or merely hedonistic practice of the self. It was rather a force that created conditions of possibility for Titcomb's politics, her will to interrogate inequalities and be active in earthly demands around her working conditions. As noted in her biographical sketch 'when the evening drawing class doubled in size, she informed the school committee that she was unable to handle so many students' (Jarzombek, 1998, p. 17). She was relieved from the evening duty and shortly afterwards her salary was significantly increased.

Titcomb's becoming has therefore been seen as an actualization of Foucault's ethico-aesthetic paradigm, a set of practices expressing a sensibility towards what is happening around us, a sort of an aesthetic rationality, founded on a capacity to perceive, through an openness to experience. This sensibility is not limited to the private sphere. It extends to the public, what is out there that one cannot stand, a sensibility to what is intolerable and unacceptable. Making connections with Guattari's thought, such an aesthetics of existence is not a personified concept. It does not relate to the artist; it is rather about following lines of flight, deterritorializing oneself, capturing the thought from the outside. The ethical implications of this paradigm relates aesthetics in self-creation with social responsibility. Guattari argues for an ethical choice 'of being not only for oneself, but for the whole alterity of the cosmos and for the infinity of times' (Guattari, 1992/1995, p. 53). Being part of a community of independent working women, travelling widely and actively seeking to reinvent her life in art were therefore practices embedded in an ethico-aesthetic orientation of 'being for oneself and the world' – the alterity of a feminist cosmos perhaps, in Titcomb's case.

Titcomb's active involvement in the Bostonian artistic community was also a passage through a range of constraints, a continuous transgression of the newly found barriers of the elite that Dimaggio has delineated (1982a, 1982b). Indeed, throughout the Brockton years, Titcomb carefully established and maintained closed relations to the Bostonian art circles. She joined the MNAS Alumni Association in 1889 and took part in their annual exhibitions and events, being awarded prizes and honorary mentions (Jarzombek, 1998, p. 4). However, knowing that MNAS was not considered to be an institution of 'serious art', she tried to connect to the Boston Art Students' Association (BASA), an alumni association for graduates of the School of the Museum of Fine Arts, becoming a member of it in 1895, when the latter opened its membership to the general artistic community. As Dimaggio (1982a) has pointed out, this openness was a strategic deployment, since the Bostonian elite very soon realized that the middle classes were becoming indispensable in their cultural project as audiences and visitors for the cultural institutions they were running:

> The Brahmin class, however, was neither large enough to constitute a public for large scale art-organizations, nor was it content to keep its cultural achievements solely to itself. Alongside of, and complicating, the Brahmins' drive towards exclusivity was a conflicting desire, as they saw it, to educate the community. The growth of the middle class during this period – a class that it was economically and socially closer to the working class and thus in greater need of differentiating itself from it culturally – provided a natural clientele for Boston's inchoate high culture. (Dimaggio, 1982a, p. 40)

Clearly Titcomb took advantage of this opportunity, which was becoming part of her logbook of movements. Her involvement in the BASA was a turning point in her life again, since it initiated her final decision to leave teaching for good and embark on a career as a professional artist. This new life path was actually initiated in 1902 when she enrolled as a student of the School of the Museum of Fine Arts at the age of 44.

What was the force that pushed a 44-year-old professional woman to leave a well-established career in education and leap into the insecurity of becoming an artist? And why should she have to go back to school to study again, after so many years of serious involvement with art education both through her professional life but also during her extended travels to Europe? Apart from her studies in MNAS, Titcomb had indeed studied with Jules Lefebvre (1895), at the renowned Julian Academy in Paris – one of the few private academies that accepted women.

Dimaggio's analysis of the significance of the Museum of Fine Arts and its educational mission in the formation of the new cultural hierarchies in Boston becomes at this point very pertinent in understanding Titcomb's decision to study at its school. Titcomb was by then very well experienced to see that entering the cultural elite would have to be done through the gate of art education and particularly through the School of the Museum of Fine Arts (SMFA) which was geographically so close and yet socially so far away from the MNAS where she had already studied. Or was it? What I want to argue here is that viewing SMFA and MNAS as two different worlds within the highbrow–lowbrow binarism is a simplistic dichotomy that does not facilitate a deeper understanding of the process of Titcomb's movements within different geographical, social and cultural worlds. It is only if the two schools are to be placed within what Deleuze and Guattari would delineate as the machine of art education, a complex assemblage of interrelations between social structures, economic conditions, power/knowledge relations, architectural and spatial arrangements, forces of desire and pleasure seductions, that Titcomb's becoming an artist emerges as an effect of disparate, co-existing elements, producing the real: subjects and their social milieus.

As already discussed, newspaper and journal articles of the period have painted idealized pictures of the artistic world that Titcomb had begun inhabiting: annual balls, theatrical performances, concerts, exhibitions and festivals as the Arabian nights festival depicted below, which Titcomb attended in the company of three women friends, former fellow students from MNAS and in the understanding that they were part of the few and advantaged: 'the rain came down in torrents, but that did not interfere with the attendance, for those who were fortunate enough to possess tickets counted themselves highly favoured, more than 200 people having been disappointed'.[10] Indeed in attending the festival, Titcomb was not only becoming part of the elite, she was being further initiated in the dream world of the Grundman studios that would very shortly become her own world, her home and workspace, a room/studio of her own:

> The atmosphere of the place is impregnated with artist life; the quaint little studios which were thrown open for the reception of guests and later became the scenes of private banquets were cozy and inviting ... the secret of it all was that this is the home of this delightful art colony.[11]

In being included in 'the favoured few' of the artists' festivals of the elite, Titcomb together with her three women friends and fellow students from MNAS were transgressing social, cultural and gendered boundaries; they were living the dream of becoming an artist. However, it was the MNAS years and experiences that had created conditions of possibility for these becomings. Although initially conceived and established as an educational institution that would serve the purposes of the industrialists, MNAS had deterritorialized its mission and its students and had opened up fields of forces for lines of flight to be released and new subjectivities to emerge, irrespective of the fact that these new women would soon be reterritorialized within the segmentarities of the social formations and cultural institutions of the elite. As Deleuze and Guattari have pithily noted: 'molecular escapes and movements would be nothing if they did not return to the molar organization to reshuffle their segments, their binary distributions of sexes, classes and parties' (1980/ 1988, pp. 216–217). It is precisely because power centres cannot be located once and for all, but can always be traced at the borders of segmented formations and lines of flight, incessantly transforming the one into the other, that Deleuze and Guattari have so persuasively argued that 'power centres are defined much more by what escapes them or by their impotence than by their zone of power' (1980/1988, p. 217). It is in this light that the machinic assemblage of Deleuze and Guattari's philosophies becomes an effective analytical tool in charting disparate elements beyond restrictive binarisms and closed causalities. Titcomb's becoming an artist is not necessarily linked to a dualistic opposition – high–low art distinction – and is not restricted within a closed causality: she was a teacher, then she became an artist. Her becoming is rather viewed as an event in the fold between life and art, a cartography of movements of a nomadic figure: Titcomb, the artist AND teacher AND student AND single woman, making rhizomatic connections with disparate elements of the machine of art education, passing through subject positions but never really permanently inhabiting any of them. As Deleuze has noted, 'even if there are only two terms [woman and artist], there is an AND between the two, which is neither the one nor the other, nor the one which becomes the other, but which constitutes the multiplicity' (Deleuze & Parnet, 1977/2002, pp. 34–35). In this sense, dualisms can be dispersed working in the intermezzo between any two terms: what is happening in the middle, becomings between being a woman and an artist, lines of flight between teaching and art, deterritorializations between Boston and Europe, connections between solitude and communication – the experience of being single but part of extended women's networks.

Spaces for art or disciplining art?

As I have already suggested, Titcomb's spatiality is marked by displacement, lines of flight, deterritorialization: the turning point of her life was the moment of her decision to leave New Hampshire and go to Boston. Her consequent involvement with the Bostonian art circles opened up the macro-world of European travelling and the micro-world of the Grundman and later Fenway studios. By establishing these studios the Bostonian elite was supporting the artists at the same time as hijacking and taming the bohemian imaginary. Indeed, beyond the rhetoric of the media representations, as in the *Sunday Herald* article that initiated the discussion of this paper, the Bostonian art circles were seriously preoccupied with creating art spaces within which they would contain and control artistic creativity and production. Safeguarding single women's respectability was highly regarded in this agenda of disciplining art:

> Grundman Studios housed a colony of women artists ... some of whom have left luxurious homes for the sake of their profession, while others have no home except that which they have provided for themselves here ... The feminine contingent is delighted with the quarters, and enjoys to the full the privilege of cultivating 'bachelor quiet or bachelor conviviality' at their own sweet will ... She can command at will the solitude, said to be so necessary to the development of genius, or, if she longs for companionship, she has but to open her door to the miniature world around her.[12]

The right to be single and lonely, the excitement and force of having a room and a studio of her own, the importance of living within a community of like-minded artists, almost everything that women had dreamt of or written about seem to become materialized in the spatial configuration and arrangements of the world of the Bostonian studios. However, being under the surveillance and control of the city's cultural elite, these artistic spaces seem to be more like Bentham's panopticon: governed spaces of creativity and freedom. Or do they? What I suggest is that such a view can hold if social institutions are only seen as striated spaces, mere effects of relations of power and domination – which they often are. Deleuze and Guattari's idea of the *machinic assemblage*, however, destabilizes monolithic views about what society or social institutions are and introduces desire, chaos and contingency as constituting forces of the social. Disciplined and programmed as they undoubtedly were, the artists' studios were also open territories, smooth spaces for creative forces to be unleashed, lines of flight to take off. In this light, the whole network of the Bostonian studios as well as the artists' colonies of Provincetown and Marblehead, where Titcomb would spend her summers, should be conceptualized in terms of the conjunctive syntheses of the concept of the Deleuzo-Guattarian assemblage, rather than the disjunctive syntheses or dialectical oppositions of molar social formations. As Deleuze and Guattari have stated: 'the assemblage has both *territorial sides*, or reterritorialized sides, which stabilize it and *cutting edges of deterritorialization*, which carry it away' (1980/1988, p. 88, original emphasis). The 'territorialized sides' of the Bostonian studios and the artists' colonies were defined by the strategic practices, discourses, desires and intentions of the elite: discipline and control of the artworld, keeping the boundaries of the high–low art binarism, monitoring gender relations and particularly 'the freedom' women artists were allowed to experience. But because 'there is always something that flows and flees', Titcomb's tactics can be registered in 'the cutting edges of deterritorialization' that have created interstices and ruptures in the segmentarities of discipline and control and have opened up nomadic passages for becoming-other. It is, as I have argued, the Deleuzo-Guattarian concept of assemblage that has created possibilities for a microanalysis of the minutiae of social relations, the microphysics of power to come under scrutiny, the microsociological project to be at work. Indeed, in suspending a priori unities and predefined causalities, in focusing on the heterogeneous elements and meshwork of social relations and in reinvesting desire within social formations, 'the assemblage replaces and reconfigures the staple sociological and philosophical concern: the relationship between man and his [sic] world' (Buchannan, 2000, p. 120).

What therefore emerges as particularly powerful in the history of the Bostonian studios is that the community of the artists who resided there created conditions of possibility for forces to be unleashed and transgressions to occur. The spatial politics of the artists' studios constitutes a plane of consistency for the deployment of a social analytics of becomings as it brings together antagonistic power/knowledge relations, uneven economic structures in a state of flux, institutional regulations, architectural arrangements and forces of artistic desire; it is indeed a milieu for a social analytics of transgressing 'the segmentation of the libidinal economy and the political economy, desire production and social production' (Fuglsang & Sørensen, 2006, p. 1), Deleuze and Guattari's project par excellence.

Machinic assemblages, narratives of nomadic becomings

In exploring connections between women, art education and spatial relations, Mary Titcomb's case emerged as an event whose multiplicities have become the object of social analytics mapped on the microsociological project of Gabriel Tarde, a grey figure of the sociological discourse overshadowed by Durkheim's all too dominant sociological image of thought. Foucault's microphysics of power and Deleuze and Guattari's analytics of desire have sided with Tarde's microsociology and have demonstrated the need to interrogate what Durkheimian sociology has taken for granted:

> Durkheim's preferred objects of study were the great collective representations, which are generally binary, resonant and overcoded. Tarde countered that collective representations presuppose exactly what needs explaining, namely 'the similarity of millions of people'. That is why Tarde was interested in the world of detail, or of the infinitesimal: the little imitations, oppositions and inventions constituting an entire realm of subrepresentative matter. (Deleuze & Guattari, 1980/1988, pp. 218–219)

The microsociological analytics looks closer into the effects of differentiation and scrutinizes the heterogeneity and meshwork of social relations, institutions, formations and subjects themselves. In this light, Titcomb's world was not so much defined by its contradictions: the high–low art distinction of the Bostonian society, the teacher–artist differentiation, the democratic Massachusetts Normal Art School as opposed to the elitism of the School of the Museum of Fine Arts. More important seem to have been its lines of flight: feminist networks that opened up time and space for women to imagine themselves differently; the teaching profession that gave them the time and money to live independently and travel to Europe; the democratic project of the Arts and Crafts movement that opened art to the masses – despite its narrowness and disciplinarian vision; the open spaces of the Bostonian studios and the artists' colonies that allowed forces of passion and creativity to be expressed. In this context the Deleuzo-Guattarian concept of *machinic assemblages* has emerged as a useful analytical tool for making sense of women's complex interrelation with their social milieus in the process of becoming other. It is precisely the need for a social analytics of becomings that has made Tarde's microsociology so relevant to the theoretical discussion of this paper. As Maurizzio Lazzarato (2006) has commented, the dominant discourse in the social sciences have given a wide range of analyses on how disciplinary societies function and reproduce themselves but they have almost nothing to say on becomings:

> The social sciences which legitimated the constitution and action of these [disciplinary] institutions function by equilibrium (political economy), integration (Durkheim), reproduction (Bourdieu), contradiction (Marxism), struggle for survival (Darwinism) or competition, but know nothing of becoming ... The time of the event, the time of invention, the time of the creation of possibles must be curtailed and fenced in within rigorously established procedures and deadlines ... For his part Tarde had already shown why economic and social sciences exclude any theory of invention and creation, and how they constitute themselves as theories of reproduction, as is still the case with the sociology of Bourdieu. (p. 176)

Within the microsociological project, the concept of the *machinic assemblage* has been useful in accounting for the formation of women artists as nomadic subjects, since as Manuel deLanda (2006, p. 253) has pointed out, subjectivities themselves are to be conceptualized as assemblages of sub-personal components. It is in the process of how a subject crystallizes as an assemblage that the Foucauldian conception of the self as an effect of the interweaving of certain historical and cultural practices or technologies has made connections with the Deleuzo-Guattarian conceptualization of the self as a threshold, a door, a becoming between multiplicities, the nomadic self par excellence. Moreover, the Foucauldian ethico-aesthetic paradigm has been related to Guattari's conceptualization of subjectivity as a continuous creation, a constant mobilization of forces and vectors expanding beyond the subject/object and individual/society divides.

Looking back into the event of Mary Titcomb's becomings, a positive force seems to be emerging: social formations and subjects are mostly defined by their lines of flight and in this light it is – as Foucault (1986) has suggested – possible, desirable and politically sustainable to live and keep imagining and reinventing our lives as works of art. After all, gender and education is a theoretical and political field par excellence where striated and smooth spaces are continuously transversed and translated into each other, a site of intense struggles and antagonistic relations at play but also an open space continuously creating conditions of possibility for deterritorializations to occur, lines of flight to be released, events and nomadic subjects in their vicinities to emerge. If, as Deleuze has argued, it is only in narratives that events can leave their marks (2001, p. 73), tracing events and following lines of nomadic becomings by way of narratives is a new, rich and undoubtedly contested area in the field of gender and education yet to be explored.

Acknowledgements

Earlier versions of this paper were presented at the sociology seminar series of the University of Surrey in November 2006 and at the Gender and Education Conference at Trinity College Dublin in March 2007. I would like to thank the participants of these events for their helpful comments and suggestions, and particularly Victoria Alexander at the University of Surrey for the illuminating discussion we had regarding Dimaggio's work. My thanks also to Paul Dobbs, Library Director of the Massachusetts College of Art, for all his support and guidance during my visit to the Massachusetts College of Art Archives in March 2006. I am indebted to the current owner of the Mary Bradish Titcomb painting for giving me permission to reproduce the image. Special thanks to the Vose Galleries in Boston and particularly to Christopher Greene for facilitating the permission process.

Notes

1. The paper draws on an on-going research project entitled 'In the fold between life and art: a genealogy of women artists'. The project was funded by AHRC and the University of East London, and I am thankful to both of them.
2. See Tamboukou and Ball (2002) for a more elaborated discussion of these notions in general and of nomadism in particular.
3. For a critical overview of this tradition, see amongst others, Tamboukou (2003a), particularly chapter 1, 'Writing herself'.
4. See Tamboukou (2008) for a detailed discussion of a genealogical approach to narratives.
5. Signs in Deleuze's analysis of Proust's work (1964/2000) are not perceived within the signifier–signified relation. They are not something that we can recognize. They are rather encounters that can only be sensed or felt through a form of violence that they exercise on our thought. Put simply, signs force us to think differently.
6. Mary Titcomb has been included in the catalogue of the inaugural exhibition 'American Women Artists, 1830–1930' of the National Museum of Women in the Arts (Tufts, 1987, cat. no. 54); there is a passing reference to Mary Bradish Titcomb as a landscape painter 'who favoured views of Marblehead' accompanied by a black and white image of one of her paintings 'View Looking Towards Gloucester Mass, 1915' in a publication on women artists in Boston (Hirshler, 2001, p. 144) and the most comprehensive presentation of her life and work is a biographical sketch included in the already-mentioned exhibition catalogue of the Vose Galleries.
7. *Boston Evening Traveller*, 22 March 1886, cited in Jarzombek, 1988, p. 2.
8. See, amongst others, Adkins and Skeggs (2004).
9. *Brockton Daily Enterprise*, 14 January 1888, p. 1, cited in Jarzombek, 1988, p. 3.
10. *Boston Daily Globe*, 13 December 1894, p. 1, cited in Jarzombek, 1998, p. 4.
11. *The Bostonian 1*, vol. 4, January 1895, p. 4, cited in Jarzombek, 1998, p. 4.
12. *Providence Sunday Journal*, 11 December 1898, cited in Jarzombek, 1998, p. 15.

References

Adkins, L. & Skeggs, B., (Eds.) (2004). *Feminism after Bourdieu*. Oxford: Blackwell.

Barbee-Babson, M. (1914, March 1). Studios of some who have made Boston famous in the world of art. (Boston) *Sunday Herald*, Special Features section, p. 3.

Buchanan, I. (2000). *Deleuzism: a metacommentary*. Edinburgh: Edinburgh University Press.

Colebrook, C. (2002). *Gilles Deleuze*. London: Routledge.

Davidoff, L. (1995). *Worlds between: Historical perspectives on gender and class*. Cambridge, UK: Polity.

De Certeau, M. (1988). *The practice of everyday life*. London: University of California Press.

Dean, S.M. (1924). *History of the Massachusetts Normal Art School, 1873–4 to 1923–4*. Boston: MNAS Alumni Association.

DeLanda, M. (2006). Deleuzian social ontology and assemblage theory. In M. Fuglsang & B.M. Sørensen (Eds.), *Deleuze and the social* (pp. 250–266). Edinburgh: Edinburgh University Press.

Deleuze, G. (2000). *Proust and the signs* (R. Howard, Trans.). Minneapolis: University of Minnesota Press. (Original work published 1964)

Deleuze, G. (2001). *The logic of sense* (M. Lester, Trans.). London: Continuum. (Original work published 1969)

Deleuze, G. (2004). *Difference and repetition* (P. Patton, Trans.). London: Continuum. (Original work published 1968)

Deleuze, G., & Guattari, F. (1984). *Anti-Oedipus: Capitalism and schizophrenia* (R. Hurley, M. Seem, & H.R. Lane, Trans.). London: The Athlone Press. (Original work published 1972)

Deleuze, G., & Guattari, F. (1988). *A thousand plateaus: Capitalism and schizophrenia* (B. Massumi, Trans.). London: The Athlone Press. (Original work published 1980)

Deleuze, G., & Parnet, C. (2002). *Dialogues II* (H. Tomlinson & B. Habberjam, Trans.). London: Continuum. (Original work published 1977)

Denzin, N.K. (2000). Foreword. In M. Andrews, S.D. Sclater, C. Squire, & A. Treacher (Eds.), *Lines of narrative* (pp. xi–xiii). London: Routledge.

Dimaggio, P. (1982a). Cultural entrepreneurship in nineteenth-century Boston: The creation of an organizational base for high culture in America. Media. *Culture and Society, 4*(1), 33–50.

Dimaggio, P. (1982b). Cultural entrepreneurship in nineteenth-century Boston: The creation of an organizational base for high culture in America, part II: the classification and framing of American art. Media. *Culture and Society, 4*, 303–322.

Foucault, M. (1986). On the genealogy of ethics: An overview of work in progress. In P. Rabinow (Ed.), *The Foucault reader* (pp. 340–372). Harmondsworth, UK: Peregrine.

Foucault, M. (1987). A preface to transgression. In D.F. Bouchard (Ed.), *Language, counter-memory, practice: Selective essays and interviews* (pp. 29–52). Ithaca, NY: Cornell University Press.

Foucault, M. (1988). Technologies of the self. In L. Martin, H. Gutman & P. Hutton (Eds.), *Technologies of the self* (pp. 16–49). London: Tavistock.

Foucault, M. (1991). *The archaeology of knowledge* (A. Sheridan, Trans.). London: Routledge. (Original work published 1969)

Fuglsang, M., & Sørensen, B.M. (2006). Deleuze and the social: Is there a D-function? In M. Fuglsang & B.M. Sørensen (Eds.), *Deleuze and the social* (pp. 1–17). Edinburgh: Edinburgh University Press.

Guattari, F. (1995). *Chaosmosis: An ethico-aesthetic paradigm* (P. Baines & J. Pefanis, Trans.). Sydney: Power Publications. (Original work published 1992)

Jarzombek, N.A. (1998, May 30–July 31). *Mary Bradish Titcomb and her contemporaries, the artists of Fenway Studios* [Exhibition catalogue]. Boston: Vose Galleries.

Hirshler, E. (2001). *A studio of her own, women artists in Boston, 1870–1940*. Boston: Museum of Fine Arts Publications.

Korzenik, D. (1987). The art education of working women, 1873–1903. In A. Faxon & S. Moore (Eds.), *From pilgrims and pioneers: New England women in the arts* (pp. 33–42). New York: Midmarch Arts Press.

Latour, B. (2002). Gabriel Tarde and the end of the social. In P. Joyce (Ed.), *The social in question. New bearings in history and the social sciences* (pp. 117–132). London: Routledge.

Lazzaratto, M. (2006). The concepts of life and the living in the societies of control. In M. Fuglsang & B.M. Sørensen (Eds.), *Deleuze and the social* (pp. 171–190). Edinburgh: Edinburgh University Press.

Levine, L. (1988). *Highbrow/lowbrow: The emergence of cultural hierarchy in America*. Boston: Harvard University Press.

Massachusetts College of Art Archives (1998). *Visionary education: 125 Years of Massachusetts College of Art* [Pamphlet]. Boston: Author.

Massey, D. (2005). *For space*. London: Sage.

Nietzsche, F. (1990). Twilight of the idols or, how to philosophize with a hammer: The anti-Christ (R.J. Hollingdale, Trans.). London: Penguin. (Original work published 1895)

Patton, P. (2006). Order, exteriority and flat multiplicities in the social. In M. Fuglsang & B.M. Sørensen (Eds.), *Deleuze and the social* (pp. 21–38). Edinburgh: Edinburgh University Press.

Stankiewicz, M.A. (1992). From the aesthetic movement to the arts and crafts movement. *Studies in Art Education, 33*(3), 165–173.

Tamboukou, M. (2003a). *Women, education and the self: A Foucauldian perspective*. Basingstoke, UK: Palgrave, Macmillan.

Tamboukou, M. (2003b). Interrogating 'the emotional turn': Making connections with Foucault and Deleuze. *European Journal of Psychotherapy, Counseling and Health*, 6(3), 209–223.

Tamboukou, M. (2008). Re-imagining the narratable subject. *Qualitative Research*, 8(3), 283–292.

Tamboukou, M., & Ball, S.J. (2002). Nomadic subjects: Young black women in Britain. *Discourse: Studies in the Cultural Politics of Education*, 23, 267–284.

Tarde, G. (1899). *Social laws: An outline of sociology* (H.C. Warren, Trans.). London: Macmillan.

Tarde, G. (2006) Monadologie et sociologie [Monadology and sociology]. In G. Tarde, *Essais et mélanges sociologiques* [Sociological essays and combinations] (pp. 309–389). Boston: Adamant Media Corporation. (Original work published 1895)

Tufts, E. (1987). *American women artists, 1830–1930*. Washinghton DC: The National Museum of Women in the Arts.

Vicinus, M. (1985). *Independent women: Work and community for single women 1850–1920*. London: Virago Press.

Williams, J. (2003). *Gilles Deleuze's difference and repetition: A critical introduction and guide*. Edinburgh: Edinburgh University Press.

When the familiar is strange: encountering the cultural politics of Hawaii in the college classroom

Hannah M. Tavares

Introduction

Women of color have been consistent in bringing attention to the power relations inherent in spaces of teaching, often speaking from the *lived* social relations they encounter as professors in the college classroom (hooks, 1989, 1994). As a result, there is a large body of scholarship that troubles the nurturing, caring, and safe environment promoted in feminist pedagogy (Belenky, Clinchy, Goldberger, & Tarule, 1986; Goldberger, Tarule, Clinchy, & Belenky, 1996) and the themes of mastery, voice, positionality, and authority cultivated in the feminist classroom (Maher & Tetreault, 1994). Most important, women of color have shown that feminist pedagogic theories advanced as being universally applicable to all women appear upon closer examination limited to *particular* women. The fractured discourses that surround feminist pedagogy expose the power differentials embedded in its framework, particularly around issues of embodiment, and, at the same time, insist upon a treatment of racialization, the fact that not all women enter into spaces of teaching on equal footing.

Although what I attend to in this essay is grounded in a very specific socio-political and historico-cultural context, the central concerns that are raised have broader implications for disclosing the complex intersections of gender, ethnicity, racialization and privilege. The specific moment – an encounter in the college classroom where the impact of racial–ethnic allegiance and repudiation meet – serves as a catalyst for the questions posed herein. These are questions that not only trouble knowledge-producing discourses concerning teaching/learning, but complicate discourses pertaining to gendered difference as well.

Before moving to the details of that traumatic moment and its significance for troubling gender, it is necessary to acknowledge the context and cultural politics to which it is a part. I will do this by entering into an academic debate that began in the mid-1990s that called into question the *canonical* narrative of the local Asian American subject as the *agent* of historical change in Hawaii. This route, although it may appear circuitous to the topic, will permit me to do two things. First, it will situate for readers a needed context of the Pacific, one that differs from the familiar representation of the region as culturally isomorphic. Najita's (2006) construct of the Pacific in terms of its 'decentered rhizomatic geography' and 'history of multiple and different (neo)colonizations' produces a more complex and disjunctive order to locate Hawaii and its cultural politics (p. 7). Against this backdrop, I hope to initiate readers into the complex distribution of racial relations formed across a range of social, economic, and cultural privileges. Second, the debate will set the stage for me to move into the details of the classroom encounter which serves as a catalyst for a theoretical consideration of the intersection of the racial and sexual symbolic in subject formation and the cultural politics of Hawaii. The explicit and implicit racial references to my 'teaching style' are suggestive of the cultural fantasies of racial *difference* that lay at the surface of the teaching/learning environment in the Pacific.

Bounded histories, bounded memories

'I' am what insiders to Hawaii would call 'local'. The 'local' subject emerged within a specific context that effected, to use Anderson's (1983) seminal phrase, a new form of an 'imagined community' among both immigrant groups and Hawaiians beginning in the last decades of the 1800s. It is a term which signified a difference, that is, a set of experiences and shared structural positioning that marked a laboring and socially subordinate class (Chinese, Filipino, Japanese, Korean, Okinawan, Portugese, Puerto Rican, and Hawaiian) from a predominantly Euro-American ruling class of planters (sugar and pineapple) and merchants and their beneficiaries. Moreover, it is a term that exposed the class positioning inherent in capitalist social relations of production. The 'local' subject, in effect, materialized out of an encounter with a white planter and merchant oligarchy. The disparate alliance developed across class, racial and ethnic lines has been central to the salience of the term and its subsequent transformation into a cultural identity in the islands.

Since the mid-1990s, primarily in academic writing, the term has come under critical examination. Chang's (1996) treatment of the historicity of the term and its signifying trajectory can be credited for provoking a critical 're-viewing of the Local' subject (p. 8). In his important essay, 'Local knowledge(s): notes on race relations, panethnicity and history in Hawaii', Chang traced the term's connection to the emergence of ethnic and race social relations of production in Hawaii; its development as an epistemological and ontological category through the production of 'local' literature; its grafting to a national narrative of American exceptionalism; as well as its potential for designating, not consensus, but a multiplicity of views.

Presently, however, the strand of American exceptionalism connected to the term that put the heroic (read Japanese Americans) local subject at the center of the social and political history of the islands in Hawaii, is under crisis. As put by Chang a decade ago, 'The Local did not seek separation from the colonial power; it sought absorption into the body of America' (1996, p. 14). Extending Chang's critique even further, Hawaiian Studies scholar and leader of the Hawaiian sovereignty movement, Haunani — Kay Trask's (2000) essay, 'Settlers of color and "immigrant" hegemony', charged the 'local' Asian American subject with collaborating in the subjugation of Native Hawaiians. As Trask put it:

> Today, modern Hawaii, like its colonial parent the United States, is a settler society. Our Native people and territories have been overrun by Non-Natives, including Asians. Calling themselves 'local', the children of Asian settlers greatly outnumber us. They claim Hawaii as their own, denying indigenous history, their long collaboration in our continued dispossession, and the benefits therefrom. (2000, p. 2)

I want to note that in Trask's critique, she cites the published works of six Japanese American men in a footnote. That such works, and by extension particular bodies, are cited, brings attention to another layer of cultural history and production of difference that cannot be sequestered from American racial dynamics. While it is crucial that Trask's critical confrontation aims to critique a dominant script that is told and retold *as if* it is uncontested it is equally crucial to discern how the various textual forms of the 'model minority' ideal underpinning the story, but also located across ethnic and cultural milieus, comes to have so much significance.

In *Immigrant Acts*, Lowe (1996) points out that 'Asia' (both within and outside of America) is a site on which the anxieties of the American nation-state have been figured (in Cheng, 2001, p. 23). Developing this link further, Cheng (2001) notes how the project of nation-making in the USA cannot be bracketed from the racialization of Asian Americans and African Americans. 'In the background of – and at times *as* the foil to – black civil rights struggles gripping this country', writes Cheng, 'Asian Americans have come to occupy a curious place in the American racial imaginary, embodying both delight and repugnance' (p. 23). As Cheng (2001) so insightfully notes:

> The very history of Asian immigration (itself far from homogenous), has often been solicited to inflect, on the part of the Asian immigrant, a manic relation to the American Dream. This strain of Asian euphoria in America in turn serves to contain the history of Asian abjection, as well as to discipline other racialized groups in America. (p. 23)

In a different place, Cheng draws attention to what that strain of Asian euphoria conceals and sanitizes when she asks, 'What would it mean to reside within inassimilable difference and incommensurability, to experience one's ontology as constantly at odds with the available cultural dressing? *That* is of course the very condition of pain that this euphoric vision is fending off' (2001, p. 71). Cheng's psychoanalytic lens onto the production of racial differences opens up rather than forecloses a line of thinking that has possibilities for engaging a 'haunted racial identity' that the narrative of ethnic euphoria works to deflect. Although the origin of the cultural construction of the Asian American model minority can be dated to a 1966 publication titled, 'Success story: Japanese-American style' in the *New York Times Magazine*, what Lowe and Cheng draw out in their analysis is not only the political cost of the construct, but its disciplining function.

Presently the histories of Asian and Asian American abjection are not only buried beneath the dominant strain of ethnic euphoria, but displaced by the primary political concerns of Native nationalism in the Hawaiian archipelago. As Trask (2000) firmly states:

> If Hawaiians have a pre-contact, pre-invasion historical continuity on their aboriginal territories ... 'locals' do not. That is, 'locals' have no indigenous land base, traditional language, culture, and history that is Native to Hawaii. Our indigenous origin enables us to define what and who is indigenous, and what and who is not indigenous. We know who the First Nations people are since we were, historically, the first people in the Hawaiian archipelago. Only Hawaiians are Native to Hawaii. Everyone else is a *settler*. (p. 6, emphasis added)

Although these questions concerning the local subject and its political relation to indigeneity are grounded within specific socio-political and historico-cultural conditions in Hawaii, the dispute has broader implications for it underscores a theoretical tension, not easily resolved, around the structure of the political act and the *fiction* of the essential subject (Burgin, 1996; Collins, 1991; Gilroy, 1993). Crucially, the broader issues of this dispute need and do have wider resonances. Concretely, the grievance draws attention to shifting relations of power involved in processes of remembering, of omission and forgetting, as well as to the political, ethical, and practical insights that may be gained and cultivated as a result. Presently it seems that such terms as 'local', 'native', 'immigrant', and 'settler' are designations that have not only been cast as *absolute*, but *placed* in opposition as well as rigidly circumscribing what is possible within the rationality of its structure.

In the subsequent sections I explore the exponential repercussions of the oppositions, and by extension the logic of identification it presumes. I ask, as Butler (2004) has, about a different set of terms, what it offers for the possibility of thinking, of language, and of embodiment (p. 176). Specifically, I inquire into how contemporary social relations in Hawaii interface with the psychic landscape where the process of identification comes into play. I do this through recounting an incident in the classroom where 'I' was forced to remember. It goes without saying that taking such a route has much to do with a desire to understand my own relation to the terms 'local', 'native', 'settler', 'immigrant'. But there are other reasons as well. I hope to make use of the openings from a body of critical work that has thought through the complex logics of *ressentiment*. Further, I hope to invigorate thinking on the politics of the classroom (historically a space of pastoral guidance and spiritual discipline) where bodies, gender and racial differences, and the dynamics of identification converge in complicated ways (see Hunter, 1996).

Unsettling lessons

> Something in the behavior of the other – speech, glance, posture . . . *some thing* – seems laden with significance . . . but, I do not know what it is . . . Nor does the other know. (Burgin, 1996, pp. 269–270)

My body is a body already preassigned as a deficit; *placed* as 'minority' (both female and racialized) signifying an undesirable subject. In the college classroom, my body lacks 'canonical recognition', residing outside of the cultural meaning and dynamics associated with the 'university professor' (Sylvester, 1998, p. 45). In the context where I teach, my body is often made (intentionally or not) a point of reference for other capabilities. A case in point is when I asked a 'senior' colleague to observe and give me feedback on my undergraduate teaching. I was both puzzled and amused when my colleague said that I had an 'Asian' teaching style. Although what that 'means' is far from self-evident; that my teaching could be reduced to *a* 'teaching style' and, moreover, that it is in accordance with the racialization of my body was perplexing. After all, what exactly does an 'Asian teaching style' look like? How does one disentangle the purportedly 'Asian' attributes from the *seeing* and *saying* which must take place *in/as* language already saturated with norms of recognition by which 'Asian' is constituted (Butler, 2004; Scott, 1995)?

The incident that caused me to grieve occurred while I was teaching a course required for teachers who were enrolled in the department's summer Masters' leadership cohort program. The program is housed in a public research-intensive university. Course work is offered in the summer with approximately 25 students. Reconstructing that moment,

I recall telling a couple of people how pleased I was with the way the course was moving. I woke up that morning in a generous mood and stopped at my neighborhood coffee shop to pick up muffins and pastries for my class. I planned to return my students' first writing assignment and distribute the next one. In the process of handing back their papers, I mentioned that more than half of the class neglected to answer all the parts of the question. I explained that re-writes would be accepted, and then proceeded to return their papers and distribute the new writing assignment. Some students began to raise questions about the new assignment. These questions were, for the most part, from the group of students who received lower marks on their papers for not responding to the entire question. After explaining several possible ways to respond to the assignment, the questions continued.

One student asked if she was to answer the essay question in such-and-such a way would it be correct. It occurred to me that a handful of students associated their low grade on their assignment with a lack of clarity on my part. One student brought up the fact that I did not have 'rubrics' and, therefore, knowing what was expected of them was unclear. Another student was quick to remind me that they were doing really well and getting good grades in their other classes.

In attempting to address these complaints, I reminded them what was minimally expected – answering all parts of an essay question – followed by a reminder that they were enrolled in an accelerated degree program. As I was attempting to calm their anxieties one of my students raised her hand. Tears streaming down her cheeks she exclaimed: 'I don't appreciate how you are talking to my cohort, I love these people!' It was followed by something very close to, 'You seem to think we are attacking you' and, then, she began to incriminate me for neglecting the different 'learning styles' in the classroom.

As I looked around the classroom I noticed at least two other women in tears. Although I must admit I did feel 'attacked', I was also surprised by their reactions. I began to talk about the various ways in which I thought I was attentive to their needs. For example, the numerous adjustments I made to the syllabus that included eliminating readings and reducing the number of assignments. I also reminded my student, who implicitly charged me of withholding my love, how I was attempting to accommodate her request to miss a day so that she could attend a family reunion on the neighbor island. After specifying some of the ways in which I symbolically 'loved' them, I found myself apologizing for my bad behavior. I apologized for the way I responded to their questions; for the way I spoke; for the tone of my voice; for my lack of clarity; a litany of apologies.

Whenever I replay that scene, I still have trouble comprehending how I was able to proceed with teaching. The course format is a seminar which incorporates class discussion around assigned readings. I realized I had to find the wherewithal to gather my self and shift from being a spectacle of humiliation to becoming their teacher. After class, as I walked back to my office, I was overtaken by both emotional and intellectual disorientation. A colleague appeared at my door shortly afterwards. Assuming that he got wind of what happened, I began to recount what had happened. While I was retracing the sequence of unsettling events, one of my students came to the door. In another time she would have called herself 'local' Japanese American, but after recovering her indigeniety she now identifies herself as Native Hawaiian. She came to tell me that she appreciated my 'teaching style' and that she valued my efforts to get the cohort out of their 'comfort zone', as she put it. She then said that I had an 'East Coast' teaching style, one that she was familiar with having gone to college somewhere in the eastern part of the US continent. Struck by the timing of her comment, I turned to my colleague who had framed me in a similar manner, and said 'Well, that's interesting because he thinks that I have an "Asian" teaching style'.

I have recounted this story many times to many different people – friends, relatives, colleagues, and my partner – as I sought to bring language to process the raw emotions and reconstruct adequately what happened that day. While I knew about the often hostile experiences women academics of color face in the classroom, I was still stunned by the confrontation and my response to it. After all, wasn't this *my* imagined community? Some of my colleagues attribute the crisis to the idiosyncracies of the cohort and logistics of the program. They have suggested that the unpreparedness of the students, the timing of my course (it was the last one in a series of four), the lack of contact time with the cohort prior to our scheduled class meeting, and my inexperience working with cohorts, can impact the teaching setting in unfavorable ways. While I knew that all of these dynamics matter tremendously, I also believe that what transpired in my classroom cannot be reduced to such technical and instrumental explanations. What remains unexamined is an entangled racial–ethnic–gender dynamic of identification at the surface of the confrontation. In the proceeding section I return to Cheng (2001), but this time to her elaboration of the psychoanalytic concept, *identification*. I do this for two reasons. First, her treatment reworks the concept and provides valuable insight into its logic and the difficult work that is required to both apprehend and transform its structural paradox. Second, I believe that the encounter helps illuminate the process of identification in which the racial and sexual symbolic operates.

Complicated loves

Cheng reminds us that the psychoanalytic origin of identification 'denotes the elaborate, mediating process that relates self to other, subject to object, inside to outside' (2001, p. 176). Elaborating further on this process, she says:

> Identification ... denotes an intricate psychical process underlying subject formation ... Identification is crucially *not* the same as identity, although it is what secures for the latter its mythology of integrity. Identification organizes and instantiates identity ... [A]s the mechanism that subtends the possibility and limit of any given identity, identification serves as the vehicle for interpersonal negotiation. (p. 176)

More significantly, the apparatus for interpersonal navigation inaugurates in conceptualizations of grief.

> First there existed an object-choice, the libido had attached itself to a certain person; then, owing to a real injury or disappointment concerned with the loved person, this object-relationship was undermined ... but the free libido was withdrawn into the ego and not directed to another object. It did not find application there, however, in any one of several possible ways, but served simply to establish an *identification* of the ego with the abandoned object. (Freud, quoted in Cheng, 2001, p. 177)

In this procedure worked out by Freud (the fundamental relationship between identification and the compensation of loss), Cheng maintains that identification may be '*literally* an expression of grief' (2001, p. 178). Tracing the views of other psychoanalytic thinkers (Diana Fuss, Judith Butler, and Elin Diamond) that acknowledge the fundamental role of melancholic identification to psychic development, Cheng (2001) elaborates a theoretical account that foregrounds race; she calls it, *racial* melancholia.

> [I]f melancholic identification is 'routine' (Fuss) or 'constitutive' (Butler) to psychic development, then racial melancholia – a melancholic structure of identification played out in the sociohistorical realm of race relations – complicates practically all of the explicit and implicit terms of that routine: compensation and loss, love and its inverse, subject and object, incorporation and rejection ... [W]hen these terms get played out as sociohistorical relations, then they leave devastating, material effects on the lost or denied 'object,' the racial other. (p. 179)

Cheng's account of racial melancholia resonates closely with Fanon's (1967) disclosure in *Black Skin, White Masks* of 'an unfamiliar weight' burdening his body upon meeting 'the white man's eyes' (p. 110). Fanon perceptively links his blackness *as* an abhorrent visual imago to a 'historico-racial schema' formulated *not* by Fanon, but instead from 'a thousand details, anecdotes, stories', or 'legends, stories ... and above all historicity' (1967, pp. 111–112). Both recognize that difference is produced *and* crafted in time. The concept of 'racial melancholia' as discussed by Cheng provides a useful lens to help disentangle the difficult nexus of racial, cultural, ethnic, sexual, gendered, political difference dramatized inside and outside of my classroom.

I am willing to wager that the teaching attributes that were assigned to my body, such as 'Asian', and then 'East Coast', although couched in a seemingly neutral discourse of 'teaching style', reveal a much more complicated set of significations. To unpack the terms we need to take them out of their neoliberal, corporate and educational psychological frame and connect them to the specificity of the (neo)colonial context and to a framework that foregrounds otherness in racialized and sexualized terms. When we locate those representations within the context of the 'American racial imaginary', to use Cheng's expression, the two utterances function as exact opposites (2001, p. 108). The former equates Asian-ness with passivity and femininity, the latter image to aggression and masculinity (2001, pp. 108–110). Both images, furthermore, marshal racial and gender assumptions about stereotypical attributes of Asians and Caucasians. But, apart from the culturally normative apprehension of 'Asian-ness' and 'whiteness', there is yet another dimension that seems to suggest that it does *matter* who is doing the looking. When my Caucasian colleague *looks* he *sees* a body that signifies 'non-whiteness', and when my Native Hawaiian student *looks* she *sees* a body that signifies 'whiteness'. It is not my desire to suggest that their *seeing* is 'wrong' and if they really would *look* more carefully they would see the 'truth' or 'essence' of my specifically embodied identity. Rather, I prefer to think about these utterances as highlighting how looking is *fractured* through socio-cultural, racial, and gender histories (Cheng, 2001, p. 182). These heterogeneous histories, including my own, is what Diamond (in Cheng, 2001) calls 'historical contradictions' (p. 181). It is a construct that is useful for thinking about the incommensurability between the two utterances and for thinking further about the complex workings of gendered difference.

In a beautifully written and provocative book entitled *Testimony*, Felman and Laub (1992) write that teaching 'should take position at the edge of itself, at the edge of its conventional conception' (p. 54). Felman views teaching as a transformative experience for her students. She says, 'I want my students to be able to receive information that is *dissonant*, and not just *congruent*, with everything that they have learned beforehand' (p. 53). This is what I want for my students as well, but it is clear to me that the heterogeneous histories that meet in spaces of teaching/learning can thwart such transformative aims. As we strive for such an ideal, perhaps we must also admit that 'not all racial bodies are created equal'. This of course has less to do with any 'essential or moral reasons'; rather, it is because as Cheng so insistently points out, 'all racial bodies exist within (indeed, are defined by) this history of power' (2001, p. 184).

This inequality is often manifested in a *phenomenology*, that is to say, a situation in which the student/subject is seeking, among other things, to extract confirmation for her/his personal self-making. The crisis in my classroom, to some extent, can be attributed to my body; a body that intensifies the dynamics of identification but in very complicated ways. I enter the college classroom already preassigned as a deficit. The question of credentials and competencies lay at the surface of my being. Yet, my body is familiar (working-class, ethnically Filipino, Portugese, English, Hawaiian, Tahitian, Chinese) signifying the 'local-ness'of my identity; at the same time, it is unfamiliar (PhD, cultural theorist, East Coast) making me a troubled 'ally'. It is in this sense that racialized and gendered bodies are dealing with complicated loves in the classroom.

Summary

The point of recounting this incident is motivated by several considerations. First, I am interested in the challenge it affords for showing how social relations *live* at the heart of psychical dynamics (Cheng, 2001, p. 15). This essay offers an opportunity for such exploratory work particularly as it relates to identity, grief, and postcolonial cultural politics. Second, I believe that the questions and issues raised by my narrative resonate with a wider audience. If we are patient we see that there are connections to be made between the expert systems of knowledge that constitute the institutional space of teaching/learning as distinctly rational where 'rubrics', 'learning preferences', and 'teaching styles' provide a grid of *intelligible* and, therefore, *legitimate* instruction; processes of identification where love and betrayal are dramatized; and, domains of the political where embodiment, histories, memories, and fantasy come together in complex ways. Finally, I wanted to show the significance of an analysis that weaves together feminist, psycho-analytic, and postcolonial strands of criticism for rendering how we might expand our thinking to account for the complicated loves at the surface of the teaching/learning environment. The move that I am calling for is to trouble differences (racial, gendered, and ethnic) by exploring their production in historical process (Gupta & Ferguson, 1992). As I indicated earlier, this endeavor builds on the critical work of the past few decades on language, discourse, and difference; but it is also shaped by the crucial interventions of Fanon (1967) and more recently feminist psychoanalytic theorists who have worked to trouble theorizations of gender and sexuality by interrogating the unacknowledged whiteness embedded in its frames (see Abel, 1990; Walton, 1995). The consequence of such work is the possibilities it offers for more detailed treatments of understanding the intersections of race and gender and investigating knowledge-producing discourses within global contexts and transnational socio-cultural formations.

Acknowledgements

I would like to thank the two blind reviewers and the editors, Jo-Anne Dillabough, Julie McLeod and Martin Mills, for their critical comments and suggestions. I am indebted to Kathie Kane, Grace Livingston, Alana Parpal, and Michael Shapiro for their politically insightful conversations.

References

Abel, E. (1990). Race, class, and psychoanalysis? Opening questions. In M. Hirsch & E.F. Keller (Eds.), *Conflicts in feminism* (pp. 184–204). New York: Routledge.

Anderson, B. (1983). *Imagined communities: Reflections on the origin and spread of nationalism.* London: Verso.

Belenky, M., Clinchy, B., Goldberger, N., & Tarule, J. (1986). *Women's ways of knowing.* New York: Basic Books.

Burgin, V. (1996). *In/Different spaces: Place and memory in visual culture.* Los Angeles: University of California Press.

Butler, J. (2004). *Undoing gender.* New York: Routledge.

Chang, J. (1996). Local knowledge(s): Notes on race relations, panethnicity and history in Hawaii. *Amerasia Journal, 22*(2), 1–29.

Cheng, A. (2001). *The melancholy of race psychoanalysis, assimilation, and hidden grief.* Oxford: Oxford University Press.

Collins, P. (1991). *Black feminist thought: Knowledge, consciousness, and the politics of empowerment.* New York: Routledge.

Fanon, F. (1967). *Black skin, white masks* (Trans. C.L. Markmann). New York: Grove Press.

Felman, S., & Laub, D. (1992). *Testimony: Crises of witness in literature, psychoanalysis, and history.* New York: Routledge.

Gilroy, P. (1993). *The black Atlantic.* Cambridge, MA: Harvard University Press.

Goldberger, N., Tarule, J., Clinchy, B., & Belenky, M. (1996). *Knowledge, difference, and power: Essays inspired by women's ways of knowing.* New York: Basic Books.

Gupta, A., & Ferguson, J. (1992). Beyond 'culture': Space, identity, and the politics of difference. *Cultural Anthropology, 7*(1), 6–23.

Hooks, B. (1989). *Talking back: Thinking feminist, thinking black.* Cambridge, MA: South End Press.

Hooks, B. (1994). *Teaching to transgress: Education as the practice of freedom.* New York: Routledge.

Hunter, I. (1996). Assembling the school. In A. Barry, T. Osborne & N. Rose (Eds.), *Foucault and political reason* (pp. 143–166). Chicago: University of Chicago Press.

Lowe, L. (1996). *Immigrant acts: On Asian American cultural politics.* Durham, NC: Duke University Press.

Maher, F., & Tetreault, M. (1994). *The feminist classroom.* New York: Basic Books.

Najita, S. (2006). *Decolonizing cultures in the Pacific.* New York: Routledge.

Scott, J. (1995). Multiculturalism and the politics of identity. In J. Rajchman (Ed.), *The identity in question* (pp. 3–12). New York: Routledge.

Sylvester, C. (1998). Handmaids' tales of Washington power: The abject and the real Kennedy white house. *Body & Society, 4*(3), 39–66.

Trask, H. (2000). Settlers of color and 'immigrant' hegemony: 'Locals' in Hawaii. *Amerasia Journal, 26*(2), 1–24.

Walton, J. (1995). Re-placing race in (White) psychoanalytic discourse: Founding narratives of feminism. *Critical Inquiry, 21*, 775–804.

Sex in the lesbian teacher's closet: the hybrid proliferation of queers in school[1]

Sheila L. Cavanagh

Introduction

It may seem odd that our culture could conceive of an ordinary classroom as a bordello, a place charged with exotic passion (rather than with the smell of wet wool, peed pants, and old uneaten lunches). But most of us take care to know next to nothing about what actually goes on in classrooms ... and erotic suspicion finds its best food in ignorance. Thus we both glamorize (as we ridicule) and resent (as we depend on) the teacher who seems to be 'reaching' the child, teaching her and actually gaining her attention. We might imagine that there's only one way this could be happening, and that way is sinister ... We are concerned, let's pretend, about teaching being a haven for pedophiles. (Kincaid, 1998, p. 218)

In 1993, six news reports relayed the story about a female teacher, Jean Robertson, who had been convicted of sexually abusing a former student, Brenda Johima, when the complainant was in ninth grade. As the Canadian news reports explained, the alleged victim, 31 years at the time of the media release, claimed that her year-long relationship with Robertson, who was 27 years at the time of the alleged abuse, began in a school bathroom near the physical education office, where the lesbian teacher kissed her. The teacher would allegedly lure her victim into the office to have private talks with Johima. In this office, at New Westminster Secondary School, Johima alleged that her coach would 'kiss ... and fondle her breasts'. The former student also testified that Robertson would 'fondle her during rides home from school ... give her a full body massage while she was naked and digitally penetrate her' (Hall, 1993a). Allegations were also heard that the teacher took Johima on a camping trip to Shawnigan Lake, took a sauna with the pre-teen, gave her pornography and liquor, and lay naked on top of her.

A key eyewitness in the trial, Victoria Harris (also a former student), told the provincial court that she 'saw Robertson in a sleeping bag, kissing Johima passionately, during a party for the volleyball team at another teacher's house in 1976' (Hall, 1993b). What made matters worse was that Harris also had a sexual relationship with a female teacher at New Westminster High School at the same time as the alleged affair involving Johima. Harris, now a prison psychiatrist, claimed that she told Heather Cranston, the school vice principal, about the affair between Johima and Robertson but that the female administrator did nothing: she 'shrugged and walked away', apparently having chosen not to investigate the report. Provincial court judge, Ross Tweedle, said that Cranston 'gave the appearance of a witness with something to hide ... she is covering up something serious' (Hall, 1993c). Robertson, now 45 years, was sentenced to four months in prison while maintaining, throughout the court proceedings, that the allegations were false.

Harris later pressed charges of her own against school counsellor, Murline Beltain (then known as Merle Bottaro) for gross indecency because she could 'no longer keep her feelings [about the abuse] bottled up'. The prison psychiatrist said that she was ashamed of her relationship with Beltain during her final four years of high school. The complainant recalled that the teacher used her 'troubled family history to coerce her into an illicit relationship'. She said the incidents included being 'forced to have sex with Beltain in front of another teacher while on a field trip to a volleyball championship in Courtenay'. Despite allegations of coercion, Harris admitted to the court that at the time of the affair, she moved into Beltain's condominium and gave her a copy of *The Joy of Lesbian Sex*. The former student explained that the book was a 'peace offering because she [Beltain] was so angry at me for not being aroused' (Lee, 1995).

The public are led to conclude that there was something sinister going on at New Westminster Secondary School, something diabolical, queer, and endemic to the homosocial underworld. The two sex scandals involving lesbian teachers are entwined and seen to be dangerously duplicitous. I contend that the panic about child protectionism in the Robertson and Beltain cases is a guise for a more deeply entrenched worry about the proliferation of queer identifications in school.

Using queer and postcolonial theories I explore how gender is secured by the deployment of child protectionist discourses. My analysis is indebted to Judith Butler's (1990) formulation of the heterosexual matrix and Judith Halberstam's (2005) writing on queer time and space. Both theorists analyze the ways heterosexuality underpins and secures gender formations. Butler defines the heterosexual matrix as a 'grid of cultural intelligibility through which bodies, genders, and desires are naturalized' (1990, p. 151). She focuses her analysis on the use of gender to regulate and manage bodies in the service of heterosexuality. She claims that the belief in 'opposite' sex bodies (male or female) is accomplished through the repetition and recitation of gender norms over time. Normative heterosexuality is, thus, dependent upon the reproduction of binary gender identifications (male masculinity, and female femininity).

I contend that gender norms are secured in school by appeals to student developmental growth, life-stages and presumptions about sexual innocence. Halberstam (2005) argues that 'Queer uses of time and space develop, at least in part, in opposition to the institutions of family, heterosexuality, and reproduction. They also develop according to other logistics of location, movement, and identification' (p. 1). In other words, queer time is unbounded by familial templates, normative ideas about adolescent growth, sexual innocence, and binary gender identifications. 'Queer subcultures [such as the one in New Westminster School] produce alternative temporalities by allowing their participants to believe that their futures can be imagined according to logics that lie outside of those paradigmatic markers of life experience – namely, birth, marriage, reproduction and death' (Halberstam, 2005, p. 2).

Queer time does not respect chronological age and generational differences that organize thought about the 'child', the 'teen', and the 'adult'. Part of what it means to be queer is to upset heterosexual life-stages. The coming-of-age stories we tell about who we are authenticate our gender identities and naturalize our sexual orientations. Queer tales of seduction in school upset the nature and linearity of heterosexual life-stories; they are out of time and place, rendered perverse, abusive, and criminal.

The problem of how to remember an amorous pedagogical encounter between lesbian teacher and student is complicated by the widespread use of the teenager as 'child' to solidify heterosexual narratives about abuse. Unless we remember female teacher seductions as abusive, the dominant story of heterosexual growth is interrupted. There is, as I will argue, a need to better understand how the high school instates gender binaries by appealing to heteronormative discourses about child and teen sexual development.

It is most often the case that heteronormative stories about budding teenage sexualities are deemed wholesome. Queer stories are often suspect and subject to censure. The sex panics in the above-mentioned cases are, consequently, structured by secrets, suspicions, disavowals, and projections that have little to do with the event that acts as a catalyst for the upset. The sex scandals involving lesbian teachers are saturated by the problem of knowledge, by the paradox of knowing and not knowing, by the 'relations of the known and the unknown, the explicit and the inexplicit around homo/heterosexual definition' (Sedgwick, 1990, p. 3). The female teachers in this case act on lesbian desire while maintaining an official silence, which Eve Sedgwick characterizes as living in a glass closet, noting that 'coming out is a matter of crystallizing intuitions or convictions that had been in the air for a while already and had already established their own power-circuits of silent contempt, silent blackmail, silent glamorization, silent complicity' (1990, pp. 79–80). As Beltain explained: 'It was not okay to be a lesbian teacher then or to be a lesbian teacher now', suggesting that she lived a secret, an open secret that was shielded by the pretence of ignorance on the part of colleagues and students alike.

When Beltain was questioned about why she had not told administrators that Jean Robertson was having a sexual relationship with Brenda Johima, the persecuted teacher insisted that she 'didn't have anything specific to report' (Bellett, 1995b). The trouble with knowledge is thus exacerbated by queer time zones. At the time of the affair, the teacher and student were in love, and there was nothing sinister to report. In the 1990s the affair is remembered as an instance of abuse and punishable by law. The relationship and the recollection of it are out of sync and produce a psychic schism. Teacher–student lesbian sex based on love, trust, and social consent is illegible in contemporary legal rationalist and professional discourse. It does not translate into professional time and cannot be remembered as anything but abuse. The lesbian teacher who fondly remembers and offers joyful reminiscences about the intergenerational relationship is seen to be an atavistic throwback to a queerly primordial time. She is also cast as a predatory lesbian, a danger and threat to children. In effect, the lesbian teacher is caught in a problem of educational time; how to tell of a queer moment when the teacher–student relationship was not coded as, or felt to be, predatory or abusive.

I want therefore to suggest that the pedagogical transgression was not in the time of the past but in the time of the present. The story the lesbian teacher of the 1970s has to tell the courts today about female teacher–student love and sex does not translate into contemporary professional ethics. Professional discourses and practices of the late twentieth and early twenty-first centuries are predicated upon a disavowal of Eros in the pedagogical encounter. Lesbian teacher desire in the educational milieu is even harder to validate, let alone comprehend (given its non-normative status in educational cultures), and so it is subsumed into a unifying narrative of child sexual abuse. Parents, school administrators, developmental psychologists, child advocates, and so forth, are confronted with the temporality of their insistence upon child sexual abuse as they listen to Robertson and Beltain's queer enunciations of teenage student–teacher love. The public and those invested in professionalism and child advocacy are troubled by how the idea of child sexual abuse did not register with the teenage girls in the time of the clandestine affairs. Despite the temporal rupture (child sexual abuse discourses, policies, and interventions are relatively new and specific to the late twentieth and early twenty-first centuries), the listeners are unable to contextualize the lesbian teacher sex scandals. There is resistance to questioning an overarching and ahistorical narrative 'truth' about child sexual abuse by those who have a stake in professionalism, the repudiation of Eros in the high school, and the longevity of the child sexual innocence thesis.

Lesbian teacher sex scandals: the problem of representation, knowledge, and illicit love

As a comparison case through which to explore the interlocking nature of sex panics and postcolonial anxieties about racial difference, I draw on Lillian Hellman's play *The Children's Hour* (1934) and on its Hollywood film adaptation in 1962, a play based on an actual nineteenth-century Scottish court case involving allegations of lesbianism between two teachers running a school for girls. The similarity between contemporary scandals involving lesbian teachers and *The Children's Hour* – not to mention a host of other films, including *Diabolique*, *Oleanna*, *Maedchen in Uniform*, *Therese and Isabelle*, *Picnic at Hanging Rock*, *Heavenly Creatures*, and *Notes on a Scandal* – is striking when we consider that both grapple with the problem of sexual knowledge in the postcolonial context. Speaking about *Oleanna* and *The Children's Hour*, Sauer (2000, p. 421) claims that 'both problematize the possibility of making objective judgments and thereby question the very foundation of the realistic conventions that they seem to espouse', both grapple with belated discoveries of lesbianism, and both underscore panic about queer subjects and timelines in the school.

In her discussion of the play and the later film adaptation, Mikko Tuhkanen (2002) identifies an overlapping anxiety about dissident sexuality, white-race suicide, and eugenics in the lesbian teacher sex scandal. On the one hand, white female homosexuals were not considered a threat by early eugenicists because they did not biologically reproduce themselves (unlike the so-called 'darker races'). From the eighteenth- and nineteenth-century eugenic standpoint, the homosexual *was* a congenital defect, but this defect was well contained by the biological injunction against same-sex reproduction; the homosexual could not reproduce her (or his) own kind. On the other hand, there was, as noted by Tuhkanen (2002, p. 1003), a parallel concern with biologically non-procreative coupling and eugenic worries about 'race and lineage, purity and hybridity'. Lesbians are culturally read as women who do not reproduce. Their investments in heterosexual futurity are weak at best. Of course, many lesbians of today (and yesteryear) do have children but their investment in reproduction is presumed to be secondary to the pleasure of homosexuality and the lifestyle it is assumed to engender. Those over-invested in heteronormativity wonder about the kind of parents lesbians (or gay men for that matter) make and whether or not we may be giving birth to a new generation of gender mutants or sexually hybrid and otherwise non-normative children. Lesbian teachers, therefore, stand in to mark a triadic panic about non-reproductivity (the white race will die out), non-normative reproductivity (the children of gays, lesbians, bisexuals, transgendered peoples, etc., will not be normal), and symbolic reproductivity (lesbian teachers will make the nation's otherwise normal girl students into lesbians).

Lesbian teachers do not always reproduce biologically, and when we do our families tend not to be seen as normative. Regardless of the extent to which a particular lesbian mother may wish to enter into a normative time-space continuum structured by heterosexual appeals to the future, the good citizen, the nation, dominant tropes of whiteness and the like, her family composition is often read as an aberration. The monstrosity of lesbianism is difficult to recoup into the terrain and time of white reproductive futurity. A postmodern eugenic concern about the heterosexual future maps itself onto the body of the white lesbian teacher. But this eugenic panic is not of the same ilk as those that flourished in the late nineteenth and early twentieth centuries. The contemporary eugenic panic is concerned not only with biological but symbolic reproduction. Queer lessons learned in class today are subjects of concern and on the homophobic radar. The proliferation of queer identified students in school is seen not so much a problem of breeding (or in terms of congenital defects), but as problems of teaching. Queer pedagogies, erotic counter-transferences, and sex educations (official and not) are seen to be dangerous and threatening to reproductive futures. This is because they are about desire and the present; not the future and its calls for abstinence. Queer identifications are seen to be products of erotic educations that do not respect the future or the heterosexual mandates central to it.

The contemporary sex panics involving lesbian teachers are laced with secrecy and disavowal because it is symbolic contagion that is of paramount concern. As Robert Young argues in *Colonial Desire* (1995), homosexual generation – 'recruiting', as the contemporary homophobe would call it – is 'silent, covert and unmarked'. The contagion is about the circulation of queer knowledge. Students are thought to be infected by knowledge. The idea of childhood sexual innocence is bolstered by adult refusals to recognize the knowledge students already have and actively seek out. These refusals place the teacher in a difficult position. She is supposed to be sexually pure and innocent even as she is a sexual subject invested with a heteronormative and colonizing mandate. Her whiteness depends on a defensive legacy of purity, morality, and sexual innocence. White femininity is structured by a negation of the horrors and colonizing initiatives actualized through recourse to the caring function (Stoller, 1997, 2000). The white woman is positioned as mother, teacher, guardian of the white race, and as an agent of love, care, and devotion unsullied by desire and carnal knowledge (Dyer, 1997). The lesbian teacher seems to refuse this positioning and shows the public and profession how it is riddled with desires and identifications, on the part of individual teachers, that are not virtuous or benign.

Tuhkanen (2002, p. 1003) argues, in relation to *The Children's Hour*, that the concern about breeding – where 'racial otherness infects white femininity with illicit sexual knowledge – [is connected] to "reading" [or acquiring knowledge of, a devious order and that] the danger of ... contamination of the adolescent female mind' is key to unpacking the scandal of lesbianism in the Scottish school. Those who receive and can understand deviant sexual knowledge become vulnerable to homosexual contagion, an infection caught through the spread of illicit knowledge. The sex scandals involving lesbian teachers are upsetting because they seem to achieve a symbolic victory over reproductive futurity. White female teachers know about non-procreative lesbian sex and seem to actively recruit.

There is a distain for the reproductive future, the white race, and its investment in citizenship, nationality, and nuclear-family forms. Conservatives do not so much panic about child welfare as they do get upset about what Tuhkanen calls the 'hybrid proliferation of queers' (2002, p. 1003). Tuhkanen explains that 'homosexuality is at once completely barren *and* intensely fecund; it signals the dying out of the race *and* a generation of unforeseen hybridities' (p. 1002, original emphasis). The white race does not really die out but it undergoes a permutation, a hybrid transmutation inaugurated by queer circuits of knowledge, desire, and timelines spread in the school.

Sexual contagion, foreign 'others', and the problem of knowledge

> Homosexual desire is the ungenerating-ungenerated terror of the family, because it produces itself without producing. (Guy Hocquenghem, quoted in Tuhkanen 2002, p. 1001)

As in the contemporary Jean Robertson case, the conviction in the Scottish verdict depended, in part, on statements given by a female student, Jane Cummings, who was said to possess intimate knowledge of a devious order. In the Scottish verdict, so well documented by Lillian Faderman (1983), the child witness, having been born in India by a South Asian mother, was thought to have come into contact with deviant sexual knowledge that a Scottish-born child would supposedly not be able to comprehend, so her testimony, which was based on 'half-heard whispers and faint, indescribable noises' (Tuhkanen, 2002, p. 1007), was not only admissible but also instrumental to the conviction. The child could understand the noises in the teacher's bedroom suite as indicative of a deviant act because her genetic breeding, her 'Indianness', and its association with foreign eroticism, fetishistic sexuality, and carnal knowledge enabled a kind of recognition that was allegedly incomprehensible to British-born children. The foreignness of the child leaves her vulnerable to contagious knowledge about deviant – in this case, lesbian – sexuality.

As observed by Mikko Tuhkanen (2002), p. 1007), in the original case on which the *The Children's Hour* was based, there continued to be epistemological uncertainty following testimony given by Cummings: 'The bewildering disparity between Jane Cummings's seeming innocence and her graphic accusations, repeatedly stated in the transcripts, suggests a concomitant anxiety that the East elicited in confounding such easy legibility of content from form'. Tuhkanen draws on Victorian stereotypes about Eastern women documented by Simeran Man Singh Gell to conclude that there was a binary between 'British middle-class women who were supposedly readable' (p. 1007) and Eastern women – characterized by the Indian student – who were secretive and deceptive. South Asian women could, allegedly, split their inner and outer worlds with apparent ease.

The evidence given by Cummings, based on sounds heard in the night, offset the demand for visual evidence, proof that could be uncontested. 'The clues from which Jane Cummings had drawn her conclusions were based on things not seen: the room had always been dark, the women covered with bedding, or, when she had slept in a separate bed, a curtain had been hung between the beds' (Tuhkanen, 2002, p. 1007). The difficulty lay in the fact that the illicit sex could not be ascertained by the British onlooker; it required a special, transgressive, foreign, or queer knowledge circuit that seemed to be lost to the white heteronormative subject.

According to Tuhkanen, deceptive traits – powers of knowledge acquisition that are foreign, wanton, and illicit – were also to be found in lesbian or closely knit same-sex female friendships in the school. Thus, it should not be surprising that in the contemporary case, former student Victoria Harris was also seen to be a reliable witness in the suit against

Jean Robertson because she had experiential access to lesbian sexuality; her affair with Beltain enabled her to stand as an educated eyewitness. Harris observed an illicit kiss between Robertson and Johima. As Jim McDowell (1995) wrote in the *BC Report*: 'She knew what the kiss implied because she was having a lesbian affair with her counsellor-volleyball coach, Murline Beltain, then thirty-six'. Harris worried that 'her lesbian relationship might be brought up and damage her credibility as a witness. So she disclosed the affair to the court'. To her surprise, her proximity to lesbianism enhanced her credibility and ensured her positioning as someone in the know. Her credibility was further buttressed by the fact that she was a prison psychiatrist at King County Prison for Women who worked with those incarcerated who had been sexually abused as children. Harris believed that if she 'was to help her clients she had to resolve her own conflicts first'.

To recognize homosexuality where it cannot be seen by the heterosexual mainstream is to admit that one is also a homosexual or, at the very least, to reveal a fluency in the language of queer culture. The capacity to read lesbianism where it cannot be seen by the heterosexual majority is to have learned the signs and symbols of the closet, an epistemology that depends on heterosexual ignorance. As Sedgwick (1990) explains: 'Insofar as ignorance is ignorance of a knowledge – a knowledge that may itself, it goes without saying, be seen as either true or false under some other regime of truth – these ignorances, far from being pieces of the originary dark, are produced by and correspond to particular knowledges and circulate as part of particular regimes of truth' (p. 8). To be ignorant of homosexuality (as the dominant heterosexual mainstream claims to be) is to be entrenched within a regime of truth that cannot tolerate homosexual knowledge without injury. 'The double-edged potential for injury in the scene of gay coming out ... results partly from the fact that the erotic identity of the person who receives the disclosure is apt also to be implicated in, and hence perturbed by it' (1990, p. 81).

Victoria Harris – as an eyewitness – is caught within a difficulty of knowledge. She cannot know about the Jean Robertson affair without herself having participated in a similarly licentious relationship, and she cannot escape persecution for having once loved another woman without disavowing her lesbian past. The disavowal is accomplished by remembering the four-year live-in relationship as abuse and admitting to shameful feelings for having had such a relationship. Harris told police that in 1977 the accused teacher 'lured her into a sexual relationship which, sixteen years later, she finally realized was a case of sexual abuse' (McDowell, 1995).

The remembrance is questionable when heard alongside the confession given by Beltain. With tears in her eyes, the accused teacher told the court that Harris 'came to her apartment in March 1977 and talked about being upset by her attraction to an older person'. Shortly thereafter Beltain realized that the student was speaking about her. The teacher and student admitted their love, and Beltain told the court that they 'fondled each other' (McDowell, 1995). Recalling the beginning of the affair in 1977, the teacher said that it was a 'joyous day ... exciting to be in love, a buoyant, exuberant time – standing here saying this – it just sounds tawdry' (Bellett, 1995a).

It would be foolhardy to suggest that there are not ethical or professional questions to be asked about teacher–student sex. Eros does permeate the pedagogical encounter (Cavanagh, 2004, 2005, 2007; Gallop, 1995, 1997; Jagodzinski, 2002), and we must consider its impact on students, teachers, and the learning environment. I do not mean to argue that Harris's recollections and testimonies are fabrications or lies or that her narrative testimony should not be taken seriously. Nor do I suggest that belated accusations of sexual abuse are without substance. I am, however, suggesting that the truth as Harris understands it might be constrained by the master narrative of child sexual abuse, which cannot comprehend an intergenerational teacher–student affair based on social (as opposed to legal) consent. If we lived in another time and place where sexuality was subject to another ruling regime – one not so upset by intergenerational and queer sex – might Harris have a different story to tell? Given that she enjoyed and sought out a sexual relationship with Beltain in her teenage years, lived with the accused teacher, and saw herself as an active party in the formation of the relationship, might the discourse of abuse in the present be playing a queer trick? There seems to be a queer lapse in time, memory, and narrative that cannot be substantiated by the evidence of abuse brought to court by Harris. In fact, there was no evidence of abuse at all, except for the difference in age, which, for the courts, is evidence of abuse in and of itself. Legal consent has nothing to do with what the younger party wants or does not want. It is beholden to the idea that sex between someone designated under-age and an adult is de facto abuse. Questions about gender, context, choice, love, safety, maturity and so forth are not only sidelined but deemed irrelevant.

Beltain openly acknowledged the intergenerational affair and was consequently found guilty of gross indecency involving a minor. The teacher insisted that she and Harris were in love and that the relationship, at the time of the affair, was not understood to be abusive. Beltain tried to explain that what is seen as gross indecency today was not seen as abusive in the 1970s. Beltain testified that there were 'differences in attitude between the 1970s and the 1990s concerning student–teacher relationships ... [and that] terms like sexual abuse, boundary violations, these are common in our language' today, but they were not talked about at the time of the relationship (Bellett, 1995b). The convicted teacher also testified that at the time of the affair, she was in love, but today she grieves and seeks forgiveness because of how the relationship is narrated through the discourse of abuse, the regime of truth intelligible to the courts.

Johima is also caught in a similar problem of knowledge demanding disavowal. The former student confessed to going along with the affair with Robertson because she was in love and kept the liaison secret because her 'dad would have [had] a fit'. The complainant explained that she 'knew it was something she had to keep secret'. Paradoxically, Johima said to the court: 'Then I thought I was in love with her. I was a kid and thought that's what love was ... I didn't define it as I see it now – as sexual abuse'. Because of the affair, Johima told the judge that she had difficulty trusting people and that she had intimacy-related struggles in her adult life. To demonstrate the residual harm caused by the affair, the former student testified that 'she feels ill every time she hears a Karen Carpenter song, Close to You, because it brings back memories of her former high school volleyball coach sexually abusing her' – the teacher used to sing the song to her. Upon hearing the tune, the alleged victim reports, 'I feel like vomiting' (Hall, 1993a).

Getting sick is, in itself, an act of expulsion. Johima speaks about illness and nausea upon remembrance. In the film *The Children's Hour*, the lesbian protagonist responds to her aunt's innuendos about her niece's unnatural proclivities by saying: 'You are making me sick' (Tuhkanen, 2002, p. 1014). The knowledge of lesbianism, in both the historical and contemporary cases, is nauseating. But this sickness is a hysterical reaction to contagious knowledge about female homosexuality: it cannot be about me, and if you say that it is, I will throw up. Heterosexual mainstreams refuse to acknowledge that maybe the teenage girls involved in the lesbian teacher sexual improprieties were less than innocent and naive. Perhaps Harris remembers her year-long, live-in relationship with Beltain as abusive even though the original incarnation was based on love and social consent. The sex might be abusive only in retrospect. The relationships seem to be more traumatic for the adults remembering the intergenerational affairs than they were for the teenagers who had the affairs. I suggest that the sex scandals involving lesbian teachers might be products of *adult* identificatory trauma. 'The adult narrator overlays his own remembered experience with another narrative, one that renders him victim. Significantly, that victim narrative is the only one available to him – and to us, in our culture. We lack the possibility to narrate a pedophilia that will have been benign (let alone benevolent, in the Greek way)' (Bruhm & Hurely, 2004, p. xxix). The memory, as opposed to the seduction, is the source of trauma. 'To the degree that the remembered child is the child who liked the sexual contact, the child is killed off; the narrative brought to define him is one of fear, power, abuse, and shame' (Bruhm & Hurley, 2004, p. xxix).

Kevin Ohi (2004), p. 82) makes a similar point in his discussion of the queer child. He writes: 'Panics about childhood sexuality concern above all the adult's fears about his or her own desire, the threat posed by the sexual child to the serenity of adult self-understandings ... To say that children aren't queer is a way of asserting that we know what children are and that we therefore know what adults are'. Adult dis-identification with the queerness of our teenage years is accomplished by the paradoxical insistence upon an innocent heterosexuality: the child or teen cannot be seen as queer because the adult does not see her or himself as queer, so anything queer about the child must not be about the child or teen, but about a queer-like adult pedophile.

The refusal to avow the queerness of our younger selves produces the child as a future heteronormative citizen. In so doing, we discount the child's own legitimate claim to queer and non-procreative sexualities. By refusing to avow the queerness of our younger selves we ward off memories at odds with adult heterosexual identification. As we disown queer remembrances we lay claim to an officially sanctioned developmental sequence that might not have been our own – one that leads organically to heterosexual citizenship. In so doing, we discount the complexities of our own sexualities along with those of school-age youth who are in many ways non-normative. If anything, children and teenagers are queer and non-normative (as opposed to innocent). They do not have domesticated desires and sexualities but profoundly ambiguous and polymorphously perverse sexualities. 'If there is anything "natural" about children it is their curiosity about bodies and pleasure, their desire to make stories that are not the colonizing narratives of heteronormativity' (Bruhm & Hurley, 2004, p. xxi).

The sexual openness of children and teens is, for some, incongruent with a more stable adult heterosexuality, so recollections of intergenerational and queer seductions can be traumatic because they render our adult sexual identities less than coherent. Recollections of adolescent and teenage lesbian sexualities are anachronistic. They queer the developmental timelines that heterosexually identified grown-ups often use to consolidate their relation to adulthood. In an effort to manage anxious heterosexual identifications shadowed by memories of queer desires, polyamorous pleasures, and engagements with adolescent bodies not yet developed into clearly demarcated gendered and sexual subjects, the adult condenses the otherwise nuanced character of an intergenerational lesbian teacher affair into an instance of abuse.

I suggest that many of the sexual relationships between lesbian teachers and students reported in the North American news were not traumatic at the time of the affair. They are, however, sometimes traumatic for the adult who lacks a conceptual template to process lesbian teacher love outside the master narrative of child sexual abuse. Time and the insistent rhetoric of abuse play a queer trick on all parties involved: love is perverted into abuse, teenagers into children, and teachers into sexual predators.

Members of the profession and the public presume that sex between teacher and student is necessarily harmful because they are beholden to the master narrative of child sexual abuse. Like all master narratives, it delimits what can be thought and legitimately said in court. If the teenager speaks about love, she (or he) has sadly mistaken abuse for love; if the teenager seeks out teacher sex the student is said to be emotionally unstable – probably abused in the family home – in need of guidance and psychological counselling; if the teenager moves in with her teacher, it must be under duress, and the relationship cannot be in any way good for the younger party. In all cases, the teacher should know better, and the teenager (imagined to be a vulnerable child) is said to be harmed. Of course, any of these things *could* be emotionally harmful and detrimental to teenage academic development but the point is that they are not necessarily so. By failing to consider the politics of social consent and teenage sexual agency we criminalize those who may have only been unprofessional as measured by present-day standards. The master narrative forecloses upon alternative explanations and counter-discourses that would trouble the absolutism now saturating discussions about intergenerational and homoerotic desires in school.

In the USA four sex scandals involving lesbian teachers have been reported in the new millennium. In none of these cases has the narrative testimony brought forth by the teenagers been validated by the courts, school professionals, parents, or psychologists. In each case, the students insisted that the relationships were loving and consensual. For example, in January 2006, Amy Lilley, a 36-year-old Florida teacher at Citrus County High School, was charged with 'lewd and lascivious battery on a child' stemming from her 18-month relationship with a female student. Lilley was said to have special access to students because she coached the girls' basketball and softball teams. The teenager did not view the relationship as harmful or coercive; she insisted that the two were in love and was heartbroken to learn that Lilley – in the early stages of the criminal investigation – denied that they had a sexual relationship. 'The girl was "very distraught" when investigators told her that Lilley had initially denied having any sexual contact with her. The two loved each other, the girl told investigators' (Ramirez & Reiss, 2005). Lilley later pleaded no contest, admitting to the sexual relationship with a minor. The judge sentenced Lilley to house arrest, eight years of probation and banned her from seeing the student in question. According to media reports, the alleged victim asked the judge, with tears streaming down her cheeks, to remove the stipulation that Lilley cease contact with her as part of her sentence. The judge refused.

Only two days later, another Florida teacher, Jaymee Lane Wallace, was alleged to have had an 18-month relationship with a female student on her softball team. She had been put on administrative leave until the sheriff's investigation could be completed. The alleged victim was 16 years old at the time of the relationship. The teacher was 27 years old. Wallace is charged with 'lewd and lascivious behaviour', which carries a maximum sentence of 15 years in prison. The teacher and student exchanged love letters, kissed in the teacher's car, stroked each other's genitals, and had oral sex. The student offered what might appropriately be called social consent. She wrote in her police statement that she initiated both the sex and the relationship with Wallace. The 17-year-old student destroyed love letters so that they could not be used as evidence against Wallace in court. According to media reports, the relationship proceeded according to the teenager's interests and desires – the teen asked for sex (not the teacher) – and the student saw herself as an active and consenting participant.

Perhaps the most sensational case, of late, involves a 36-year-old American teacher at South Haven's Baseline Middle School, Elizabeth Miklosovic, who was accused of sexually assaulting a 14-year-old girl and marrying her in a deep-woods, pagan ritual. Both Miklosovic and the student professed their mutual love, and the student told the judge that

Miklosovic was a wonderful woman and that she, as a student, was neither manipulated nor taken advantage of in her relationship with the teacher. Even police agreed that both parties understood the relationship to be consensual. The judge disagreed. He insisted that consent was impossible. Miklosovic was sentenced to serve from 5 to 25 years in prison. Even pagan communities, which hold more liberal ideas about sexuality, shunned Miklosovic and went to great lengths to condemn her while dissociating themselves from the sensational press, which portrayed her as a lesbian pedophile. Both the teacher and the teenaged student felt that many people, themselves especially, had been hurt by the homophobic and sensational coverage of their case. The student was said in the news media to have gone to great lengths to protect the teacher and their relationship, and to wrestle her interpretation of events from the courts.

In the vast majority of cases, it is the publicity and criminalization of the relationships (and the teachers) that causes anxiety, distress, and emotional upset to the youth involved in the teacher sex scandals.

The idea of the 'child' and the pedagogy of sex scandals

Kincaid (1998) argues that '"the child" is a product of ways of perceiving, not something that is *there*' (p. 19, original emphasis). In the sex scandals involving lesbian teachers, there is a curious temporal slippage; teenaged girls (alleged victims) are *seen* to be children. Even though Victoria Harris was 16 when the affair began and was said to have initiated the affair by kissing the teacher on the lips following a counselling session, her case was seen to be synonymous with *child* sexual abuse. Justice William Selbie sentenced the teacher to jail time so that the conviction would be a 'deterrent to other teachers, counsellors or professionals entrusted with *children*' (*The Vancouver Sun*, 1995, emphasis added). Johima was also said to be a 'vulnerable *kid*' (Hall, 1993b, emphasis added) even though she was a teenager. Negating her earlier feelings of love for the accused, Johima similarly positioned herself as a 'kid' who confused abuse with love. Referring to the Mary Baxter sex scandal in the USA, which involved an adult female teacher and a 17-year-old boy-student, Kincaid (1998, p. 31) documents how in the court proceedings a 'smart and active older adolescent is shrunk into a child, a generic "essence-of-child", by this cultural story [of pedophilia], remoulded as passive, innocent, and guileless. His actual age, activities, and particularities are melted away to fit our needs' so that we can see the teenager as a child.

While age differentials are exaggerated in panic about pedophilia, child and teenage sexual wishes and inclinations are largely ignored. It is exceedingly difficult to theorize child and teen sexualities without evoking the phantom of the pedophile, not coincidentally rendered queer in homophobic discourses. While many believe that the pedophile exploits child sexuality, I suggest that the positioning of the teenager as 'child' is harmful to student sexual and emotional health. It is only the young who have their legitimate rights to sexual exploration prohibited for 'their own good'. That many queer people have their 'initial sexual experiences with older men or women, experiences they will probably not define as traumatic or exploitative as they reflect on them later' (Bruhm & Hurley, 2004, p. xxvi) is an enigma that North American cultures tend to ignore.

But it is not only the reproduction of heterosexuality that is secured through the mythology of the sexually innocent child; postcolonial power structures are stabilized as well. Alternative sexualities bring about different ways of being together, as Foucault (1997) claims, but they also enable new sexual cultures to proliferate in postcolonial contexts. For example, Kincaid (1998) shows us how our cultural investment in erotic innocence is mapped onto the child's body, and without overtly acknowledging it, he shows us how the use of whiteness, as a racialized technique of representation, is central to the accomplishment of an ideal of childhood virginal purity:

> Baby-smooth skin is capable of inciting desire; unsmooth, or contoured skin is not: is this because flatness is innately more titillating than texture, or because flatness signifies nothing at all and thus doesn't interfere with our projections? In the same way, desirable faces must be blank, drained of color; big eyes round and expressionless; hair blond or colorless; waists, hips, feet, and minds small. (Kincaid, 1998, p. 17)

The images employed to construct a fantasy of innocence depend heavily on whiteness as a visual trope. There is something invisible or perhaps ultra-visible and thus unspeakable about whiteness, youth and its imagined innocence. As Richard Dyer (1997, p. 13) observes in his book on whiteness in popular film culture, white heterosexuality structures desire as dark, so I wish to claim that the mythology of childhood sexual innocence is also structured by a contemporary concern about the proliferation of sexual appetites that are not conducive to white heterosexual breeding.

Conclusion

I conclude that hegemonic gender identifications are secured, in part, by ideas about childhood sexual innocence, developmental growth and life-stages. In order to better understand the regulation of gender and sexuality in high school it is necessary to question the use of child protectionist narratives. While ages of consent laws are important we must guard against the indiscriminate use of them to police non-normative sexual exploration. The purpose of challenging child protectionist discourses is, of course, not to make students sexually available to teachers, but to wrest youthful (often queer) sexualities from the clutches of adult projections and false-fantasies of abuse. I submit that adult investments in protection are often about reproducing normative gender and sexual identifications, and less often about child welfare.

Much of what happens between lesbian teachers and students is not well understood in studies of education because the transgressions are over-determined by the master narratives of abuse. Consequently, we know little about how normative gender identifications are consolidated by prohibitions placed on queer sexual expressions in school. Those of us committed to educational studies need to think critically about how ideas about developmental time, growth and sexual innocence are deployed to regulate gender. New directions in gender theory and education must be able to navigate the sexual politics of Eros in the pedagogical encounter. By condemning and criminalizing teachers in one fell swoop we miss opportunities to better understand the function of desire in our lives and in education. We need to make better use of queer and postcolonial theories of gender to understand the matrixes of heterosexuality secured in school.

Note

1. This essay is a substantially revised version of a chapter published in S.L. Cavanagh, *Sexing the teacher: School sex scandals and queer pedagogies* (University of British Columbia Press, 2007).

References

Bellett G. (1995a, January 13). Pupil started lesbian affair, teacher says. *The Vancouver Sun*.
Bellett, G. (1995b, January 16). Counsellor feared being found out. *The Vancouver Sun*.
Bruhm, S., & Hurley, N. (Eds.) (2004). *Curiouser: On the queerness of children*. Minneapolis: University of Minnesota Press.

Butler, J. (1990). *Gender trouble: Feminism and the subversion of identity.* New York: Routledge.

Cavanagh, S.L. (2004). Upsetting desires in the classroom: School sex scandals and the pedagogy of the femme fatale. *Psychoanalysis, Culture and Society, 9,* 315–332.

Cavanagh, S.L. (2005). Sexing the teacher: Voyeuristic pleasure in the Amy Gehring sex panic. *Social Text, 23*(1), 11–34.

Cavanagh, S.L. (2007). *Sexing the teacher: School sex scandals and queer pedagogies.* Vancouver and Toronto: University of British Columbia Press.

Dyer, R. (1997). *White.* London: Routledge.

Faderman, L. (1983). *Scotch verdict: Miss Pirie and Miss Woods v. Dame Cumming Gordon.* New York: W. Morrow.

Edelman, L. (2004). *No future: Queer theory and the death drive.* Durham, NC: Duke University Press.

Foucault, M. (1997). Friendship as a way of life. In P. Rabinow (Ed.), *Ethics: Subjectivity and truth* (pp. 135–140). New York: New Press.

Gallop, J. (1995). *Pedagogy: The question of impersonation.* Bloomington and Indianapolis: Indiana University Press.

Gallop, J. (1997). *Feminist accused of sexual harassment.* Durham, NC: Duke University Press.

Halberstam, J. (2005). *In a queer time and place: Transgender bodies, subcultural lives.* New York: New York University Press.

Hall, N. (1993a, Februrary 23). Tune brings abuse memories, witness says. *The Vancouver Sun.*

Hall, N. (1993b, February 25). Former teacher denies sexual relationship. *The Vancouver Sun.*

Hall, N. (1993c, March 17). Vice-principal faces probe in suspected cover-up. *The Vancouver Sun.*

Jagodzinski, J. (2002). *Pedagogical desire: Authority, seduction, transference, and the question of ethics.* Westport, CT: Bergin and Garvey.

Kincaid, J.R. (1998). *Erotic innocence: The culture of child molesting.* Durham, NC: Duke University Press.

Lee, J. (1995, January 11). Counsellor 'lured high-school student' into abusive lesbian relationship. *The Vancouver Sun.*

McDowell, J. (1995, February 20). Counselled with lesbian sex: A teacher is convicted. *BC Report.*

Ohi, K. (2004). Narrating the child's queerness in *What Maisie Knew.* In: S. Bruhm & N. Hurley (Eds.), *Curiouser: On the queerness of children* (pp. 81–106). Minneapolis: University of Minnesota Press.

Ramirez, E., & Reiss, D. (2005, November 3). Praise halts for teacher ... *St. Petersburg Times.*

Stoller, A.L. (1997). Making empire respectable: The politics of race and sexual morality in twentieth-century colonial cultures. In A. McClintock, A. Mufti & E. Shohat (Eds.), *Dangerous liaisons: Gender, nation, and postcolonial perspectives* (pp. 344–373). Minneapolis: University of Minnesota Press.

Stoller, A.L. (2000). *Race and the education of desire: Foucault's history of sexuality and the colonial order of things.* Durham, NC: Duke University Press.

Sauer, D.K. (2000). *Oleanna and The Children's Hour*: Misreading sexuality on the post/modern realistic stage. *Modern Drama, 43,* 421–441.

Sedgwick, E.K. (1990). *Epistemology of the closet.* Berkeley and Los Angeles: University of California Press.

The Vancouver Sun. (1995, March 18). Ex-counsellor jailed over sex with student.

Tuhkanen, M. (2002). Breeding (and) reading: Lesbian knowledge, eugenic discipline, and The Children's Hour. *Modern Fiction Studies, 48,* 1001–1040.

Young, R. (1995). *Colonial desire: Hybridity in theory, culture and race.* London: Routledge.

'Girls hit!' Constructing and negotiating violent African femininities in a working-class primary school

Deevia Bhana

Tisha [Teacher] says that the girls who hit are 'grabbers'[1] because the girls are better than boys. The boys are 'skelms' [criminals] so the girls mustn't hit like boys. But the girls hit! (Interview with Nompilo,[2] an eight-year-old girl at an African working-class township school called KwaDabeka Primary School, Durban, South Africa)

South African schoolgirls have often been depicted as victims of and vulnerable to the African vanguard – violent boys and men. Yet, in contrast to this static approach, eight-year-old Nompilo presents a somewhat different perspective. She argues that despite the teacher's attempt to regulate acceptable feminine identities which exclude violence, 'girl's hit'. Nompilo positions African[3] schoolgirl femininity within the dominant discourse of docility (and victimization). Alternate expressions of femininity in the study of gender and school violence in South Africa (and Africa more generally) are uncommon and even less examined is the study of violence amongst primary schoolgirls. There is of course a strong case to be made for the continued focus on boys (and men) doing violence, given that recent studies have focused on violence in African schools as an inhibitor of gender equality (Unterhalter, 2007). There has been much feminist research on men's and boys' violence, including within schooling (Connell, 1995; Jordan, 1995; Kenway & Fitzclarence, 1997; Mills, 2001; Salisbury & Jackson, 1996). This has been an important feminist project, and in the context of South Africa (as with most other nations) the project still remains relevant.

Feminist research on women's violence is not new (Alder & Worrall, 2004; Macdonald,

1991). Disrupting violence as a male domain, feminist research shows how women who do violence are often constructed as monstrous and more ruthless than men reproducing rigid gender binaries. Violent women, it is argued, break with the natural gender order and often are seen as pathological (Macdonald, 1991). Younger girls' violence has been under-theorized in feminist research, and by drawing on primary school ethnographic work this paper makes a case for such theorization and begins such work.

South Africa has the worst statistics on gender and sexual violence in the world. At least one in three South African women will be raped in her lifetime, and one in four will be beaten by her domestic partner (Jewkes, Levin, Mbananga, & Bradshaw, 2002; Moffett, 2006). In South African schools, pernicious forms of gender violence have been recognized by the Human Rights Watch in its descriptive accounts of violence:

> I was scared. The last day at school came and he beat me like he never did before. He told me he was going to kill me. I apologized and he beat me again and asked me to kiss him and I did because I was scared. (Interview with a 17-year-old African schoolgirl in a township school in South Africa; Human Rights Watch, 2001, p. 55)

While little quantitative measure of the extent of the violence exists, the Human Rights Watch acknowledges the widespread phenomenon of gender violence in schools. The violence includes physical and sexual assault and rape and harassment perpetrated by male classmates and teachers. That men and boys are actively involved in making schools unsafe for girls, increasing their vulnerability to violence and HIV/AIDS, has been recognized as an important concern in African schools (Bhana, 2005a; Dunne, Humphreys, & Leach, 2006; Leach et al., 2003; Mitchell & Smith, 2001; Morrell, 1998; Pattman & Chege, 2003; World Health Organisation, 2002; Wolpe, Quinlan, & Martinez, 1997). Examining these trends, researchers tend to dwell mainly on the ways in which girls are victims of male violence, which is hardly surprising given the South African context of violence (Wolpe et al., 1997). Significant questions are raised about the social and cultural milieux in which school violence takes place and about the social and economic factors in South Africa which permit such gender violence (Morrell, 1998, 2001). However, while focusing on the ways in which patriarchal structures work to the detriment of African women and girls, hardly any attempt has been made to investigate the ways in which girls navigate the context of violence in schools.

Because of the grim picture of gender violence in South African schools and effects of such violence on girls, the inclination of many researchers is to see African girls as victims who fit into the good girl/bad boy representation of gender relations. This suggests an innate opposition and a certain rigidity between a dangerous and fearsome African masculinity and an innocent African femininity. Scholarly work in gender and schooling in South Africa (and this has resonance beyond the continent) sees violence chiefly as an area where boys and men are supposed to realize themselves as masculine just as girls are meant to understand themselves as being 'better than boys', passive, and quiet. Similarly, Skelton's (2001) UK study of primary schoolgirls notes that they saw themselves as selfless and sensible.

Viewing African schoolgirls simply as victims of violence not only fragments our knowledge about their schooling experiences, as Nompilo attests to, but also creates an analytically unhelpful dichotomy which reduces girls to homogeneous stereotypes and ignores the possibility of multiple forms of femininities, just as there are multiple forms of masculinities (see Connell, 1995). Breaking with gender binaries, Halberstam (1998) argues that gender ambiguous constructions are often pathologized and suggests that female masculinity can be an empowering model in gender relations.

It is especially important to challenge static representations of African schoolgirls, particularly in popular discourse which portrays young African men and boys as vicious killers, diseased and vectors in the spread of HIV/AIDS leading to a racist image of a 'whole sub-continent of Lord of the Flies' (Barker & Ricardo, 2006; Grout, 2002). In the context of the frightening reality of the gendering of HIV/AIDS[4] and the South African government's efforts to ensure gender equality, these racist analogies remain major tropes in the analysis of gender identities in schools where African boys are consistently seen as bad (Pattman & Bhana, 2006). Thus instead of addressing the nuanced and complex understandings of gender violence and the social context within which violence emerges, many educational researchers look no further than African boys in their articulation of violence. Notions of gender identity are static, and girls are given the status of victims with narrow (and polarized) conceptions of gender, assuming that the changing South African context has not altered or modified patriarchal dynamics.

Primary schoolgirls are rendered particularly invisible in patterns of gendered school violence, and this research caveat extends beyond the African continent. (See Alder & Worrall, 2004; Bright, 2005; Burman, Batchelor, & Brown, 2001; Currie, Kelly, & Pomerantz, 2007; Jackson, 2006; and Simmons, 2002, for emerging work on girls and secondary school violence, though none of these feature schoolgirls in primary school.) Part of the neglect in researching gender and school violence in the junior years of schooling stems from longstanding tropes of childhood innocence, which posit children primarily as objects of concern and in need of protection (Connolly, 1998; Epstein & Johnson, 1998; Jordan, 1995; MacNaughton, 2000; Renold, 2005). Not only are girls placed under the gaze of innocence, but their innocence – more than boys' – is eroticized, vigorously policed and reinforced. Young girls who are sexually explicit, for example, are seen as stained and forgo the prized status of innocence (Walkerdine, 1999). Within this conceptualization of girls' innocence (and docility), there is little place for making girls' violence visible. In the African context of war, famine, poverty, and social and economic upheaval, it is women and girls who are rendered most visible, not in terms of their resilience in conditions of social and economic vulnerability, but as objects of pity. The presence of African schoolgirls in the study of gender and schooling is thus mostly passive, framed by their need for protection from violent boys and men.

These framings are necessary but not, as this chapter argues, sufficient. They do not provide an explanation of the ways in which young primary school girls actively participate in school cultures of violence whilst also being victims of it (see Bhana, 2005a, 2005b). Research in African contexts and in South Africa has been quick to seize upon the discourse of 'poor African schoolgirls' as the only way of understanding gender relations, which makes it imperative to challenge any static representation of girls as simply victims of violence as opposed to complicit with the gender regime and the respective gender positioning within schools. This point has been noted by Dunne et al. who suggest that the limited research evidence of girl-on-girl violence in developing contexts tends to present girls as innocent victims without agency (2006, p. 85). In my view, research scholars have not placed sufficient weight on girls' strategies of survival. Taking issue with the dominant construction of young girls as passive and dependent, proponents of the new sociology of childhood attribute greater agency to young children (James & Prout, 1998; MacNaughton, 2000; Thorne, 1993). This development is particularly important in the African context, given the mythical representation of girls as innocent and pitiful.

This chapter attempts to build on these themes by drawing on elements of a primary school ethnography which emerged from a study of the construction of gender identities in an African township school in Durban (Bhana, 2002). The data for this chapter build on

Nompilo's testimony of girls' violence. The research is geographically situated in KwaZulu-Natal, a province in South Africa where political violence of the 1980s and 1990s received wide media coverage. Whilst there are remnants of political violence, such violence has now largely been overtaken by violent crime (Bonin, 2000; Terreblanche, 2002). Nompilo, like other girls in the study, attends KwaDabeka Primary School located in an African township, one of many sites of rising unemployment and social inequalities, poverty, HIV/AIDS, and violence. Rooted in the uneven provision of housing for Africans under colonialism, informal settlements have mushroomed around urban areas (Hunter, 2007). Townships in South Africa most vividly illustrate the vast patterns of racial and social inequalities in that they are mainly working-class Africans who inhabit what are commonly referred to as one-roomed *imijondolos* (or 'shacks'). This is a population without income security, with fragile family structures, with reported HIV rates twice as high as those in rural and urban areas (Human Science Research Council, 2002; Pettifor et al., 2004), and also a context of school dynamics which increase the propensity of violent gender relations.

It is part of the pathos of South African history that race and class overlap to the extent that they do. The social context of KwaDabeka Primary School bears testimony to the interconnected trends of rising unemployment and deepening social inequalities and the increasing scale of gender violence. The association between poverty and violence is strong although violence is clearly not caused by poverty alone – although violence is increased where race, class and gender intersect (Barker, 2005; Morrell, 2001). Social divisions have widened in post-apartheid South Africa, particularly as the market-led economic policy has accentuated inequalities, and income distribution remains highly unequal (Terreblanche, 2002). The climate of chronic unemployment and deepening social differentiation has significantly affected relationship patterns, increased gender violence, and the formation of African masculinities prone to violence (Morrell, 2001). Given South Africa's social context, the study of violence and the issue of masculinity have been given careful treatment. However, it is important to recognize as Dunne et al. (2006) do, that gender violence in developing contexts – unlike the north – is embryonic, and remains an under-researched topic resulting in violence in schools remaining invisible and unrecognized.

Arguably, a more capacious view of primary school girls, alert to their agency, and informed by the broader social conditions of their self-creation, can provide a fresh perspective on the study of schooling and gender violence in South Africa, not simply as victims of violence. This approach, developed through an ethnographic study of the making of gender (and sexual) identities amongst African boys and girls aged between seven and nine, situates young girls' experience of violence and the use of violence within specific dimensions and conditions of power, social class structures and cultural contexts. The approach views girls not simply as muted victims of Africa's vanguard, but also as active participants in everyday school life within larger contexts of persistent violence and social inequalities.

To evoke and contextualize this approach, this chapter argues that young African working-class primary schoolgirls are not victims of violence; they are agents too, albeit shaped by material and social deprivation and gendered inequalities. Showing how feminist social historians are reframing the image of African working-class women (and girls) as politically active agents during apartheid resistance, the chapter goes on to argue that such nuanced analysis disrupting gender polarities has yet to reach into studies of violence and schooling in South Africa (and beyond). The purpose of this section is not to provide a comprehensive report on the work of feminist social historians in South Africa but to point to the ways in which African working-class women take on gender roles beyond that which are normatively ascribed to them. After noting the complete silence on younger girls' agency within South African historiography, the chapter points out that there is scant focus on younger children in the study of violence and gender. Young children are not considered to be properly gendered, and as MacNaughton (2000) argues, myths prevail about the aptness of addressing gender in junior years of primary schooling/early childhood since children are regarded as blank slates without the capacity to think, know and feel. Next, the chapter focuses on the method and the research context of KwaDabeka and adds rich data to the understanding of the recurring patterns of violence and the economic, social, and cultural forces that help to account for them. The latter part of the chapter focuses on elements of schoolgirl violence as articulated by Nompilo, before concluding that the research on girls, violence and schooling is under-theorized and too narrowly defined.

South African context of gender and political resistance

Ideas about African women's and girls' involvement in resistance and violence under conditions of social and political vulnerability are undergoing revision, though this has not yet been imported into education. Notwithstanding the tendency of research scholars to position African women as objects of pity, the history of resistance against apartheid celebrates the example of children (boys and girls) as political actors. Whilst there is little examination of the agency of younger girls under 10, the work of social historians is beginning to redefine the roles of women and adolescent girls in political resistance (Gasa, 2007; Hassim, 2005; Meintjes, 2007). These scholars argue against the tendency to construct South African women as a homogenous group who exclusively perform conventional gender roles. Younger women in certain situations were able to play the roles normally assigned only to men – aggressors. While this section of the chapter does not attempt to delve deeply into the work of feminist social historians, the main line of argument here is that South African historiography demonstrates that African women and girls, whilst victims of violence, were also supporting and organizing violence of various kinds in the turbulent history of racial oppression and resistance (Gasa, 2007). Bonin (2000), Hassim (2005), Suttner (2007) and Cherry (2007) argue that whilst there has been an attempt to downplay or ignore the ways in which women resisted traditional classifications of gender in South African historiography, the evidence suggests that rigid male–female dualisms do not explain the resistance history in South Africa and women's involvement in political protest: 'it means that you are fighting, even though you don't have a weapon ... and now you have broken this characteristic of a women who is quiet and doesn't involve herself in fights' (Bonin, 2000, p. 315).

Bonin describes the experiences of women who took charge in the tumultuous period of conflict between the apartheid state and the resistance movement. In the mid-1980s, for example, the mass African movement came increasingly into violent confrontation with the apartheid state but these clashes were mainly confined to African townships. Within these contexts, African working-class women emerged as a powerful force for change within their communities, taking charge and transgressing gender roles. Older women, the literature argues, were less open to changing roles; generational differences between older and younger women and adolescent girls are thus highlighted (Gasa, 2007). About younger girls, however, there remains complete silence.

What is the significance of this theorization of women in the political struggle for the young school girls in this study? One of the most interesting aspects of African working-class women in the political struggle was the ways in which gender identities were being presented. In the first instance, African township women were identified according to traditional gender roles; they were expected to nurture and protect their families even as they too were victims of the apartheid state violence. But this was not the only violence that they faced. Morrell (2002), for example, argues that whilst African men challenged race and class inequalities, they were simultaneously defending their masculinity which also involved efforts to re-establish and reinforce power over women, often in violent ways. On the other hand, the political protests created space for women to challenge these gender roles. Young African women activists were militant and proactive, though fewer women than men participated in leadership structures and militant structures. Women's involvement in resistance campaigns was not merely supportive, but women actively encouraged dissemination of information, persuasion and even coercion (Cherry, 2007). In other words, the perception of violence as a masculine domain and women as passive victims of male violence goes against African women's experiences and is in reality far more complex and varied than this. However, young men were more likely to perpetrate violence particularly in the context of the dominance of traditional gender roles, the domestic division of labour, and apartheid's vicious entrenchment of gender and racial inequalities (Gasa, 2007). Shedding assumptions about the fixity of gender roles, South African historiography of African working-class women resists the stereotype of poor women (and girls). The latter were actors, who were not just supportive but taking the lead and offering resistance, and using physical violence in the process of transition to warrior femininities (Gasa, 2007). Thus the particular political, social and economic circumstances created the space for alternate forms of femininities.

Another important example of women's agency was the extent to which African working-class women were able to use their bodies and sexuality as social power to fend off attacks from the apartheid police. Meintjes (2007) shows how women and girls resisted the apartheid police from demolishing their shacks – the only source of shelter for many disenfranchised, unemployed African men and women – by stripping naked. The tradition of African women using nakedness as a signal of anger and as a means of cursing perpetrators for unacceptable behaviour, has a long history. Meintjes (2007) argues that it is hard to imagine men using their bodies in a similar act of protest; this example of sexuality, body and gender within specific race and class contexts raises fundamental questions about agency and struggles over fundamental material needs. Their actions showed their agency, their strategic understanding of their position, and the ways in which they used sexuality to recast attention to themselves by mobilizing their vulnerability as a tool, and using the cultural and social capital of sexuality to make claims for their right to shelter.

There is little space here to demonstrate that young girls aged seven and eight can and do use their sexuality to fend off violent space invading boys at the school under study (see Bhana, 2005b). By 'showing boys their panties', young girls use their sexual capital to embarrass and humiliate boys and momentarily gain freedom from invasion of their play space at school. Feminist-orientated historiography in South Africa has been important in disrupting the binary opposition of innocent women and girls versus violent males and argues for a more sophisticated and nuanced analysis of women's role in resistance, defying the boundaries set up for them as women. Importantly, such work is helpful in arguing that South Africa's girls are not a homogeneous group, and that violence is not the exclusive domain of men. In the current political context, African women's broader engagement has challenged politics in South Africa and intensified challenges to gender identities and practices. While South African women's successes have been widely celebrated, particularly in terms of one of the most progressive constitutions in the world, translating gender equality into reality is a formidable endeavour (Walsh & Scully, 2006). Not only do these changes produce innovations and resistance to gender roles, but they also show the inflexibility of gender roles reflected in the heightening rates of violence against women and girls. Publicity about gender violence in South Africa is growing, and there is now evidence to suggest increasing levels of violence and that perpetrators and victims are getting younger and younger (Meintjes, 2007). Yet for all the richness and complexity of this literature on women (and girls) as political actors, there is silence on the ways in which younger girls were/are agents and resilient actors.

It is to this missing information in primary school that the rest of the chapter turns after describing the research method and context.

School context and method

The analysis presented here derives from a completed doctoral project exploring the salience of gender through the accounts by, and the observations of, boys, girls and their teachers in the first two years of primary schooling (Bhana, 2002).[5] The principal data that this chapter draws upon were produced over a period of a year at KwaDabeka Primary School. With little existing South African research into how children between the ages of seven and nine construct their gender identities, I embarked on a qualitative study using ethnographic methods, including observations, unstructured exploratory group interviews, and individual interviews, to explore the process of gendering in the junior years of schooling. I sat with boys and girls in their classrooms, and outside their classrooms as they ate lunch and in the playground. I observed and chatted with them and heard their voices. As in many ethnographic studies, the flexibility of the research process meant that I was with children in the process of constructing their identities while they engaged in the everyday routines of school life. In addition, interviews with teachers were also conducted. This chapter draws attention to the conversation with Nompilo in her portrayal of violence. What is offered is not a comprehensive or a representative account of African working-class young girls; it does not try to generalize about the role of African working-class young girls in school violence. Instead, it posits an understanding of African working-class primary schoolgirls as being constructed through contestation in everyday primary school life in situations where material and cultural contexts are inseparable from the experiences and formations of gender. Testimony to the links between schooling and material and social inequalities and violence is indicated in one of the teacher's portrayal of the children's lives at KwaDabeka:

> Mrs I: It's a hard life here. The government is trying to make it better with the feeding scheme but how much can it help? Some can afford a little. Then there are those who cannot afford anything. They say to me 'Tisha we have nothing to eat at home'. Sometimes they have no food in the morning, no food at home after school.[6] The meal they eat at school is the only meal for most of them. The neighbours sometimes help and the grandparents. The parents are 20 years old, sometimes 23, very young. Siyanda's mother is 19. The mother is unemployed and I don't think he knows who his father is ... Fathers have died fighting. Velile's father died, the police killed him just recently. The father was in the taxi, the police were after that taxi and shot him...

Unemployment, the rising number of very young teenage mothers, pervasive patterns of poverty, crime and violence, are central to understanding the context from which young boys and girls at KwaDabeka Primary School emerge. Elsewhere the ways in which primary school boys use violence against girls at the same school has been described in greater detail (Bhana, 2005a, 2006). Such work shows how young boys use their bodies and their size to hit and verbally abuse girls, deploying sexually harassing performances for claims to power – including the claim to material rewards such as pencils and food. This research, however, also highlights the fact that boy-against-girl violence is only one form of violence. South African schools have historically been violent places where corporal punishment was and is frequently still used, despite legislation that abolishes it (Morrell, 1998; Department of Education, 1996). The use of corporal punishment in this school is no exception, and used by women against children as young as six and seven (see Bhana, 2006, for full illustration of its use). Corporal punishment is not the domain of men alone. Women's use of violence stretches outside the school:

> Mrs G: These kids live a hard life. Thobeka's mother died of paraffin burns. She was fighting with another woman about her boyfriend. The other one threw paraffin on her and she died in hospital. Now the granny does not know who Thobeka's father is ... There are cases where the girls can be aggressive and they behave like men. I went to court last week and heard the story of this lady who is a jailbird. She stole a bottle of liquor from Liberty Liquors. They said that when they caught her she fought and she kicked like a man. There are cases like these jailbirds.

Not only are African working women victims of male violence but in a context of declining economic conditions, material insecurity and urban crime, women are both victims and offenders, a point noted by Zimudzi (2004) in her study of violent crime amongst African women in Zimbabwe. It is argued that under certain circumstances women might become masculinized. Masculinity is not confined to men. Women who are strong and assertive (and violent) defy the boundaries imposed by femininity and as Connell (2000) argues, are making excursions into masculinity and are recognized as laying claims to social power. The girls in this study are all too familiar with violence and have to make sense of it routinely in their lives, incorporating it, resisting it and rejecting it.

The rest of the chapter considers the complex negotiation of violence amongst young primary schoolgirls as an important strategy for survival.

'I'm not scared of girls because the girl is wearing a pantie like me'

Under the specific material, social and cultural conditions prevalent at KwaDabeka Primary School, the girls' use of violence is highly strategic and embedded within the knowledge of their vulnerability to violent boys. Violence inheres in the everyday life of many girls – they avoid it, negotiate it and indulge in it, but always within the broader social context which sets limits to their identities as girls. These material and ideological conditions thus create the conditions for relations of power, making girl-on-girl violence an important means through which to attain social and material reward. The rest of the discussion focuses on Nompilo who constructed her femininity in ways that defied the traditional version of docility, whilst simultaneously recognizing the limits of her agency in relation to violent boys. She was most often with a group of girls, including Zama; together they routinely played clapping and rhythmic games often associated with junior years of schooling. These games allowed a variety of gendered and heterosexual positionings which included moments during which they could mock and tease the boys (Bhana, 2005b). Boys would often harass the girls and invade their spaces and hurt the girls, including Nompilo. But there were contradictions. As a tall girl with a commanding voice, Nompilo carved out a sense of identity which defied gender boundaries (see Thorne, 1993). Her voice, her size and her bullying practices meant that she was able to share lunch with boys who used violence against other boys and girls (Bhana, 2005a). I often observed how Nompilo would share her lunch with Andile (a nine-year-old boy who often committed violence against other girls), and how he would share his lunch with her. This sharing has important meaning as boundaries of gender-defined friendships and alliances were broken (see

Thorne, 1993). Significantly, Nompilo was able to use her transgressive femininity in ways that meant collusion and collaboration with other boys who were often avoided by the majority of girls. Nompilo developed a strong position with her group of girl friends:

Nompilo: Zama, she hits the other girls if they don't share lunch with her.
Researcher: What does Zama want?
Nompilo: She wants their lunch or anything they have. Zama hit Amanda. Amanda told Tisha [teacher], and Tisha hit Zama, but Zama hit Amanda after school, and then Amanda told sir [reference to male teacher], and sir hit Zama, then Zama hit Amanda in the break. So I hit Zama, and then Zama cried.
Researcher: Why did you hit Zama?
Nompilo: Because Amanda is my friend and Zama hit her.
Researcher: I thought it was only the boys who hit?
Nompilo: No, the girls learn from boys. If the boys say, 'Can I go on that side' and the girls say 'no' because the boys didn't say please, the boys hit the girls and that's how the girls learn to hit. Tisha says that the girls who hit are 'grabbers' because the girls are better than boys. The boys are 'skelms' [criminals] so the girls mustn't hit like boys. But the girls hit.

Breaking the myth that girls are often victims of violence, Nompilo confirms the extent to which school girl violence is connected to the overall climate in the school and the social context (see Alder & Worrall, 2004). Within the matrix of violence described, is the recognition of the material basis in and through which the violence arose. Avoiding the image of innocent girls, Nompilo is complicit in violence and within the school regime. Boys and teachers are not alone in perpetrating gender violence – girls do so as well although, as Bright (2005) argues, it is important to recognize that when compared to boys' physical aggression, girls' violence often goes unrecognized and is made invisible through the narratives of the good girl versus bad girls ('grabbers') image. Resisting simplistic forms of analysis which offer little in the way of understanding the complex dynamics of girl-on-girl violence, the overall climate at the school, its gender regime, the prevalence of boys' violence and teachers' use of corporal punishment are all co-factors in making sense of girl-on-girl violence. It is true that African working-class girls enter schools under social, material and emotional conditions which are extremely unfavourable to the development of gender equality. Nevertheless, girls like Nompilo and Zama arrogate to themselves the authority and power to express violence in these very conditions. Violence causes humiliation and hurt for both the perpetrator and the victim. Nompilo's defence of her friend, Amanda, must be seen in the light of these conditions of deprivation, where violence flourishes as a tool in the negotiation of power. Violence is a claim to power, and Nompilo uses it not only to stake her claim but also to create solidarity amongst her girlfriends, whilst at the same time positioning herself with authority and power over other girls. As suggested later in this section, friends might be the chief resource in navigating the hardships of poverty, food insecurity, lack of parental care and support both within and outside school. Nompilo's strategy of coming to her friend's defence must be seen within these circumstances. Significantly, it was not Amanda who initiated violence – a fact which highlights the multiple ways in which some girls in the same context avoid violence and at times use it. It was therefore not surprising to see other 'gentler' girls align themselves to Nompilo where the sharing of lunch and snacks was crucial in the maintenance of friendship groups. There were always benefits for gentler girls and to be seen in alliance with a hard girl who did the dirty job of hitting, and defending and (re)producing the violent girl status. Against the backdrop of harsh material inequalities and unemployment, violence is therefore a significant means to attain material rewards as well as social and emotional rewards. Gentler girls also attain reward in the form of protection and friendship. Both Zama's and Nompilo's use of violence reinforces their power position against more fragile and delicate femininities like Amanda's. Zama has little to lose and much to gain by shifting to violence in order to get 'lunch' and 'anything they have'. Violence is thus not about boys, although it is necessary to see the context of the male gaze in the gendering of violence. Violence is connected to the site of massive structural inequalities, where social conflict shifts speedily to violence and where children with limited access to alternative patterns of conduct resort to violence (and succeed) in the fight for survival. It is therefore not surprising that girls too incorporate this conduct into their repertoire. Violent contexts produce not only violent masculinities but violent expressions of femininities although it is the girls who more generally bear the main burden of male violence. The girls' use of violence is tenuous and the strategy is intimately linked to their overall vulnerability in asymmetrical relations of power:

> Researcher: Do they [boys] hit the girls, then?
> Nompilo: Yes they do but I hit them. I beat them too.
> Researcher: Who do you hit?
> Nompilo: You see him? (Pointing to Mncedo). He is a hitter. He is a boss of hitting.
> Mncedo: She lies. She hits me.
> Researcher: Do you hit the girls also, Nompilo?
> Nompilo: *I'm not scared of girls because the girl is wearing a pantie like me.* They have a private part like me. The boys ... ai ai ..., they got a underwear. I touch my panties not theirs. ... (emphasis added)

The above quote demonstrates the ambiguities and contradictions through which Nompilo forges her identity. The extent of her power is relative. She refers to Mncedo, a violent lad, as the 'boss of hitting', which establishes the patterns of hierarchy. Asymmetrical relations of power are reinforced as Mncedo is positioned as 'boss', raising the point that girls bear the main burdens of boys' violence. Nompilo does hit boys, but she is alert to her limits as a young girl at KwaDabeka Primary School. Nompilo states that she is 'not scared of girls because the girl is wearing a pantie', whilst the boys 'they got underwear'. Nompilo sexualizes the difference between boys and girls (although she transgresses it), but the polarity works to underscore the acute sense of recognition of the enormity of male violence. Some boys present for Nompilo the threat of, and the capacity for, violence. The reference to 'private part' also refers to boys' potential for sexual violence and her vulnerability as a South African girl (Richter, Dawes, & Higson-Smith, 2004). Nompilo is thus alert to the general pattern of boys' (and men's) violence against women and girls and to the diffused nature of power. The indulgence in violence is thus severely circumscribed by the threat of, and actual, violence–both physical and sexual (see Human Rights Watch, 2001). Within the structure of gender relations and the dynamics of the school and broader social context, the regulation of girls' use of violence is thus evident. Alternate forms of femininities are thus always in ebb and flow, contesting, challenging, and reproducing and forming patterns of hierarchy and exclusion:

> Nompilo: I'll hit the girls if they are hitting me. Pindile is naughty and so I hit her. She takes our names and tells her friends stories about me and my friends and so I hit her.
> Researcher: I don't understand. Tell me again.
> Nompilo: It's like this. Pindile and her friends were talking about us and we heard them. I asked her why she did that, and then Pindile cried.
> Researcher: Why does she cry?
> Nompilo: She is not my friend. She shouts at us and she doesn't share lunch with us.
> Researcher: Did you hit her?
> Nompilo: I only hit if she hits me.

Me: Did you hit her?
Nompilo: I'll hit her again.

Currie et al. (2007), in their study of adolescent girls, suggest that girls, who lack economic and social power, find a resource in peer status groups. Nompilo is able to assert her power amongst her peers by challenging and using violence. Lloyd (2005) notes that friendship is an important resource for girls; they use it to define and mark out the 'other'. In the above context, the other is constructed as the rival – Pindile – whose power is squashed through Nompilo's questioning of her. Nompilo's expression of femininity is callous and insensitive. Telling stories or gossiping is seen as an attack on Nompilo's status and leaves Pindile open to attack: 'Pindile and her friends were talking about us and we heard them. I asked her why she did that and then Pindile cried'. Through the othering of Pindile, Nompilo could publicly defend and maintain her position, thus reinforcing her reputation and status amongst her group of friends, and excluding others. The exclusion, however, is not simply based on gossiping or shouting but is embedded within the material context of poverty and the extent to which food (lunch) was shared. Nompilo says that Pindile 'doesn't share lunch with us'. The sharing of lunch was key to forming and maintaining friendships and exclusion. In the context of deep poverty and food insecurity, Nompilo has much to gain in the expression of violent femininity, not only friendships, and a claim to social power but to the most basic necessity – food – supported by sharing with other girls in friendship groups. The litmus test of friendships is thus the ability to share food. In Thorne's (1993) study of boys and girls in the primary school material objects like lip gloss, cars and trucks can become the focus of provocation and dispute, through which friendship alliances are launched and disrupted and become painful markers of exclusion and hierarchies. At KwaDabeka, the sharing of lunch was significant in the construction of friendship alliances. Within an impoverished context like KwaDabeka Primary School, shouting, gossiping and not sharing lunch are key areas that can diminish respect and leave girls like Pindile open to attack, violence, exclusion and pain. Femininities are constructed within and against each other in the constant battles for power in the context of wider social and economic inequalities where the most basic necessity (food) is lacking. The violent expressions of femininity, its location within the broader social context of inequalities including food insecurity and poverty, its relation to violent masculinities and the formation of friendships and friendship hierarchies complicates and contributes to the understanding of girls' violence.

Conclusion

While uncommon, violence is more than simply a one-dimensional expression of male power expressed in African secondary schools. This conception alone betrays the complex fabric of young working-class African primary schoolgirl experiences in the mobilization of violence. Arguing against dominant depictions of the poor African schoolgirl, this chapter has demonstrated how violence (mainly hitting) is negotiated as a strategic ploy to stake a claim for power in the presence of material and social impoverishment. The coming together of specific cultural and material domains, as attested to by the school context of KwaDabeka, together with the violent gender regime, allows violence to flourish, including the violent expressions of femininity. Violence is unquestionably part of African working-class primary schoolgirl experiences, not as victims of boys and teachers alone, but also as agents as they struggle to secure power, friendship, respect and food from other girls. Analysis rooted in the agency of African primary schoolgirls – rarely featuring in debates about gender violence – has an important role to play in replacing stereotypes with accounts that recognize the complex and contested processes through which violence is constructed. As Lisa Vetten (2000) in her study of gangs in South Africa argues, the emphasis on women as victims reinforces stereotypes of women as passive and living on terms dictated by men. While Nompilo in this study has an acute awareness of the extent of her agency in relation to boys with 'underwear', it is clear that this is only part of the picture.

In the last decade, emerging work on the study of gender, schooling and violence in South Africa (Morrell, 1998; Wolpe et al., 1997) has correctly stressed the deep social roots of violence. It is undoubtedly true that gender violence in school extends beyond the school for, as many researchers inside and outside of South Africa argue, violence intersects with race and class to produce specific gender relations (Mac an Ghaill, 1994; Mills, 2001; Morrell, 2001). But so too must feminist scholars begin to re-assess what is meant by violence as the chief domain of masculine formations. This chapter has given attention to girl-on-girl violence in the primary school, suggesting that such violence not only defies gender polarities so often used in making African girls victims of male violence, but also situates violence in an area of schooling that is not featured in research around gender and school violence. There is very little work in the area of violence, primary schoolgirls and agency, and theoretical work needs to begin exploring primary school girl agency and its relationship to violence. Gender violence in African schools can no longer be simply conflated with male power, and this has implications for feminist research. Girls are not simply passive recipients of male violence. They engage with violence, use it, and resist it. Linking masculinity to maleness and to power and domination does not cover the ambiguous ways in which power is manifest in gender relations. As this study has shown, the complexity through which power is deployed by young working-class African girls contests the rigid binary definitions that separate boys from girls. Halberstam (1998) affirms the ambiguous figure of the masculine woman. Criticizing an essentialist relationship between men and masculinities, Halberstam attempts to restore some of the complexities of gender relations by focusing on masculine women (particularly lesbian women) and the pathologization of those representing gender ambiguities. Empowering models of female masculinity have been neglected or misunderstood because of cultural intolerance towards gender ambiguity that the masculine woman represents. The possibility of a conjunction between female and masculinity that challenges the pathology associated with transgressive women and applied to young girls in this study makes it possible to argue that African women are not waiting to become victims. In other words, female masculinity can be empowering and suggests that multiple forms of power and domination are not the exclusive preserve of boys and men.

In a democratic South Africa, the need to eradicate gender violence remains a pressing concern. The remarkable successes with policy and the Constitution have created new gender ideologies, but these successes have not been matched by greater efforts that link job security, eradication of poverty, housing and social equality to the heightening prevalence of gender violence in schools including girl-on-girl violence. This chapter has touched on these interconnected relationships which mean that ending girls' violence also involves ending the worsening social and economic inequalities in South Africa. At the same time when Nompilo says: 'The boys ... ai ai ... they got a underwear. I touch my panties not theirs', is an indication of the capacity to know when to commit violence and when not to. This requires that despite the ongoing material crisis, schools can and do have a part to play in working with girls and boys in ending violence. However, aggressive behaviour amongst girls is often unrecognized, and in the junior phases of the primary school research into the construction of gender violence remains a neglected field (Connolly, 2004). Discourses of childhood innocence remain powerful in these sectors, making gender invisible and gender violence a minor concern (Jordan, 1995).

Notes

1. This word is used in a way that suggests wildness that is boisterously assertive, which stands in contrast to a gentle femininity.
2. Names of places and people in this chapter have been changed throughout to ensure anonymity.
3. Apartheid classified people according to race: Black/African, Indian, white and coloured. Race continues to be significant in post-apartheid South Africa and is important in marking out the social landscape in the country. In this chapter I use the term African to refer to the participants in this study.
4. Between 1990 and 2005, HIV prevalence rates in South Africa rose from 1% to around 29% with the highest rates of infection located amongst the 15–24 year age group. There is considerable gender disparity in prevalence rates. Pettifor et al. (2004) indicate that among young adults aged 20–24 years, 21.5% of women are infected compared to 7.6% of men.
5. The broader study included one predominantly white middle-class school (Westridge Primary), one predominantly Indian, middle to working-class school (Umhlatuzana Primary), an African poor township school (KwaDabeka Primary) and one African rural poor school (Umbumbulu Primary). Altogether I visited 12 classrooms (and 12 teachers, Mrs A to Mrs L) – four white teachers in Westridge, two Indian teachers in Umhlatuzana, three African teachers in a township school KwaDabeka, and three African teachers in a rural school in Umbumbulu.
6. In terms of nutrition in schools, the School Feeding Scheme has been implemented as part of the progressive realization of social and economic rights for poor children. The Primary School Nutrition Programme was introduced by former President Nelson Mandela in 1994, with the explicit aim of improving the quality of life of all South Africans, in particular the poorest and most marginalized groups of the community. The programme targets impoverished communities where hunger has been an important factor hindering the development of children at school.

References

Alder, C., & Worrall, A. (2004). *Girls' violence: Myths and realities.* Albany: State University of New York Press.
Barker, G. (2005). *Dying to be a man: Youth, masculinity and social exclusion.* London: Routledge.
Barker, G., & Ricardo, C. (2006). Young men and the construction of masculinity in Sub-Saharan Africa: Implications for HIV/AIDS, conflict and violence. In I. Bannon & M. Correia (Eds.), *The other half of gender* (pp. 159–195). Washington, DC: The World Bank.
Bhana, D. (2002). *Making gender in early schooling: A multi-sited ethnography of power and discourse: from grade one to two in Durban.* Unpublished PhD thesis, University of Natal, Durban.
Bhana, D. (2005a). Violence and the gendered negotiation of masculinity among young black boys in South Africa. In L. Ouzgane & R. Morrell R (Eds.), *African masculinities* (pp. 205–221). London: Palgrave Macmillan.
Bhana, D. (2005b). 'Show me the panties': Strategies of girls' resistance in the playground. In C. Mitchell & J. Reid-Walsh (Eds.), *Seven going on seventeen: Tween studies in the culture of girlhood* (pp. 163–173). New York: Peter Lang.
Bhana, D. (2006). Doing power: Violent masculinities in the primary school. In F. Leach & C. Mitchell (Eds.), *Gender violence in and around schools: Strategies for change* (pp. 171–181). Stoke-on-Trent, UK: Trentham Books.
Bonin, D. (2000). Claiming spaces, changing places: Political violence and women's protests in KwaZulu-Natal. *Journal of Southern African Studies, 26*, 301–316.
Bright, R. (2005). It's just a Grade 8 thing: Aggression in teenage girls. *Gender and Education, 17*, 93–101.
Burman, M.J., Batchelor, S.A., & Brown, J.A. (2001). Researching girls and violence: Facing the dilemmas of fieldwork. *British Journal of Criminology, 41*, 443–459.
Cherry, J. (2007). We were not afraid: The role of women in the 1980s township uprising in the Eastern Cape. In N. Gasa (Ed.), *Women in South African history* (pp. 281–315). Cape Town, South Africa: HSRC Press.

Connell, R.W. (1995). *Masculinities.* Cambridge, UK: Polity Press.

Connell, R.W. (2000). *The men and the boys.* Cambridge, UK: Polity Press.

Connolly, P. (1998). *Racism, gender identities and young children: Social relations in a multi-ethnic, inner-city primary school.* London: Routledge.

Connolly, P. (2004). *Boys and schooling in the early years.* London: RoutledgeFalmer.

Currie, D.H., Kelly, D.M., & Pomerantz, S. (2007). 'The power to squash people': Understanding girls' relational aggression. *British Journal of Sociology of Education, 28*(1), 23–37.

Department of Education. (1996). *South African Schools Act.* Pretoria, South Africa: Department of Education.

Dunne, M., Humphreys, S., & Leach, F. (2006). Gender violence in schools in the developing world. *Gender and Education, 18*, 75–98.

Epstein, D., & Johnson, R. (1998). *Schooling sexualities.* Buckingham, UK: Open University Press.

Gasa, N., (Ed.) (2007). *Women in South African history.* Cape Town, South Africa: HSRC Press.

Grout, E. (2002). Keep awake: AIDS in the world. A series of essays toward a general convention. Retrieved from http://www.rci.rutgers.edu/lcrew/dojustice/j025.html

Halberstam, J. (1998). *Female masculinity.* Durham, NC: Duke University Press.

Hassim, S. (2005). *Women's organisations and democracy in South Africa: Contesting authority.* Madison: Wisconsin University Press.

Human Rights Watch. (2001). *Scared at school: Sexual violence against girls in South African schools.* New York: Human Rights Watch.

Human Science Research Council. (2002). *Nelson Mandela HSRC study of AIDS.* Cape Town, South Africa: HSRC Press.

Hunter, M. (2007). The changing political economy of sex in South Africa: The significance of unemployment and inequalities to the scale of the AIDS pandemic. *Social Science and Medicine, 64*, 689–700.

Jackson, C. (2006). 'Wild girls?' An exploration of 'ladette' cultures in secondary schools. *Gender and Education, 18*, 339–360.

James, A., & Prout, A. (1998). *Constructing and reconstructing childhood: Contemporary issues in the sociological study of childhood.* London: RoutledgeFalmer.

Jewkes, R., Levin, J., Mbananga, N., & Bradshaw, D. (2002). Rape of girls in South Africa. *Lancet, 359*, 26.

Jordan, E. (1995). Fighting boys and fantasy play: The construction of masculinity in the early years of school. *Gender and Education, 7*, 69–86.

Kenway, J., & Fitzclarence, L. (1997). Masculinity, violence and schooling: Challenging 'poisonous' pedagogies. *Gender and Education, 9*, 117–133.

Leach, F., Fiscian,V., Kadzamira, E., Lenani, W., & Machakanja, P. (2003). *An investigative study of the abuse of girls in African schools* (DfID Education Research Report No. 54). London: Department for International Development.

Lloyd, G. (2005). *Problem girls: Understanding and supporting troubled and troublesome girls and young women.* New York: RoutledgeFalmer.

Mac an Ghaill, M. (1994). *The making of men, masculinities, sexualities and schooling.* Buckingham, UK: Open University Press.

Macdonald, E. (1991). *Shoot the women first.* New York: Random House.

MacNaughton, G. (2000). *Rethinking gender in early childhood education.* London: Paul Chapman Publishing.

Meintjes, S. (2007). Naked women's protest, July 1990: 'We won't fuck for houses'. In N. Gasa (Ed.), *Women in South African history* (pp. 347–369). Cape Town, South Africa: HSRC Press.

Mills, M. (2001). *Challenging violence in schools: An issue of masculinities.* Buckingham, UK: Open University Press.

Mitchell, C., & Smith, A. (2003). Sick of AIDS: Literacy and the meaning of life for South African youth. *Culture, Health & Sexuality, 5*, 513–522.

Moffett, H. (2006). 'These women, they force us to rape them': Rape as narrative of social control in post-apartheid South Africa. *Journal of Southern African Studies, 32*, 131–144.

Morrell, R. (1998). Gender and education: The place of masculinity in South African schools. *South African Journal of Education, 18*, 218–225.

Morrell, R., (Ed.) (2001). *Changing men in Southern Africa.* Pietermaritzburg, South Africa and London: University of Natal Press and Zed Books.

Morrell, R. (2002). Men, movements and gender transformation in South Africa. *The Journal of Men's Studies, 10*, 309–319.

Pattman, R., & Bhana, D. (2006). Black boys with bad reputations. *Alternation: Interdisciplinary Journal for the Study of the Arts and Humanities in Southern Africa, 13*(2), 252–272.

Pattman, R., & Chege, F. (2003). *Finding our voices gendered and sexual identities in HIV/AIDS education*. Nairobi: Unicef.

Pettifor, A.E., Rees, H.V., Steffenson, A., Hlongwa-Madikizela, L., Macphail, C., Vermaak, K., & Kleinschmidt, I. (2004). *HIV and sexual behaviour among young South Africans: National survey of 15–24 year-olds*. Johannesburg, South Africa: Reproductive Health Research Unit, University of Witwatersrand.

Renold, E. (2005). *Girls, boys and junior sexualities: Exploring children's gender and sexual relations in the primary school*. London: RoutledgeFalmer.

Richter, L., Dawes, A., & Higson Smith, C. (Eds.) (2004). *Sexual abuse of young children in southern Africa*. Cape Town, South Africa: HSRC Press.

Salisbury, J., & Jackson, D. (1996). *Challenging macho values: Practical ways of working with adolescent boys*. London: Falmer Press.

Simmon, R. (2002). *Odd girl out: The hidden culture of aggression in girls*. New York: Harcourt Press.

Skelton, C. (2001). *Schooling the boys: Masculinities and primary education*. Buckingham, UK: Open University Press.

Suttner, R. (2007). Women in the ANC-led underground. In N. Gasa (Ed.), *Women in South African history* (pp. 233–257). Cape Town, South Africa: HSRC Press.

Terreblanche, S. (2002). *A history of inequality in South Africa, 1652–2002*. Pietermaritzburg: University of Natal Press.

Thorne, B. (1993). *Gender play: Boys and girls in school*. Buckingham, UK: Open University Press.

Unterhalter, E. (2007). *Gender, schooling and global social justice*. London: Routledge.

Vetten, L. (2000). Invisible girls and violent boys: Gender and gangs in South Africa. *Development Update, 3*(2), 40–54.

Walkerdine, V. (1999). Violent boys and precocious girls: Regulating childhood at the end of the millennium. *Contemporary Issues in Early Childhood, 1*(1), 3–23.

Walsh, D., & Scully, P. (2006). Altering politics, contesting gender. *Journal of Southern African Studies, 32*, 1–12.

Wolpe, A., Quinlan, O., & Martinez, L. (1997). *Gender equity in South Africa: Report of the Gender Equity Task Team*. Pretoria, South Africa: Department of Education.

World Health Organisation. (2002). *World report on violence and health*. Geneva.

Zimudzi, T.B. (2004). African women, violent crime and the criminal law in colonial Zimbabwe, 1900–1952. *Journal of Southern African Studies, 30*, 499–517.

The politics of veiling, gender and the Muslim subject: on the limits and possibilities of anti-racist education in the aftermath of September 11

Wayne Martino and Goli M. Rezai-Rashti

Introduction

> ... the veil has a history far more complex and multilayered than its current signification with oppression or Islamic fundamentalism. (Najmabadi, 2006, p. 250)

> Islamic fundamentalism has become a generic signifier used relentlessly to single out the Muslim other in its irrational, morally inferior, and barbaric masculinity and its passive, victimized, and submissive femininity. (Moallem, 2005, p. 8)

In this paper we draw on important feminist, queer and postcolonial analytic frameworks as a basis for outlining the pedagogical implications for addressing the politics of gender and representation surrounding the West's construction of the essentialized, veiled, Muslim subject (Abu-Lughod, 2002; Ahmed, 2005; Moallem, 2005; Mohanty, 2003; Najmabadi, 2000, 2006; Razak, 2004; Shohat, 1998). The preoccupation with veiling, as a transcendental signifier of patriarchal oppression, is presented as an exemplary instance of what Said[1](1997, 2003) has identified as the political enterprise of Orientalism, which has intensified in the post-September 11 aftermath of the demonization of Islam and the Muslim subject. As Mahmood (2005) argues, 'the veil more than any other Islamic practice, has become the symbol and evidence of violence Islam has inflicted on women' (p. 136). Moallem (2005) also points out, 'the Western trope of the Muslim woman as the ultimate victim of a timeless patriarchy defined by the barbarism of the Islamic religion, which is in need of civilizing, has become a very important component of Western regimes of knowledge' (p. 20). She further adds that the

> need to engage with the gender underpinnings of Orientalism is no longer a rhetorical gesture of postcolonial criticism but its sine qua non, since it is under the sign of the veiled woman that 'we' increasingly come to recognize ourselves not only as gendered and heteronormative subjects but also as located in the free West, where women are not imprisoned. (Moallem, 2005, p. 20)

Abu-Lughod (2002), for example, argues that women's oppression in Afghanistan was a justification for US bombing and intervention to make a case for the 'war on terrorism'. Further, she quotes Laura Bush stating that:

> Because of our recent military gains in much of Afghanistan, women are no longer imprisoned at home. They can listen to music and teach their daughters without fear of punishment. The fight against terrorism is also a fight for the rights and dignity of women. (p. 784)

In this sense, we are concerned to tease out the pedagogical implications of veiling and unveiling. This involves, we propose in this chapter, a necessary examination of the reception regimes that are governed by an Orientalist and neoliberal dogma which dictates the terms of 'a well-organized sense' that the Muslim subject is not like 'us' and, hence, does not subscribe to *our* democratic and supposedly enlightened values (Said, 2003, p. xx). We examine the pedagogical significance of this imperialist and neocolonial gaze as a basis for thinking further about what it means to be addressing the politics of gender and racialized difference in schools in the aftermath of September 11 when 'territorially reductive polarizations like Islam v. the West' seem to have intensified (Said, 2003, p. xxii; see also Rizvi, 2005).

   This focus is particularly important given the research-based literature on pedagogical reform in schools. For example, proponents of what has been coined the productive pedagogies approach to school-based reform stipulate that teachers need to *work with and value difference* alongside providing an intellectually demanding and relevant curriculum within the context of building a supportive classroom learning environment (see Darling-Hammond, French, & Garcia-Lopez, 2002; Hayes, Mills, Christie, & Lingard, 2006).[2] What is required in terms of the *valuing difference* dimension of productive pedagogies, we argue, however, is a knowledge about the politics of difference and identity that is informed by postcolonial, feminist and queer analytic perspectives which draw on a more nuanced understanding of the intersecting power relations involving issues of gender, race, ethnicity and sexuality (see Hall, 1996; Omi & Winnat, 2005). As Mohanty (2003, p. 191) emphasizes, what is required is a commitment to thinking through and theorizing what it means to engage with more nuanced notions of difference in terms of moving to a deeper understanding about the politics of identity. This becomes pertinent, particularly in relation to addressing Islam, gender relations and the politics of schooling, as we will illustrate through a focused discussion and critique of the *veil* as a signifier of an essentialized or monolithic Muslim identity (see Rezai-Rashti, 1999).

The limits of anti-racist education

Research into the experiences of Muslim students in schools has been unable to satisfactorily address the contradictions and tensions that arise as a result of the coalescing of power relations pertaining to colonialism, compulsory heterosexuality, gender, class and racial inequalities in their historical specificity (see Alvi, Hoodfar, & McDonough, 2003; Ruby, 2006; Zine, 2007). For instance, while we argue for the need to move beyond, and indeed to interrupt, reductive and simplistic attempts to cast the Muslim subject in terms which reify and invoke binaries of impugned fundamentalist Islam and the idealized West as 'the standard for enlightened modernity' (Said, 1997, p. xxix), it is necessary to address the internal dynamics of gender relations for men and women on both sides of this problematic Orientalist divide. Anti-racist approaches to addressing equity and social justice issues in education must address such tensions and internal forms of hierarchical power relations within minority communities involving homophobia, heterosexism and sexism, while still addressing broader systemic forms of oppression perpetuated by the imposition of Orientalist and neo-colonialist frameworks for conceptualizing the marginalized/racialized *other* (see Kumashiro, 2001; Said, 1997). As Rezai-Rashti (1999) argues, 'Anti-racism proponents, even when their awareness of institutional racism and power differences is acknowledged, are unable to move beyond reductive concepts of culture and community and examine the intertwining and complex relationships between sexism and racism' (pp. 47–48).

As Rattansi (1992) also points out, we need to avoid resorting to reductive notions of culture and ethnic essentialism in developing an anti-racist framework capable of addressing racial inequality, while simultaneously entertaining a critique of other hegemonic power relations involving class, gender and, we would emphasize, compulsory heterosexuality (see Britzman, 1995, 1998; Kumashiro, 2001; Rich, 1980). These tensions have been thrown into particular relief in the September 11 aftermath of global uncertainty and market-driven neo-liberal economic and social policies (see Giroux, 2002). Such a context involving a *crisis of democracy* has fuelled a particularly virulent form of Islamophobia that has been propelled by an Orientalist dogma invested in the politics of fear and a particular form of truth-making vis-à-vis the representation of Islam and the essentialized Muslim subject (Ahmed, 2003; Thobani, 2003). This sort of politics, which is grounded in 'repressive binary logics' (Giroux, 2006), forecloses informed historical commentary and directs attention away from examining the specificity of emergent neocolonial forms of power and their investment in a politics of truth-making:

> much of what one reads and sees in the media about Islam represents the aggression as coming from Islam because that is what 'Islam' is. Local and concrete circumstances are thus obliterated. In other words, covering Islam is a one-sided activity that obscures what 'we' do, and highlights instead what Muslims and Arabs by their very flawed nature are. (Said, 1997, p. xxii)

In this sense, we draw attention to how discourses about veiling have functioned to confirm particular beliefs or Orientalist truths about Muslim women's oppression and, more generally, Islam. We also engage with specific empirical work on the veil in North America to draw attention to the limits of the critiques provided of Orientalist representations of Muslim women vis-à-vis the burden of signification that has been imposed on the *hijab* in the West (see Alvi et al., 2003). In so doing, we highlight how such anti-racist frameworks deployed by these researchers are limited in their capacity to raise crucial issues about the complex internal dynamics of gender relations, masculinities and sexuality in Muslim women's lives (see Mohanty, 2003). As Brah and Phoenix (2004) argue, 'the need for understanding complexities posed by intersections of different axis of differentiation is as pressing today as it has always been' (p. 75). In this sense, we emphasize that knowledge about the historical specificity of gender-based and racialized identities, particularly as they relate to the politics of veiling as a putative monolithic or transcendental signifier, need to be introduced or incorporated into a critical dialogue and interrogation of intellectual and political frameworks for addressing anti-racist education in schools.

The politics of the veil and Muslim women's narratives of veiling

North American scholars have made a significant contribution to providing a critique of the Orientalist depiction of Muslim women and girls in education, particularly as it relates to wearing the *veil* (Rezai-Rashti, 1994). For instance, Alvi et al. (2003) have edited an entire anthology addressing this specific issue in Diasporic Muslim communities in North America. In their introductory chapter they highlight how the aftermath of September 11 has further intensified the West's scrutiny of the Muslim female subject in terms of veiling and dress codes, which have spurred intense Islamophobia in what they portray as a 'post-Cold war reality of the demonization of Islam, and by implication, Muslims' (Alvi et al., 2003, p. xi). Alvi et al. (2003) are concerned to provide access to empirical research which illuminates a counter-hegemonic political project committed to challenging the Orientalist enterprise of truth-making about veiled Muslim women as the quintessential symbol of patriarchal oppression. Ahmed (2003) also highlights the extent to which there is a need to interrogate 'the hegemonic norms that govern the reproduction of social life', particularly as they relate to or inform our understanding of the politics of truth that are 'deeply bound up with gendered histories of imperialism and capitalism, in which violence against the bodies of subaltern women is both granted and taken for granted in the making of worlds' (p. 385). Thus it is this focus on elaborating a critique of the Orientalist categorization of the Muslim subject that best characterizes this body of literature and that which attempts to articulate an anti-racist approach to addressing Islamophobia in schools (see Zine, 2003). In fact, Alvi et al. claim that very little research has been devoted to providing the space for Muslims themselves to voice their own concerns, issues and priorities. As a result, they provide such a political space in their book for documenting Muslim women's various interpretations of veiling, which serves as a politicized act of providing research-based knowledge that is not so much *about* as it is *for* Muslim women (see Kumashiro, 2000).

There are several Canadian studies which document Muslim women's and school girls' experiences of veiling as a basis for calling into question the colonialist construction of these subjects as oppressed and subjugated by Islamic patriarchy (see Hoodfar, 2003; McDonough, 2003; Rezai-Rashti, 1999, 2005; Ruby, 2006; Zine, 2007). These studies, in their efforts to address the limits of Orientalist constructions of Muslim women/girls as backward and oppressed, provide important knowledge that illuminates the significance of agency in the negotiation of Muslimness and gender identity management which defies simplistic and reductive stereotypes. Hoodfar (2003), for example, uses the narratives of Muslim women to provide a more nuanced analysis of their veiling practices, which defies the limits imposed by hegemonic discourses that treat the veil as merely a reductive symbol of patriarchal oppression. This is consistent, she claims, with the Western scholarly tendency and the colonial impulse to present 'a one-dimensional image of Islam, encompassing a seamless society of Muslims', which has precluded any analysis of the socio-economic significance of veiling practices throughout history (which we will take up in the following section), as well as overlooking 'the actual variations in the way Islam has been and is being practiced' (Hoodfar, 2003, p. 11). For example, Hoodfar mentions that many feminists and Quebec nationalists in Canada have advocated the banning of the veil in public schools on the basis that it will free young women from oppression imposed on them by their families. However, she claims that she did not find any support for such claims among the participants in her study. In fact, to the contrary, Hoodfar asserts that many of her participants actively chose to wear the veil, despite objections from their parents and specifically their mothers who did not associate the practice of veiling with Islam. Alternatively, the majority of women in Hoodfar's study chose to wear the veil because they identified it as part of their religion, which was consistent with their desire to be *good Muslim women*.

From the outset, the women's narratives are used as a means by which to counteract and interrupt hegemonic understandings of veiling that have been shaped by 'persistent colonial images of Muslims' (Hoodfar, 2003, p. 17). Thus veiling is presented in terms which identify it as a political practice and a 'voluntary act with a multiplicity of meanings' (p. 38). For example, the Muslim women in Hoodfar's study claim that it has allowed them to participate in public life without necessarily compromising their religious beliefs or apparently forcing them to subscribe to patriarchal values and practices that have been imposed in the name of Islam. Many of the participants talked about how veiling, in being equated with a certain Muslim morality, guaranteed them a certain degree of freedom socially which otherwise would have been denied to them by their parents. However, Mahmood (2005) raises important questions about the need to rethink agency in relation to Muslim women as entailing not only the act of resisting norms but also in terms of how they inhabit and enact those norms:

> If the ability to effect change in the world and in oneself is historically and culturally specific (both in terms of what constitutes 'change' and the means by which it is effected), then the meaning of agency cannot be fixed in advance but must emerge through an analysis of the particular concepts that enables specific modes of being, responsibility, and effectivity ... In this sense, the capacity for agency is entailed not only in acts that resist norms but also in the multiple ways one inhabits norms. (p. 119)

In this sense, such forms of agency need to be understood in terms of how Muslim women inhabit particular norms that should not be cast in terms of their failure to realize an emancipatory feminist politics which invokes the 'self-regulating liberal subject' (Moallem, 2005). What is required is the need to avoid casting agency in binary terms as caught between the poles of oppressive patriarchal structures of subordination and the promise afforded by feminism of liberation from such structures. Hence, Mahmood (2005) argues that:

> the liberatory goals of feminism should be rethought in light of the fact that the desire for freedom and liberation is historically situated and its motivational force cannot be assumed a priori but needs to be considered in light of other desires, historical projects, and capacities that inhere in a discursively and historically related subject. (p. 135)

Macdonald (2006) highlights the extent to which the media's fixation on veiling is caught within such a symbolic order which refuses the play of difference in its representation of the veiled Muslim woman. In this sense, the media's preoccupation with images of the veiled woman, which, she argues, intensified following 9/11, is more symptomatic of 'the residual influence of colonial discourses'. Within such discursive and representational frameworks, the veil becomes a signifier or rather a central trope of the atrocities enacted on the bodies of women by the Taliban and its function is to confirm the narrative of barbarity, primitiveness and violence that is ascribed to all things Muslim (Said, 1997). Macdonald indicates that this has led to the proliferation of a discourse – post-September 11 – which emphasizes the need to rescue Muslim women from Islamist patriarchy, with the media becoming obsessed with unveiling 'as a symbol of the success of Western interventionism' (2006, p. 11).

Zine's (2007) research, like Hoodfar's (2003), highlights the extent to which veiling was adopted as a feminist protest against the objectification of the female body and the tyranny of beauty that has been further intensified by the commodification of women for the 'edification of patriarchal capitalist values' (p. 243). In this sense, for some Muslim women, the veil represents a means by which to divert the gaze of men away from sexualizing the female body (see also McDonough, 2003). This leads to the liberal humanist assertion, on the part of several participants in Hoodfar's research, that the veil is a means by which to present themselves as a *person* rather than as a sex object. Such criticisms need to be situated alongside an investigation into the persistence of patriarchal and colonialist discourses in the West vis-à-vis the effects of the commodification and marketization of the gendered body, with the implications for interrogating the policing and self-regulation of the female body in the West being brought to the fore (see Macdonald, 2006; Moallem, 2005). This contributes to a more nuanced analysis of new and resurgent forms of sexism and racism in the West that continue to be framed by 'representational practices of "othering" and the identitarian claims of "we-ness"', which, as Moallem (2005) argues, 'are inseparable from the modern history of race, gender, religion, and nation' (p. 9). For example, Omi and Winant (2005) identify the need to focus on 'resurgent Islamaphobia and the increasing racialization of white identities' in the North American context, which, we argue, have resulted in an intensification of hegemonic masculinities grounded in an oppositional politics organized around the demonization of Islam.

In accordance with this view, Moallem (2005) argues that 'such representations reinvent new religious identities by attributing barbarism and otherness to Islam and Muslims' (p. 12). The effect of this, we propose here, is a form of displacement that involves averting the analytic gaze away from those representational practices and apparatuses in the West which continue to support and legitimate white hegemonic heterosexual masculinity, male violence and the persistence of patriarchal power, sexism and the racialization of bodies. As Moallem (2005) points out vis-à-vis Western representational practices 'the dichotomous notions of the veiled Muslim woman and the Western woman, and their juxtaposition as signifiers of unfreedom and freedom, respectively, are incorporated into consumer capitalism' (p. 16). Thus, what is needed, we argue, are analytic frameworks which illuminate both the local and the broader context of globalization for understanding the racialized practices of de-gendering and re-gendering, as they pertain to the politics of remasculinization in post-industrial times. However, the effect of the obsessive focus on the veiled Muslim subject in the the West, where the veil has come to signify 'backwardness, oppression and even terrorism' (Zine, 2007, p. 245), is to divert attention away from examining manifestations of patriarchal ideologies as they are embedded in the representational and regulatory apparatuses of late capitalism, particularly in terms of their capacity to define appropriate and desirable femininity.

Thus, feminists such as Moallem (2005) draw attention to the need to interrogate new and persistent forms of sexism in a consumerist culture alongside an analysis of the perpetuation of colonialist discourses for inscribing the veiled Muslim subject as the epitome of the denial of female sexual agency. Engaging with such analytic frameworks does not preclude a critique of oppressive gender relations in other cultures. Rather it highlights the need for a discussion of gender issues that is extricated from Orientalist frames of reference for othering the veiled Muslim subject as a victim of Islamist patriarchy. As Rezai-Rashti (2005) has already argued, this can be achieved with the complexity, coherence and cultural sensitivity that is required to avoid the tendency to reinforce distorted information and to over-generalize based on fixed notions of Muslim female identity and repressed sexuality.

The significance of historical knowledge of veiling practices

More informed perspectives on the historically situated practices of veiling are needed as a basis for challenging Imperial fictions and the politics of truth-making about Islam and the veil in the West. This is important given that much discussion about Islam in the the aftermath of September 11 continues to be one-dimensional in its tendency to cite reductive and simplistic stereotypes which rely on 'assertions of homogenizing concepts' of Muslimness, while ignoring actual 'discontinuities of history' (Said, 1997, p. 170). Knowledge about such historical perspectives, particularly as they relate to illuminating the cultural norms governing the practices of veiling, are instrumental in exposing the fiction of the end of colonialism in the 'West'. In addition, it provides further insight into what *valuing and working with difference* might look like in terms of foregrounding the knowledge that is needed to inform pedagogical practices committed to addressing the politics of difference, particularly as it relates to more accurate and informed perspectives on Islam. This is consistent with Said's call for *antithetical knowledges*, which he understands as an incitement to a very different discourse about Islam. He identifies the need for a kind of knowledge produced by people who consciously see themselves as writing against the prevailing Orientalist orthodoxy which perpetuates 'the idea that Islam is medieval and dangerous, as well as hostile and threatening to "us"' (1997, p. 157). The literature on documenting historically specific practices of veiling provided in this section is understood in these antithetical terms.

Hoodfar (2003) provides an overview of the historical specificity of the veil, which she asserts 'was never viewed as a symbol of Muslim culture' prior to the nineteenth century: 'Historically, veiling – especially when accompanied by seclusion – was a sign of status and was practiced by the elite in the ancient Greco-Roman, pre-Islamic Iranian and Byzantine empires' (p. 6). Najmabadi (2000) also cautions against resorting to ahistorical general-izations of Islam and feminism in any attempt to explain the politics of modernity vis-à-vis the politics of veiling and modernity in Iran, for example. She documents the diversity of women's rights discourses in Iran and traces the historical forces at play behind debates about veiling and unveiling practices there. In this way she demonstrates how these debates and tensions get framed in terms that are wrought as a consequence of conflating Islam with tradition and an anti-modernist cultural project that is set in opposition to embracing secular modernity.

For example, Najmabadi illustrates how the project of modernization, initiated under Riza Shah's government, needs to be understood in light of this historical legacy. She illustrates the deep division that ensued among women in Iran in 1936 over the government's official ban on veiling and points out that such divisiveness was not characteristic of other feminist political reform initiatives at the time, such as those pertaining to women's education, marriage and divorce laws. Girls were withdrawn from schools and kept at home, while many teachers who refused to unveil either resigned from their positions or were dismissed. Schools which had previously functioned as sites for coalition building among women became divisive in terms of the potential for fostering alliances between secular feminists and those drawn from Islamist ranks. While the latter simply vacated the political space for alliance building, Najmabadi is concerned to illustrate that 'the beginnings of Iranian feminism were not marked by a boundary, setting Islam to its beyond' (2000, p. 35). In fact, for some women, unveiling was perceived to be part of an imperialist agenda in which Riza Shah was merely a pawn. In short, the situation of the 1936 ban illuminates that women were not only divided on the issues of un-veiling, but they also differed in terms of their political views and engagement with Riza Shah's centralized and autocratic government.

As an over-determined sign, Najmabadi argues that it is difficult to imagine how the veil might be successfully renegotiated, given that meanings have become so solidified and caught between opposing poles of representation – women's oppression under Islamist patriarchy versus religious difference as a challenge to the secularism of modern states. As Scott (2005) reiterates, the veil has become constituted as a 'sign of intolerable difference' in its capacity to signify 'everything that is wrong with Islam' (p. 110). However, one way of interrupting such modes of signification, Najmabadi proposes, is to trace the historical legacy of the 'heterosexualization of desire' as it relates to mapping the emergence of Middle Eastern men's beards as 'a visible public sign of belonging' in the nineteenth century. This phenomena of the male body in its capacity to signify Islamic masculinity and desirability, she claims, needs to be understood as a historical shift which occurred in relation to the attention that was directed to women's bodies and their clothing as signs of cultural difference (Najmabadi, 2006, p. 244).

For example, Najmabadi indicates that the self-monitoring of Muslim men's public appearance, in terms of the shape and size of their beards, as well as their overall dress, was governed by the extent to which they resembled or deviated from the appearance of European men. She highlights that for some men becoming modern involved advocating a different change of dress and customs that was consistent with modern European norms, while for others looking European meant acting non-Muslim and was accompanied by a fear that the more one looked like *them* the more one became like *them*. However, as Najmabadi indicates, this latter sentiment was indeed compounded by a sexual anxiety, given that beardlessness for Middle Eastern men signified deficient or failed adult masculinity. In other words, the beard was interpreted as a sign that an adolescent boy had completed the rite of passage to achieving full manhood and, hence, had acquired the status of being more manly. Given the significance of the beard as a signifier of achieving manhood, therefore, Najmabadi highlights that the Europeanized shaven man threatened the very foundations of Middle Eastern men's conception of heterosexualized masculinity. Thus, shaving and looking more like a European man, as Najmabadi points out, invoked not only a representation of a young adolescent male as a symbol of failed, abject masculinity, but also provoked anxieties about being positioned as an object of adult male desire, with all of its shameful associations. In this sense, Najmabadi argues that 'the appearance of Europeanized men in one's own midst seemed nothing less than a sign of the end of the world' (2006, p. 245). However, despite its shameful associations, Najmabadi points out that beardlessness came to signify modernity as defined against a sense of religious backwardness that was projected onto the bearded bodies of Middle Eastern men. In this sense, she characterizes the nineteenth century as 'a time of the beard wars', whereas in the twentieth century the gaze, she claims, turned to veiling as a site for generating tensions and anxieties about Middle Eastern women.

Thus, Najmabadi argues that in the nineteenth and early twentieth centuries veiling functioned within a particular regime for inscribing gender heterosocialization and inciting heteronormalization. This occurred, she asserts, at a time when homoeroticism and same-sex practices were being increasingly reconfigured as signs of backwardness and a mark of national shame in the context of developing modernity. Achieving modernity, hence, became part of a project of 'heteronormalization of eros and sex' which required a resig-resignification of male bonding and camaraderie as asexual practices which became marked as manifestations of patriotic nationalism (2006, p. 246). In this sense, male friendships were able to be de-eroticized. However, Najmabadi, claims that, within the context of modernity, gender segregation became linked to the driving force behind men's engagement in same-sex practices with the veil emerging as 'the most visible sign of gender homosociality' (2006, p. 246). In other words, it was because men could not socialize with women that they were incited to have sex with other men. This 'unnatural sex', Najmabadi claims, was also held to be responsible for driving same-sex desire among women. It is within such a context of modernist drives to address these inimical effects of gender segregation, she argues, that unveiling emerged as a central strategy to eradicate same-sex practices. As Najmabadi points out, such readings of unveiling disrupt modernist discourses of progress and their alignment with Europeanization, in that they foreground the extent to which the heteronormalizing function of such a practice is denied in favour of privileging the apparent 'emancipatory effects of gender heterosocialization' (2006, p. 246).

According to Najmabadi, the disciplinary function of unveiling merely served to reinscribe women's bodily presence and needs to be understood in terms of its generative capacity to reinstate the heterosocializing public space of modernity as a basis for naturalizing heterosexuality. Equally, she draws attention to the work of the veil in Muslim societies as a mechanism for containing and controlling active female sexuality for fear of the threat that it would pose to men's civic and religious lives (2006, p. 247). Once again, Najmabadi's queer postcolonial perspective draws attention to the heterosexual presumption underlying such discourses about the need to contain female sexuality in Muslim societies which is predicated on the belief that heterosexuality is natural. It is in this sense, Najmabadi argues, that the veil and gender segregation cannot be treated merely as institutions for regulating heterosexuality. Rather, they are conceived by Najmabadi as generative of and as inciting heterosexuality and, in this sense, need to be understood as part of a broader heteronormative regime for regulating desire. Thus Najmabadi's historical narratives function to challenge common assumptions that both the removal of the veil was considered essential to modern progress and that all Middle Eastern reformers or modernists advocated unveiling (2006, p. 247).

The pedagogical implications of the body as signifier

The veil as a signifier of Islamist oppression against women within dominant regimes of Western knowledge raises important questions about the need for educators to challenge the authority of Orientalist worldviews of Islam and the Muslim subject. As we have demonstrated in this chapter, this requires both a particular knowledge about Islam and the historically specific practices of veiling and unveiling as well as a particular knowledge about bodies. These sorts of analytical and historical perspectives on veiling offered by postcolonial theorists such as Najmabadi (2000, 2006) and queer theorists such as Britzman (1995, 1998) draw attention to the need to engage with a politics of difference as it relates to both the racialization and sexualization of gendered bodies (see also Moallem, 2005). As Britzman (1995) reiterates in relation to her discussion of the significance of queer in education, what is needed is a pedagogical approach that is capable of engaging with concerns about the 'constitution of bodies of knowledge and knowledge of bodies' (p. 151). By contextualizing veiling and unveiling as historically contingent practices the politics of the knowledge/power relations that are mobilized in constituting the body as a site for gender regulation and for inciting heterosexuality become amplified. Such a postcolonial queer perspective highlights the need for an understanding of both the constitutive knowledge of heterosexualized and racialized bodies in terms of their signifying potentialities and the means by which that knowledge is produced and circulated through the mobilization of representational apparatuses that perpetuate Orientalist perspectives about the embodied Muslim subject. In short, what is foregrounded is that bodies need to be understood as constituted in racialized, gendered and heterosexualized terms in relation to historically specific systems or regimes of knowledge/power relations (Foucault, 1980). Hence, the focus on the Muslim subject and its representation in racialized and gendered terms vis-à-vis Western regimes of knowledge needs to inform pedagogical imperatives that are capable of fostering in students critical capacities for interrogating the Orientalist enterprise of othering. As Rizvi (2005) argues, this requires 'teachers and administrators ... find[ing] ways of not only uncovering silences that help reproduce misleading and harmful representations of Islam but also of exploring how certain organizational practices perpetuate them' (p. 168). This means, he adds, developing pedagogic strategies that enable students to 'examine Islamic beliefs and practices critically, but in ways that do not offend Muslim students with representations that are implicitly hostile to their faith, and to their sense of themselves as both American and Muslim' (p.168).

The historical narratives documented in this chapter point to the significance of mobilizing discourses capable of achieving such a pedagogical imperative that is governed by an engagement with the 'gender underpinnings of Orientalism' understood in terms of the capacity of Western representational practices to constitute the veiled Muslim subject as a sign under which '"we" increasingly come to recognize ourselves not only as gendered and heteronormative subjects but also as located in the free West, where women are not imprisoned' (Moallem, 2005, p. 20). Such hidden or forgotten narratives can be deployed to interrogate the Orientalist tendency to essentialize the Muslim subject as the oppressed other of Western feminist consciousness. This knowledge, combined with an analytic focus on the body as signifier, can do much to turn the critical gaze back on Western representational apparatuses for marketing the female body as a site for public consumption and objectification, as Tincknell, Chambers, Van Loon, and Hudson (2003) demonstrate in their analysis of the limits of what is to count as sexually desirable for women in the West. In addition, Jean Kilbourne (2000) also highlights the role of advertising as a key pedagogical site for interrogating the constitution of women's bodies in the West, in both racialized and heteronormative terms, as fetishized and sexualized objects of the male gaze.

Such a critique needs to be set alongside a critique of the Western media's obsessive focus on the veiled Muslim subject and draws attention to the role of popular and media culture as 'the primary pedagogical medium' for constructing meanings, regulating desires and inciting investments that, Giroux (2002) argues, 'play such an influential role in how students view themselves, others, and the larger world' (see also hooks, 1997):

> As a performative practice, pedagogy is at work in a variety of educational sites – including popular culture, television and cable networks, magazines, the internet, churches, and the press – where culture works to secure identities; it does the bridging work for negotiating the relationship between knowledge, pleasure, and values, and renders authority both crucial and problematic in legitimating particular social practices, communities, and forms of power. (Giroux, 2000, p. 1153)

In this sense, there is an urgent need for pedagogy to be grounded in both a knowledge of bodies as socially, culturally and historically inscribed and in bodies of knowledge that attend to the neocolonial limits of the Orientalist enterprise in its representation of the Muslim subject post-September 11. Giroux (2006) has argued that this needs to involve explicit pedagogical engagement with the public media and popular culture in an attempt to de-centre the *spectacle of terrorism*, as a basis for interrogating Western representational practices which are informed by problematic Orientalist discourses of Islamic fundamentalism. As Moallem (2005) reiterates:

> An interrogation of new frames of knowledge and representational practices is crucial for critical intervention in the ways in which the notion of Muslim is circulated along with bodies and capital in a neocolonial, postcolonial context. (p. 20)

Such perspectives highlight the need to attend to both the ways in which bodies are constituted as particular objects and the disciplinary body of knowledge/power relations that governs the analytic frameworks for thinking about bodies in racialized, heterosexualized and gender normative/heteronormative terms (Najmabadi, 2005, 2006). This has important implications for *valuing and working with difference* dimensions of the 'productive pedagogies' approach to equity and social justice issues in educational contexts (see Hayes et al., 2006). As part of our Equity and Social Justice graduate course, which attracts a considerable number of classroom teachers, we provide students with the postcolonial, feminist and queer analytic frameworks presented here. We draw on Kilbourne's lecture and a critique of the apparatus of advertising in the West as a basis for interrogating the representation of women's bodies and the knowledge/power relations of late capitalist production that govern the marketization of such bodies. This provides a forum for addressing issues pertaining to the patriarchal control of women's bodies and sexuality via Western practices of representation (Moallem, 2005). It also provides the space for interrogating the cultural and economic conditions of white supremacist, capitalist patriarchy (hooks, 1997) that produce such manufactured representations of women's bodies as objects of desire in the first place and which are framed by the male gaze. It is within such a pedagogical milieu that a critical analysis of Western representational practices of veiling, vis-à-vis the post-September 11 era of the 'threatening presence of Islamic fundamentalism', is introduced (Moallen, 2005, p. 17).

Using articles/editorial commentary drawn from local and national Canadian newspapers, we provide a forum for students to interrogate 'the dichotomous notions of the veiled Muslim woman and the Western woman and their juxtaposition as signifiers of unfreedom and freedom, respectively' and how they are 'incorporated into consumerist capitalism' (Moallem, 2005, p. 16). For example, an article for *The Globe and Mail*, a national Canadian newspaper, written by James Laxer (2006), a professor of political science at York University in Toronto, is introduced to the class. This article presents the burden of veiling as a signifier of Islamist oppression of women, through a critical lens which targets the role that liberal discourses play in framing the constitution of the Muslim subject as an alien and intolerable presence in the Canadian context. Laxer also offers counter-historical narratives of the reception of other ethnic minorities in Ontario who have also been subjected to the same sort of racialized scrutiny. For example, he recounts how the Irish Catholic immigrants, who came to Ontario in the 1850s and 1860s to escape famine in their homeland, were also considered suspect, with many people raising serious questions about their non-British ethnicity. In fact, concern was expressed about their capacity or willingness to embrace an Anglo-Canadian identity. Laxer also recounts how Chinese immigrants to Canada in recent decades have been similarly subjected to suspicion and doubt as an alien presence, with concerns also being expressed about their capacity to become *real Canadians*. Thus in addressing issues of identity, nationalism and assimilation by naming the persistence of colonial discourses about the alien immigrant presence throughout Canadian history, the analytic gaze is directed away from the essentialized Muslim subject to the systemic colonial forces at play in constituting other ethnic and religious minorities in these terms.

Such critical perspectives are juxtaposed against those offered by columnists for *The Globe and Mail* such as Margaret Wente (2006), which are grounded in the very liberal discourses that Laxer identifies as problematic. For example, in referring to veiled women in Canada, and specifically those who dress 'entirely in black ... with only a slit for the eyes', Wente begins her column by asserting: 'Whenever I see a woman in veil walking down the street, I get a chill'. This leads throughout the column to a discussion of veiling as a sign of radicalization that invokes discourses of Islamic fundamentalism and barbarism which are couched firmly in Orientalist notions of the Muslim subject. This results in the journalist imploring Muslim women to unveil and by so doing to succumb to the civilizing influences of the West. Wente, in fact, draws on familiar tropes of the Muslim subject as the *alien other* through invoking discourses about veiling as a signifier of radical Islam. In this sense, Muslim veiled women are presented as failing to assimilate to *our* ways of life and customs and, in this sense, are cast as refusing to integrate into Canadian society.

By juxtaposing various ideological standpoints as they are articulated via the representational apparatus of the public media, spaces of resistance can be created in public schools and universities where students can be encouraged to develop a more critical media literacy that is capable of addressing the persistence of colonial discourses in the post-September 11 context. As we have outlined here this can be achieved by engaging with postcolonial and queer bodies of knowledge that engage with the historical significance of racism as a basis for interrogating the persistence of colonial practices and the heterosexualization of desire (see Najmabadi, 2005, 2006). This needs to be undertaken, pedagogically speaking, in conjunction with knowledge of the body as a signifier. This can be achieved, we believe, by inserting the sort of counternarratives on veiling provided by Najmabadi into the pedagogical space of resistance that we have outlined in this section. As Najmabadi (2006) argues, it is by returning to 'the nineteenth century focus on men's beards as a visible public sign of belonging' that it is possible to trace the 'the process of the heterosexualization of desire and interrelated resignification of the veil that became the ground for the shift to women's bodies and clothing as the key sign of cultural difference' (p. 244). It is in this sense that such historically contingent narratives of veiling and unveiling may 'offer us alternative usable pasts as languages for present contestations' (Najmabadi, 2006, p. 253).

Conclusion

In this chapter we have attempted to confront the politics of veiling as a basis for teasing out the significance of an anti-racist politics capable of engaging with Islamophobia, without eliding the importance of sexism and the heteronormative policing of gender relations across the Orientalist divide. Moreover, we have attempted to raise important questions about the limits of a progressive politics which resort to invoking the self-regulating liberal subject and, hence, flawed notions of resistance and agency as they pertain to our understanding of the representational practices of veiling in Muslim women's lives. We have demonstrated that such an anti-racist politics within the context of public schools and universities needs to engage with a pedagogical approach that incorporates specific bodies of knowledge and a knowledge about bodies as gendered, heterosexualized and racialized. In other words, what is needed is knowledge about the historical specificity of veiling practices that has either been forgotten or elided. Analytic perspectives informed by postcolonial, queer and feminist theories are needed to address the body as a signifier within limits imposed by representational practices that are governed by a repressive binary logic for thinking about the Muslim subject in Orientalist terms (Najmabadi, 2000, 2006). In this sense, we have tried to demonstrate that merely including the voices of Muslim women with the diversity of their perspectives on the practices of veiling and unveiling, is not enough. What is needed, we have argued, is a pedagogical approach to anti-racist education in the aftermath of September 11 that is capable of both attending to the historical specificity of veiling as a basis for interrogating current Orientalist significations of the veil and to engaging with the politics of desire, hetero-normativity and sexism as they continue to be racialized boundaries that demarcate cultural spaces of belonging and otherness.

Notes

1. Said did not engage with gender depictions of Orientalism. The work, however, has intellectually and politically inspired postcolonial feminists to engage with gender dimension of Orientalism.
2. Productive pedagogies have been defined by Hayes et al. (2006) as involving four integrated dimensions: intellectually demanding curriculum; relevant curriculum that is connected to the everyday lives of students; safe classroom learning environments and working with and valuing difference. All of these dimensions are considered integral to any pedagogical reform agenda in education.

References

Abu-Lughod, L. (2002). Do Muslim women really need saving? Anthropological reflections on cultural relativism and its others. *American Anthropologist, 104*, 783–790.

Ahmed, L. (2005). The veil debate – again. In F. Nouraie-Simone (Ed.), *On shifting ground: Muslim women in the global era* (pp. 153–171). New York: The Feminist Press at the City University of New York.

Ahmed, S. (2003). The politics of fear in the making of worlds. *Qualitative Studies in Education, 16*, 377–398.

Alvi, S., Hoodfar, H., & McDonough, S. (Eds.) (2003). *The Muslim veil in North America: Issues and debates*. Toronto: Women's Press.

Brah, A., & Phoenix, A. (2004). Ain't I a woman? Revisiting intersectionality. *Journal of International Women Studies, 5*(3), 75–86.

Britzman, D. (1995). Is there a queer pedagogy? Or stop thinking straight. *Educational Theory, 45*(2), 151–165.

Britzman, D. (1998). *Lost subjects, contested objects*. New York: State University of New York Press.

Darling-Hammond, L., French, J., & Garcia-Lopez, S. (Eds.) (2002). *Learning to teach for social justice*. New York and London: Teachers' College Press.

Foucault, M. (1980). *Michel Foucault: Power/knowledge: Selected interviews and other writings 1972–1977*. Brighton, UK: Harvester.

Giroux, H. (2002). Democracy, freedom, and justice after September 11th: Rethinking the role of educators and the politics of schooling. *Teachers College Record, 104*, 1138–1162.

Giroux, H. (2006). *Beyond the spectacle of terrorism*. Boulder, CO: Paradigm.

Hall, S. (1996). New ethnicities. In D. Morley & K. Chen (Eds.), *Stuart Hall: Critical dialogue in cultural studies* (pp. 441–449). London: Routledge.

Hayes, D., Mills, M., Christie, P., & Lingard, B. (2006). *Teachers and schooling making a difference*. Sydney: Allen & Unwin.

Hoodfar, H. (2003). More than clothing: Veiling as an adaptive strategy. In S. Alvi, H. Hoodfar & S. McDonough (Eds.), *The Muslim veil in North America: Issues and debates* (pp. 3–40). Toronto: Women's Press.

hooks, b. (1997). *Cultural criticism and transformation* [Videorecording] (Sut Jhally, producer, director, editor). Northampton, MA: Media Education Foundation.

Kilbourne, J. (2000). *Killing us softly 3: Advertising's image of women* [Videorecording] (Sut Jhally, producer, director, editor). Northampton, MA: Media Education Foundation.

Kumashiro, K. (2000). Toward a theory of anti-oppressive education. *Review of Educational Research, 70*(1), 25–53.

Kumahsiro, K., (Ed.) (2001). *Troubling intersections of race and sexuality: Queer students of color and anti-oppresive education.* Boston: Rowman and Littlefield.

Laxer, J. (2006, October 26). Veiling intolerance in liberal discourse. *The Globe and Mail*, p. A21.

Macdonald, M. (2006). Muslim women and the veil. *Feminist Media Studies, 6*, 7–23.

Mahmood, S. (2005). Feminist theory, agency, and the liberatory subject. In F. Nouraie-Simone (Ed.), *On shifting ground: Muslim women in the global era* (pp. 111–152). New York: The Feminist Press at the City University of New York.

McDonough, S. (2003). Voices of Muslim women. In S. Alvi, H. Hoodfar & S. McDonough (Eds.), *The Muslim veil in North America: Issues and debates* (pp. 105–120). Toronto: Women's Press.

Moallem, M. (2005). *Between warrior brother and veiled sister: Islamic fundamentalism and the politics of patriarchy in Iran.* Berkeley and Los Angeles: University of California Press.

Mohanty, C. (2003). *Feminism without borders: Decolonizing theory, practicing solidarity.* Durham, NC: Duke University Press.

Najmabadi, A. (2000). (Un)Veiling feminism. *Social Text, 18*(3), 29–45.

Najmabadi, A. (2005). Rules of desire. Retrieved November 5, 2007, from http://iranian.com/Najmabadi/2005/August/Hijab/index.html

Najmabadi, A. (2006). Gender and secularism of modernity: How can a Muslim woman be French? *Feminist Studies, 32*(2), 239–255.

Omi, M., & Winant, H. (2005). The theoretical status of the concept of race. In C. McCarthy & W. Crichlow (Eds.), *Race, identity, and representation in education* (pp. 3–12). London: Routledge.

Rattansi, A. (1992). Changing the subject? Racism, culture and education. In J. Donald & A. Rattansi (Eds.), *'Race', culture and difference* (pp. 11–48). New York: Sage.

Razak, S. (2004). Imperilled Muslim women, dangerous Muslim men and civilised Europeans: Legal and social responses to forced marriages. *Feminist Legal Studies, 12*(2), 129–174.

Rezai-Rashti, G. (1994). The dilemma of working with minority female students in Canadian high schools. *Canadian Women Studies, 14*(2), 76–82.

Rezai-Rashti, G. (1999). The persistence of colonial discourse: Race, gender, and Muslim students in Canadian schools. *Journal of Curriculum Theorizing, 15*(4), 44–60.

Rezai-Rashti, G. (2005). Unessential women: A discussion of race, class and gender and their implications in education. In N. Mandell (Ed.), *Feminist issues: race, class and sexuality* (pp. 83–99). Toronto: Pearson Education Canada.

Rich, A. (1980). Compulsory heterosexuality and lesbian experience. *Signs, 5*, 631–660.

Rizvi, F. (2005). Representation of Islam and education for justice. In C. McCarthy & W. Crichlow (Eds.), *Race, identity, and representation in education* (pp. 167–178). London: Routledge.

Ruby, T. (2006). Listening to the voices of hijab. *Women's Studies International Forum, 29*(1), 54–66.

Said, E. (1997). *Covering Islam: How the media and the experts determine how we see the rest of the world.* New York: Vintage Books.

Said, E. (2003). *Orientalism.* New York: Vintage Books.

Scott, J. (2005). Symptomatic politics: The banning of Islamic head scarves in French public schools. *French Politics, Culture & Society, 23*(3), 106–127.

Shohat, E., (Ed.) (1998). *Talking visions: Multicultural feminism in a transnational age.* Cambridge, MA: MIT Press.

Tincknell, E., Chambers, D., Van Loon, J., & Hudson, N. (2003). Begging for it: 'New femininities', social agency, and moral discourse in contemporary teenage and men's magazines. *Feminist Media Studies, 3*, 47–63.

Thobani, S. (2003). War and the politics of truth-making in Canada. *Qualitative Studies in Education, 16*, 399–414.

Wente, M. (2006, October 12). Let's raise the veil on veils. *The Globe and Mail*, p. A23.

Zine, J. (2003). Dealing with September 12th: The challenge of anti-Islamophobia education. *Orbit*, *33*(3), 39–41.

Zine, J. (2007). Safe havens or religious 'ghettos'? Narratives of Islamic schooling in Canada. *Race, Ethnicity and Education*, *10*(1), 71–92.

Index